Intellectual P[illegible]tion Management [illegible] Small Firms

Intellectual Property [illegible] and innovation are [illegible] today's enterprise. This timely book combines research on SMEs, IP and innovation.

Drawing on original material from the ESRC's Programme on Intellectual Property, and showing a variety of approaches to the study of IP in small firms, this book reveals that IP and innovation management are interdisciplinary areas of research. These chapters provide new evidence on IP management in specific sectors such as software, engineering, textiles, biotechnology and electronic publishing. Some also address the strategic management of IP and examine IP management in the case of university spin-offs, while others focus on the role of patents in protection and innovation.

The first major collected edition on IP and innovation management in SMEs, this book will be of interest to students, policy-makers and practitioners interested in IP and innovation.

Robert A. Blackburn (Ph.D.) is Director of Research, Kingston Business School, and HSBC Professor of Small Business Studies, Kingston University, UK. He has extensive experience of researching the smaller enterprise, using a variety of methodological approaches. He is editor of the *International Small Business Journal* and co-author of *Researching the Small Enterprise* (with James Curran). He is a member of the Institute of Small Business Affairs and the Academy of Learned Societies for the Social Sciences.

Routledge studies in small business
Edited by David J. Storey

1 Small Firm Formation and Regional Economic Development
Edited by Michael W. Danson

2 Corporate Venture Capital
Bridging the equity gap in the small business sector
Kevin McNally

3 The Quality Business
Quality issues and smaller firms
Julian North, Robert A. Blackburn and James Curran

4 Enterprise and Culture
Colin Gray

5 The Financing of Small Business
A comparative study of male and female small business owners
Lauren Read

6 Small Firms and Network Economies
Martin Perry

7 Intellectual Property and Innovation Management in Small Firms
Edited by Robert A. Blackburn

8 Understanding the Small Family Business
Edited by Denise E. Fletcher

Intellectual Property and Innovation Management in Small Firms

Edited by Robert A. Blackburn

First published 2003
by Routledge
2 Park Square, Milton Park, Abingdon, Oxon, OX14 4RN

Simultaneously published in the USA and Canada
by Routledge
270 Madison Ave, New York NY 10016

Routledge is an imprint of the Taylor & Francis Group

Transferred to Digital Printing 2007

© 2003 Editorial matter and selection, Robert A. Blackburn; individual chapters, the contributors

Typeset in Baskerville by
BOOK NOW Ltd

All rights reserved. No part of this book may be reprinted or reproduced or utilised in any form or by any electronic, mechanical, or other means, now known or hereafter invented, including photocopying and recording, or in any information storage or retrieval system, without permission in writing from the publishers.

British Library Cataloguing in Publication Data
A catalogue record for this book is available from the British Library

Library of Congress Cataloging in Publication Data
Intellectual property and innovation management in small firms / edited by Robert A. Blackburn.
p. cm.
Includes bibliographical references and index.
1. Technological innovations–Great Britain–Management. 2. Small business–Great Britain–Management. 3. Small business–technological innovations–Great Britain. 4. Intellectual property–Great Britain. I. Blackburn, Robert A., 1957–.

HD45.I553 2003
658.5′7–dc21 2003043133

ISBN10: 0-415-22884-0 (hbk)
ISBN10: 0-415-43981-7 (pbk)

ISBN13: 978-0-415-22884-8 (hbk)
ISBN13: 978-0-415-43981-7 (pbk)

Publisher's Note
The publisher has gone to great lengths to ensure the quality of this reprint but points out that some imperfections in the original may be apparent

Printed and bound by CPI Antony Rowe, Eastbourne

Contents

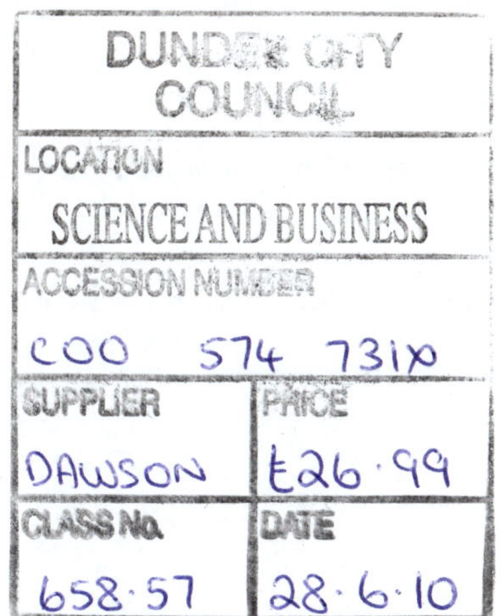
DUNDEE CITY
COUNCIL
LOCATION
SCIENCE AND BUSINESS
ACCESSION NUMBER
C00 574 731X
SUPPLIER
DAWSON
PRICE
£26·99
CLASS No.
658·57
DATE
28·6·10

Figures

Tables

Contributors

John Adams was co-ordinator of the ESRC's Intellectual Property Initiative. He has been Professor of Intellectual Property at Sheffield University since 1994 and he was also Director of the Intellectual Property Institute until 2000. He has published very widely in the field of intellectual property and commercial law generally, including *Franchising* (co-author) (4th edn, Butterworth, 1997), *Character Merchandising* (2nd edn, Butterworth, 1996), *Atiyah's Sale of Goods* (conributor) (10th edn, Pearson Education, 2000), and (with Roger Brownsword) *Understanding Contract Law* (3rd edn, Sweet and Maxwell, 2000) and (with Roger Brownsword) 'Understanding Law' (3rd edn, Sweet & Maxwell, 2003).

Robert A. Blackburn (Ph.D.) is Director of Research of Kingston Business School, Professor of Small Business Studies and Director of the Small Business Research Centre, Kingston University. His academic interests span the social sciences including sociological, regional and economic analyses of small firms. His academic output is prolific and he is editor of the *International Small Business Journal* (Sage Publications). His latest book (with co-author James Curran) is entitled *Researching the Small Enterprise* (Sage, 2001).

David R. Charles is the David Goldman Chair of Business Innovation and director of research in the University of Newcastle upon Tyne Business School. He also co-ordinates the Innovation, Learning and Knowledge research group in the Centre for Urban and Regional Development Studies (CURDS). His research interests are in innovation, regional innovation policy, clusters and the interactions between universities, industry and regional economies. He recently co-edited an OECD book on *Innovative Clusters: Drivers of National Innovation Systems* (OECD, 2001).

Anne-Marie Coles (Ph.D.) is a Research Fellow in the School of Business and Management at Brunel University. She is involved in developing a research programme for the centre for Brunel Research into Ethics, Sustainability and Enterprise (BRESE). Her research interests include management of technology, innovation and technology policy.

Keith Dickson is Professor of Technology Management and Head of the School of Business and Management at Brunel University. His research interests focus on the effective management of technological resources and innovation within organisations, particularly small 'high-tech' firms. He is Deputy Editor of *Technology Analysis and Strategic Management* (Taylor and Francis).

Matthew Hall (Ph.D.) is a Lecturer in Information and Knowledge Management at Aston University, Birmingham, UK. His research has been centred around the flow of information in an organisational context. More recently he has become involved in research in knowledge management, with a particular interest in the limits of knowledge codification.

John Kirkland (Ph.D.) is Director of Human Capacity Development at the Association of Commonwealth Universities, London, where he also directs an international universities research management programme. He was previously Secretary of the National Institute of Economic and Social Research and Head of Research Services at Brunel University. Other positions currently held include that of Executive Secretary to the Commonwealth Scholarship Commission in the United Kingdom.

John Kitching (Ph.D.) is Senior Researcher at the Small Business Research Centre, Kingston University. His research interests focus on small enterprises and, more specifically, on labour market and employment issues. Recent projects include research on small businesses and the national minimum wage, owner-manager and workforce training, and the recruitment and employment of disadvantaged labour market groups in SMEs. His publications include *The Nature of Training and Motivation to Train in Small Firms* (with Blackburn) (Department for Education and Skills, 2002).

Bernard Lefang (Ph.D.) is former Research Fellow in the Management School of the University of Sheffield. His first degree (from Bradford University) is in statistics, his Ph.D. (from Lancaster University) in computer use in small firms, a subject of direct relevance to his intellectual property research into the use of patent information by small firms. Bernard was once a member of the Cameroon football squad and he gave up academic life to become an actuary in Texas.

Stuart Macdonald (Ph.D.) is Professor of Information and Organisation at the University of Sheffield. His research is primarily into the role of information in change, and the implications of this role for policy and strategy. Recent work has looked at the importance of information flow and information networks in the context of science parks, management consultants and management methods, organisational gatekeepers, technology transfer, export controls on high technology, intellectual property rights, industrial espionage and corporate strategy. A constant theme of the research is the interaction of formal and institutional information systems with informal and personal systems. He is European Editor of the journal *Prometheus* (Taylor and Francis Publications) and his latest book is *Information for Innovation. Managing Change from an Information Perspective* (Oxford University Press, 1998).

Duncan Matthews is Senior Lecturer in Intellectual Property Law at the Intellectual

Property Research Institute, Queen Mary College, University of London. He has written widely on intellectual property rights, environmental policy and European Union law. He is author of *Globalising Intellectual Property Rights: the TRIPs Agreement* (Routledge, 2002) and (with Wyn Grant and Peter Newell) *The Effectiveness of European Union Environmental Policy* (Macmillan, 2000).

Charles Oppenheim is Professor of Information Science at Loughborough University. Previously he held posts in academia and the electronic publishing industry. He is interested in legal issues in information work, patent information, the valuing of information assets in industry, and the economics of the electronic publishing industries and of electronic libraries. He is an Honorary Fellow of the Chartered Institute of Library and Information Professionals. He is a member of the Legal Advisory Board of the European Commission. He was the Specialist Advisor to the House of Lords' Inquiry into the Information Superhighway.

Professor John Pickering is an Economic and Business Consultant. He was, until recently, Professor of Business Strategy at the University of Bath School of Management. Previously, he was Deputy Vice-Chancellor of the University of Portsmouth and before that, variously, he was Dean, Vice-Principal and Professor of Industrial Economics at UMIST. He was formerly a reporting panel member of the Monopolies and Mergers Commission, now the Competition Commission. He holds or has held various external positions of responsibility, for example as Church Commissioner.

Brian Rappert (Ph.D.) is a Research Fellow in the School of Sociology and Social Policy at the University of Nottingham, UK. His research focuses on the assessment of controversial and risky technologies. Among his publications include the co-edited *Contested Futures* (Ashgate, 2000) and the monograph *Technology, Politics and Conflict* (Frank Cass, 2002).

Margaret Sheen (Ph.D.) is Director of the Emerging Technologies Research and Assessment Centre (ETRAC) at the University of Strathclyde and a Senior Lecturer in Technology and Business Studies. Her research is mainly associated with the commercialisation of university knowledge but she also runs a programme nurturing independent thinking and fostering enterprise in undergraduates.

Puay Tang is a political scientist, with a Ph.D. in international relations from the Johns Hopkins University, Washington D.C. With 7 years of experience as a Research Fellow at SPRU, her research focuses on application and development of new information and communication technologies, software patents and the management of intellectual property rights in a digital environment. She is on the editorial board of the journal *Information, Communication and Society* (*iCS*), published by Routledge. Dr Tang is a frequent evaluator and reviewer of European Commission Framework 5 Information Society Technology proposals and projects.

Dr Sandra Thomas is Director of the Nuffield Council on Bioethics and a Senior

Fellow at the Science Policy and Technology Research Unit (SPRU), University of Sussex. She has recently been appointed to the UK Government Commission on Intellectual Property Rights. Over the past decade, she has published widely on the development of public policy for biotechnology, particularly in the area of intellectual property rights and the development and application of genomics. In 2002, she was a member of the Economic and Social Committee of the European Communities (Sections: External Relations and Agriculture and Rural Development and the Environment).

Andrew Webster (Ph.D.) is Professor of Sociology at the University of York, UK. He is Director of the Science and Technology Studies Unit (SATSU), and of a UK research programme on Innovative Health Technologies. His main interests lie in the sociology of science and technology, foresight and innovation studies, health technologies and policy, intellectual property and the commercialisation of research. Recent publications include, *Embodying New Medical Technologies* (co-author) (Polity Press, 2003) and *Capitalising Knowledge* (co-author) (SUNY Press, 1998).

Adrian Woods (Ph.D., FRSA) is Dean of Brunel University Graduate School and Professor of Management Studies. He has acted as a consultant for the EU, local authorities and other government agencies on small business development. His latest book on *Strategic Management* was published by Kogan Page in 2001. He is on the editorial boards of *Small Business and Enterprise Development* and the *Journal of Strategic Change*.

Acknowledgements

This book is based on those studies in the ESRC's Intellectual Property Initiative which sought to address IP issues in small firms. I am grateful to the authors of the following chapters for their contributions and the staff in Routledge for their guidance. I would also like to acknowledge the support of the ESRC for supporting research into small firms and IP and to John Adams for co-ordinating the Initiative. A big thank you goes to my colleagues in the Small Business Research Centre, past and present, who have helped me undertake this project, especially Dr John Kitching for his research contribution and Valerie Thorne for her administrative support. Finally, I would like to thank all those business owners 'out there', doing it, who have helped provide the empirical material on which much of this book is based.

Every effort has been made to contact copyright holders for their permission to reprint material in this book. The publishers would be grateful to hear from any copyright holder who is not here acknowledged and will undertake to rectify any errors or omissions in future editions of this book.

Introduction

The Intellectual Property Initiative

John Adams

The origins of the chapters which make up this book are as follows. For some time, concern had been expressed by a number of UK policy-makers that little empirical work had been done into how business used the intellectual property system, and especially of its relevance to the needs of small and medium-sized enterprises (SMEs). The 'intellectual property system' for these purposes principally consists of patents, trademarks, copyrights and designs, and confidential information. Which, if any, of these rights will be of interest to a particular SME will depend on the sector in which it operates? The Economic and Social Science Research Council (ESRC) held a one-day workshop for invited academics and practitioners hosted by the UK Patent Office in Newport, to explore what might be done in this area. As a result of that, the ESRC, supported by the Intellectual Property Institute and the Patent Office, decided to fund a research programme the 'Intellectual Property Initiative'. Tenders were invited, and 11 projects were selected for funding. These involved a wide range of social science disciplines. The present volume is based on the research outputs from eight of these projects. Although some of the findings confirm what specialists in the field had already suspected, having empirical confirmation for informed guesses and anecdotal evidence is proving to be of great value to policy-makers.

Unsurprisingly, the Initiative confirms that the use made by SMEs of the system depends very much on the sector in which they operate, and their size. As the Macdonald study suggests (Chapter 8), probably, for most, the patent system has little or no relevance, even though a surprisingly large percentage stress the importance of R&D to their business. But, as Thomas (Chapter 5) shows, for those engaged in research-*intensive* sectors such as biotechnology (and, I would say, electronics), patenting can be crucial. In this sector the role of an established industrial partner is very important, and the partner will have the necessary expertise to deal with the IP issues.

The Kitching and Blackburn study (Chapter 2) covered four different industrial sectors: software; mechanical engineering; electronics; and design. It suggests that SMEs have realised the importance of IPRs and know-how to manage their assets, but again supports the findings of Macdonald that SMEs are making little use of formal methods of protection, i.e. methods requiring registration such as patents. They prefer to rely on informal methods because they are successful, cheaper and within the control of the company. None showed any interest in a less formal registration system (the 'petty patent') which Germany and some other European countries have, and in relation to which the European Commission is considering a harmonisation directive.

The patent system is intended to be both a source of protection and a source of information. The Hall, Oppenheim and Sheen study suggests that for SMEs the system is seriously defective in fulfilling the latter role (Chapter 9). Hall *et al.* point out that there are four reasons for using published patent information: (a) to find out what has been done at the start of an R&D project; (b) to find out what competitors are up to; (c) to evaluate the chances of protecting an idea; and (d) to find technology to license in. Nearly all information used by SMEs is related to (c). Clearly this points to the need for patent offices to market the value of the other three uses of the information. Another suggestion made by the study is the need to involve patent agents at an early stage in an R&D project. They have the shills within the confines of the present system to use the information more fully for the benefit of their clients.

The chapter by Webster, Rappert and Charles (Chapter 7) shows that patenting has only a small role in university spin-off companies ('USOs'). It also suggests that in some sectors, such as materials, university 'parents' could do more to help their offspring. An interesting and potentially important development picked up by this study, and one which is also occurring in the United States, is 'virtual' USOs linking researchers in different university departments and different universities.

Copyright is the principal source of protection for the textile design centre. This is acquired automatically without the need to register or other formality, and it might have been expected, therefore, that much use would be made of it to prevent unauthorised copying. Surprisingly, Dickson , Coles and Woods (Chapter 4) show that many textile designers accept blatant copying, doing nothing about it in 50 per cent of the cases. This may have to change as the development of digital technology erodes market lead time on which designers have traditionally relied.

Further support for the proposition that the IPR system is of little relevance to many SMEs is lent by the chapter by Tang (Chapter 6) on the electronic publishing sector (CD-ROMs and on-line databases, but not music and software). This showed that finding a market niche, and protecting products by technical means, was much more important than copyright law (even though that is acquired automatically). Presumably the same thing applies to database right. This study is complemented by the Wallis study, reported elsewhere, of the multimedia sector. That study has proved to be prescient in suggesting the coming together of previous competitors, and the polarisation of the market between global operators and small local operators, with little left in between. Importantly, it also suggests that the commercial imperatives of convergence resulting from digitisation have been overrated and the cultural baggage of the media industries standing in the way of these commercial imperatives underrated.

In contrast to the main thrust of the Initiative, Matthews, Pickering and Kirkland (Chapter 3) focus on larger firms and provide an interesting contrast. The Matthews *et al.* chapter shows that large science- and technology-based companies recognise the importance of having an IP strategy. It also shows that the way in which financial control is assigned can have an important impact on that strategy, so that if the IP budget is devolved to R&D departments, they are likely to evaluate carefully the need to acquire and maintain rights. This, of course, may not be in the overall interests of the company, and higher strategic decision-making is important if short-term cost-cutting is not to lead to errors. This finding is of significance in relation to the Bosworth study which shows that the stock market places value on a company's IPRs (though banks, it seems, do not at present). Similarly, it shows that levels of investment in R&D are reflected in stock market values. In turn, levels of employment are linked to R&D.

Importantly, some *specific* recommendations to policy-makers can be made on the basis of the Initiative:

- The UK Patent Office (and other patent offices around the world) need to make patent databases more user-friendly.
- The Department of Trade and Industry, and other policy-makers, must accept that patent counts are not indicators of the pace of innovation, and that the patent system may be marginal to innovation outside specific sectors.
- The present emphasis at both a UK and a European level on formal mechanisms for protecting commercially valuable knowledge ignores the needs of most SMEs. Future policy must be based on the differing requirements of different industry sectors and company sizes.
- Higher education institutions (HEIs) are unlikely to provide many significant IPRs for business, or get significant rewards from this. The job of HEIs is to produce high-quality graduates who apply their skills in industry.

The findings summarised in the previous paragraph have subsequently been endorsed by the report of the European Technology Assessment Network *Strategic Dimensions of IPRs in the Context of Science and Technology Policy* (an independent report commissioned from a committee of experts by DGXII (as it was then) of the European Commission 1999).

1 Small firms, innovation and intellectual property management

The context and a research agenda

Robert A. Blackburn

This book seeks to bridge three phenomena which are central to the development of capitalism: small firms, innovation and intellectual property management. It may be argued that these areas have received growing analytical attention but few books have addressed all three together. It is a premise of the book that a study of intellectual property management cannot be adequate without a focus on innovation and small firms. This approach should add considerable value to our existing knowledge of the management innovation in small firms and owner-managers' perceptions and management of their intellectual property. In other words, whilst literature abounds on these areas of study, there has been insufficient attention on all three together.

The significance of these phenomena is highlighted in the policy literature. One common theme which recurs through the three literatures is that of *exhortation*. Innovation, we are told, is essential to the competitive performance of firms and the growth of economies (e.g. Freeman and Soete, 1997; Competitiveness White Paper, 1998). It is also considered imperative to protect the intellectual property of innovators to ensure justifiable income streams for effort and to encourage future innovations (Granstrand, 1999). This position has been strengthened in what has been described as the 'pro-patent era' (Granstrand, 1999: Ch. 1). Finally, a healthy small firms' sector and business start-up rate is increasingly regarded as important for a buoyant economy. This is a theme in the growing academic literature (Storey, 1994; GEM, 2002) and has been embedded in a range of policy initiatives including

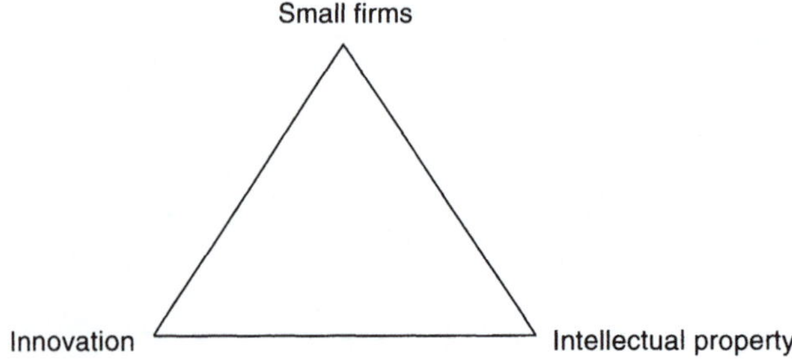

Figure 1.1 The scope of the book.

the establishment of the Small Business Service as a focal point within UK government (e.g. Competitiveness White Paper, 1998; Small Business Service, 2001).

This book does not seek to argue against these common themes: themes which are based on significant and growing literatures in their own right. Instead, it seeks to draw on the three literatures and provide new empirical approaches to understanding innovation and intellectual property management in small firms. This contextual chapter seeks to set the scene for the following more substantial contributions. It aims to provide an overview of the relevant literatures and help set out a context and agenda for subsequent chapters. Hence, the chapter seeks to answer three questions: why focus on small firms? Why study intellectual property? And why address innovation management?

Why small firms in the economy?

The significance of small firms in the economy means that investigations of intellectual property and innovation must take a SME perspective. At the start of 2000, 98 per cent of UK enterprises employed fewer than 20 people (Small Business Service, 2002). Conversely, less than 7,000 enterprises employed more than 249 people (Table 1.1).

The significance of SMEs is not merely a UK phenomenon. The Global Entrepreneurship Monitor (GEM) identified the salience of small firms in mature and developing economies, indicating a positive relationship (though not necessarily

Table 1.1 The number of enterprises, employment and employees in the whole economy by size of enterprise, 2000, UK

	Number			*Percentage*		
	Enterprises	*Employment ('000)*	*Employees ('000)*	*Enterprises*	*Employment*	*Employees*
All enterprises	3,783,429	26,758	23,190	100.0	100.0	100.0
With no employees[1]	2,612,147	3,014	288	69.0	11.3	1.2
Employers	1,171,282	23,745	22,902	31.0	88.7	98.8
1–4	756,710	2,263	1,652	20.0	8.5	7.1
5–9	216,041	1,549	1,407	5.7	5.8	6.1
10–19	114,181	1,598	1,534	3.0	6.0	6.6
20–49	48,877	1,525	1,504	1.3	5.7	6.5
50–99	16,872	1,177	1,173	0.4	4.4	5.1
100–199	8,675	1,211	1,210	0.2	4.5	5.2
200–249	1,759	395	395	0.0	1.5	1.7
250–499	3,779	1,319	1,319	0.1	4.9	5.7
500 or more	4,388	12,707	12,707	0.1	47.5	54.8

Source: Small Business Service (2002).

Note

1 Sole proprietorships and partnerships comprising only the self-employed owner-manager(s) and companies comprising only an employee director.

causal) between economic growth and business start-ups (GEM, 2002). Given the skewness in the size distribution of enterprises towards smaller firms and their importance in innovation, it could be argued that the smaller enterprise offers the crucible for the debates surrounding the usefulness of intellectual property in society.

Some basics: what is intellectual property?

As suggested, the major empirical contribution of this book is on intellectual property in small firms. The literature on intellectual property rights is extensive and here only an overview of the salient concepts of relevance to this book is presented. Those readers looking for more specialist and detailed information are encouraged to examine the Patent Office website (www.intellectual-property.gov.uk) as well as specialist law journals. Intellectual property can be defined as those legal rights, existing under national and international law, assertible in respect of the products of human intellect and creativity. Intellectual property law in the United Kingdom comprises an amalgam of statutes, rules, regulations and orders enacted by statutory instruments and common law, European Union legislation, and international treaties and conventions (Bainbridge 1996). The law offers protection from the wilful misuse of intellectual property whether in the form of theft, imitation or modification; copyright law also protects the rights of the author of a work to be identified as such. Intellectual property rights can be protected, exploited, modified and transferred through contract. Examples include licensing arrangements under which the licensee pays the licensor to exploit the right; the imposition of contractual obligations not to use or disclose information; or restrictive covenants which prohibit employees from establishing rival businesses within a specified period or geographical area.

A more laconic definition of intellectual property suggests that 'it comprises all those things which emanate from the exercise of the human brain, such as ideas, inventions, poems, designs, micro computers and Mickey Mouse' (Phillips, 1986: 3). Intellectual property rights refer to the ability to own and protect the products of human intellect. These rights may have to be applied for and granted, or in some cases, such as with copyright, this arises automatically. Formally, there are four main types of intellectual property protection and these will now be explained briefly.

Patents cover inventions of both new and improved products and processes. They are probably the most publicised and conventional form of protection. Patents are granted to cover new products and processes and in the United Kingdom last for up to 20 years. In order to be patentable an invention must meet various criteria relating to its novelty, inventiveness and industrial applicability. A patent gives the inventor the monopoly right for a limited period to stop others from making, using or selling an invention without the permission of the inventor. In return, the inventor discloses the technical details of the patent to the Patent Office which can be examined by others in society through patent searches. Patenting systems vary throughout the world and their jurisdiction is territorial. In the United Kingdom the patent is granted to the first applicant to file rather than to invent (unlike in the United States).

Patents are usually awarded 18 months after the initial application and cover the four first years from filing. If a patent is to continue after this period an annual renewal fee is required. Normally a patent cannot last beyond 20 years, when the product or process becomes 'free technology' for anyone to exploit.

Patents and levels of patent activity excite interest from government policy-makers as well as a whole patent 'industry' which assists in the filing of patents and patent searches. Estimates suggest that there are more than 4 million patents worldwide, and every year applications are filed for a further 700,000 inventions. Worldwide revenues from patent licensing is estimated at $100bn, 10 times that in 1990 (European Patent Office, 2001).

Trademarks and service marks (usually collectively called trademarks) indicate the origin of goods and services of one trader from others. They are for brand identity, giving the holder the exclusive right to market goods and services under that mark. A trademark aims to protect the reputation and goodwill of a trader. Registration of a trademark requires a sign to be represented graphically in words or pictures. The sign includes words, logos, colours, scents, slogans and shapes and may include sounds and gestures. Registration grants a statutory right, subject to certain conditions, to prevent others from using a trademark without the registered proprietor's permission. The initial period of registration is for 10 years, although this can be renewed for ever provided renewal fees are paid. If an unauthorised use of a trademark is proven then the owner may be able to sue for 'passing off'.

The commercial value of a registered trademark can be considerable, and where a product becomes dominant consumers use the trademark generically – as in thermos, cellophane and aspirin. Non-registration of a trademark does not guarantee protection from infringement although this may be pursued through common law. Registered trademarks are shown by the symbol ® whereas the symbol ™ indicates that the word/logo referred to is not necessarily registered.

Design registration covers the whole or part appearance, distinctive 'look' or 'eye appeal' of a product resulting from features including the 'lines, contours, colours, shape, texture and/or in materials of the product itself and/or its ornamentation' (Patent Office, 2002). Designs are protected by three legal rights in the United Kingdom: registered designs, unregistered designs and artistic copyright. Design registration can provide up to a 25-year monopoly, whilst unregistered designs last for up to 15 years.

Copyright provides protection for the creators of original material, including literature, art, music, sound recordings, films and broadcasts. Computer programmes and databases also come within the scope of copyright (since 1998). Copyright confers two basic rights: a moral right by which the authors (or copyright owners) are entitled to ensure that any use of their work is faithful to the original, and an economic right for their effort to make sure they are paid for the use of their work. Copyright protection is automatic as soon as there is a record, in any fixed form, and exists for 70 years (since 1996) (See Vaver, 1999a for discussion).

Copyright is infringed when an act restricted by copyright in a work is carried out without the copyright owners' permission. A court of law decides whether or not the copyright has been infringed. Copyright has received increased attention, particularly as a result of its relevance to newer industries including computer software programmes and internet-based media, particularly music. As one author highlights: 'Copying, manipulation and distribution of copyright works have been transformed into straightforward, and common, activities' (Griffiths, 1999: 285). As a response to the growth in copying, organisations such as Anti-Copying in Design (ACID) have emerged which seeks to protect members' intellectual property rights.[1] These represent the basic pillars of intellectual property protection in the United Kingdom and should provide sufficient background for what is discussed in this book. However, the area is vast, complex and constantly changing.[2]

The link between innovation and intellectual property: a new focus on small firms

Whilst there is an abundance of descriptions of different types of intellectual property law, the literature on small firms *and* intellectual property is particularly wanting. There is a vast literature on notions of intellectual property, whether protection is justified on the grounds of innovation (e.g. Mansfield, 1986; Vaver, 1999b), raising productivity (Budd and Hobbis, 1989; Greenhalgh and Longland, 2002) and for the dissemination of information (Nicholson Report, 1983). However, in relation to small firms, the literature is limited. This is partly a result of the focus on what is considered to constitute intellectual property, with its historical obsession on patent activity, but also because of the attention given to protection by the corporate sector.

Considerable debate has focused on the economic role of intellectual property in ensuring an economy's competitiveness within the global economy. Increased prominence has been given to the need to protect knowledge assets and produce innovative products in an environment where industrialised economies are exposed to increased competition, not just from each other but from emerging powers in regions such as the Pacific Rim and China. With this has come a renewed emphasis on patenting. Granstrand (1999) describes the 1980s as the 'pro-patent era', during which the economic value of patents and the amount of patent activity increased. Patent activity has excited a great deal of attention by commentators and is frequently used as a comparator for international performance. Often attention focuses on the number of patents filed and this is used as a surrogate for measuring innovative activity. As a result of this perceived connection, explicit attempts at encouraging patent activity have been undertaken by policy-makers. Several commentators have argued that, in this respect, the United Kingdom, and the European Union in general, are losing out in the race to innovate (Walker, 1991; Amendola *et al.*, 1992). Typically, attention is focused on the number of patents filed as an indication of a country's innovative performance (Schwander, 2000). Data shows that the number of first filings has grown faster in the United States and Japan than in the European Union over the past ten years. Even when national and European patent filings are counted, the number of patents and the patents filed per million inhabitants are relatively low in the EU compared with the United States and Japan (Schwander, 2000: Table 2). A striking difference is the number of first filings per million inhabitants. In 1998, Europe produced on average some 263 applications per million inhabitants, while Japan is the clear leader with 2,824 applicants per million inhabitants, followed by the United States with 482 (Schwander, 2000: 4).

Not surprisingly, the European Patent Organisation and the European Commission have been concerned that the above statistics imply that the innovative potential within Europe is not being adequately tapped. Patent offices across Europe frequently argue that the patent system is not being adequately used, leaving considerable numbers of potential innovations unprotected (Hofinger, 1996). Schwander (2000), however, is less alarmist about the data and points out that there is a different culture concerning patenting in Japan, where it is common to file a number of applications for a single invention.

This book takes the argument further and may lead to questions about the need to target SMEs with formal mechanisms for protection. It may be argued that the difference in approaches to the use of the formal intellectual property systems, identified between nation states, is also one of the distinguishing features between small and large firms. Similarly, the relatively low use of the formal systems by small firms may also mean that a reliance on patent counts, etc. is an inaccurate measurement of innovation or research activity. Hence, there is a need to 'unpack' the approaches to innovation and intellectual property management by owner-managers.

There is little evidence on owner-managers' understanding of intellectual property rights and, indeed, this is one area that this book seeks to address. However, the perceived positive link between formal intellectual property protection and innovation is not without controversy (Granstrand, 1999), and is picked up on in this book by Macdonald (Chapter 8). Empirical and theoretical research has offered several arguments in favour of weaker intellectual property protection. One argument hinges on the negative effects of monopolistic behaviour that strong protection permits. Gilbert and Newbery (1982) assert that under some conditions a monopoly may accumulate patents to preserve its power by allowing patents to 'sleep', so as to deter entry into an industry. Even if the system is not abused, it may still be inappropriate or provide too much protection. Vaver (1999b), for example, offers a stimulating discussion of the appropriateness of intellectual property rights as a stimulant to innovative activities. Given the relatively poorer resource base of smaller firms, it could be argued that the formal, fee-based protection system is of greater benefit to larger corporations.[3]

A priori, a number of issues may be identified when examining intellectual property and small firms. These include:

- the level of complexity of formal intellectual property, and conversely the level of ignorance of owner-managers of intellectual property;
- the perceived cost of engagement with the 'industry', including patent offices and patent lawyers;
- the perceived ambiguous link between formal intellectual property protection and innovation;
- the perceived inability of owner-managers adequately to administer and enforce formal intellectual property laws, especially when in conflict with larger organisations;

- the incongruity between formal, bureaucratic, state-based regulatory systems and those based on notions of informality, trust and laissez-faire so common in small firms.

The available research on small firms suggests that business owners are often reluctant to adopt formal rights, such as patents or registered trademarks, primarily because it entails money and time costs to become aware of, acquire, and enforce intellectual property rights (ACOST, 1990; ICIP, 1995; HM Treasury, 1998; Derwent Information, 2001). Other evidence suggests that SMEs rely on more informal methods to protect their intellectual property, such as maintaining a lead time advantage over competitors in bringing new products to market (e.g. Moore, 1996), or through the development of high-trust (Dickson, 1996). These alternative strategies and methods of management fit in with the broader managerial style in small firms (Stanworth and Curran, 1973; Gibb, 2000) which were identified a long time ago and are still as relevant today. An adequate study of the management of intellectual property in SMEs must therefore explore both *formal* and *informal* methods of protection and the rationales of owner-managers for the various approaches adopted.

Why focus on small firms and innovation?

The role of small enterprises in the economy has been the subject of numerous studies and debates, and there is a growing emphasis on the positive role of SMEs in economic development and innovation. Various management literatures indicate that small firms have a crucial role to play in innovation. Some have argued that SMEs provide a disproportionately high number of innovations per employee (Vossen, 1998). However, much of this literature has little or no reference to intellectual property protection and instead has focused on small firms vis-à-vis larger organisations. Schumpeter (1934) pointed out the role of small firms in the 'gales of creative destruction' necessary for innovation and thus economic advancement. However, Schumpeter also argued that larger firms would play a crucial role in 'organising' innovation because of the costs involved and their market power. This resonates with Williamson's (1985) view that alliances between innovative small firms combined with the market advantages of large firms can lead to effective innovation. 'Resource constraints' have been a recurring theme and approach in the analysis of innovation in small firms (see, for example, Hull and Kaghan, 2000).

Overall, the literature here focuses on the advantages and disadvantages for small firms compared with larger firms in the innovation process (see, for example, Rothwell, 1986: 116–17). The perceived advantages and disadvantages of small firms in the innovation process were summarised by Rothwell (1986) and are shown in Figure 1.2.

Of course, such a table is schematic and can only provide a general picture of the advantages and disadvantages for small firms of innovation. Rothwell was careful to point out that 'innovative advantage is unequivocally associated with *neither* larger *nor* small firms' (1986: 118). However, the advantages of larger enterprises tend to be

	Small firms	*Large firms*
Marketing	Ability to react quickly to keep abreast of fast-changing market requirements. (Market start-up abroad can be prohibitively costly.)	Comprehensive distribution and servicing facilities. High degree of market power with existing products.
Management	Lack of bureaucracy. Dynamic, entrepreneurial managers react quickly to take advantage of new opportunities and are willing to accept risk.	Professional managers able to control complex organisations and establish corporate strategies. (Can suffer an excess of bureaucracy. Often controlled by accountants who can be risk-averse. Managers can become mere 'administrators' who lack dynamism with respect to new long-term opportunities.)
Internal communication	Efficient and informal internal communication networks. Affords a fast response to internal problem solving; provides ability to reorganise rapidly to adapt to change in the external environment.	(Internal communications often cumbersome; this can lead to slow reaction to external threats and opportunities.)
Qualified technical manpower	(Often lack suitably qualified technical specialists. Often unable to support a formal R&D effort on an appreciable scale.)	Ability to attract highly skilled technical specialists. Can support the establishment of a large R&D laboratory.
External communications	(Often lack the time or resources to identify and use important external sources of scientific and technological expertise.)	Able to 'plug-in' to external sources of scientific and technological expertise. Can afford library and information services. Can subcontract R&D to specialist centres of expertise. Can buy crucial technical information and technology.
Finance	(Can experience great difficulty in attracting capital, especially risk capital. Innovation can represent a disproportionately large financial risk. Inability to spread risk over a portfolio of projects.)	Ability to borrow on capital market. Ability to spread risk over a portfolio of projects. Better able to fund diversification into new technologies and new markets.
Economics of scale and the systems approach	(In some areas scale economies form a substantial entry barrier to small firms. Inability to offer integrated product lines or systems.)	Ability to gain scale economies in R&D, production and marketing. Ability to offer a range of complementary products. Ability to bid for large turnkey projects.
Growth	(Can experience difficulty in acquiring external capital necessary for rapid growth. Entrepreneurial managers sometimes unable to cope with increasingly complex organisations.)	Ability to finance expansion of production base. Ability to fund growth via diversification and acquisition.
Patents	(Can experience problems in coping with the patent system. Cannot afford time or costs involved in patent litigation.)	Ability to employ patent specialists. Can afford to litigate to defend patents against infringement.
Government regulations	(Often cannot cope with complex regulations. Unit costs of compliance for small firms often high.)	Ability to fund legal services to cope with complex regulatory requirements. Can spread regulatory costs. Able to fund R&D necessary for compliance.

Figure 1.2 Advantages and disadvantages of small and large firms in innovation.

Source: Rothwell (1983).

Note: The statements in brackets present areas of potential *disadvantage*. Abstracted from Rothwell and Zegveld (1982).

in financial and technical resources (material), whilst in smaller firms they are in flexibility and adaptability (behavioural). Clearly also, in relation to intellectual property, it is asserted that small firms struggle in engaging with the patent system (Figure 1.1).

One problem with such a scheme is that it fails to account for variation. The contributions of small firms to innovation vary immensely. Small firms are *not* a homogenous category and their economic role in progress is diverse. Many small firms are not involved in innovation and instead survive by operating in specific geographic or market niches (Storey, 1994). Rothwell (1986), for example, classified small firms according to the products they manufacture and the markets they serve. These included: SMEs in traditional sectors; 'modern', niche-strategy SMEs; and new-technology-based firms (NTBFs). Rothwell also emphasised the complementarities of large and small firms in the innovation process rather than merely considering them as separate entities. A focus on NTBFs has continued with subsequent contributions from Oakey *et al.* (2000). Whilst this approach is a major contribution to understanding the different contributions that SMEs have in the innovating process, it has focused on high-technology-based enterprises, even though, as Cobbenhagen has pointed out, 'innovation is certainly not the exclusive concern of high-tech firms' (Cobbenhagen, 2000: 33). Thus, whilst making a significant contribution to understanding the innovation process, the literature has tended to focus on technology-based activities, rather than wider approaches to innovation in small firms. In addition to this limitation, criticisms of the innovation management literature have shown that it tends to be based on project-orientated studies, over-focused on manufacturing, sector-specific and limited to specific larger size types (Cobbenhagen, 2000: 32–6).

A great deal of the literature on innovation emphasises innovation networks and inter-firm co-operation. Small firms often become involved with external parties in the innovation process because of their internal resource constraints or particular expertise which is valuable to others. This literature has often alluded to the informal and embedded nature of intellectual property management within this process.

However, although the literature on 'innovation networks' is voluminous (see Johannisson, 2000; Barnett and Storey, 2000), there is little on the potential threats to a firm's intellectual property as a result of co-operating with other businesses (Biemens, 1992). Engagement with others, either informally or formally, may require some exposition of the firm's intellectual property. More recently, the networking literature has emphasised notions of 'trust'. For smaller firms in particular, trust is essential for the maintenance of these networks:

> Practitioners in general and entrepreneurs in particular rely mainly on tacit knowledge, which is mainly transmitted through metaphors, hands-on demonstrations and mentorship. . . . Elaborate tiers, such as those provided by a personal network, are needed to make the learning processes work. The trust embedded in individual tiers and the network at large generally represents social capital, which gives access to all other kinds of resources and capital . . .
>
> (Coleman, 1989)

. . . and also helps overcome institutional barriers.

(Johannisson, 2000: 371–2)

Johannisson suggests that despite these perceived advantages of networking, informal ties may be preferable to small firms than formal ties (such as having an external member on their board or even venture capital) because of the 'perceived high costs and unwillingness to disclose business secrets and the need for power and control' (p. 373). Despite such assertions, it is fair to summarise that a fundamental gap exists in the literature on how small business owners protect their intellectual property when involved with external organisations. This leads to a subsequent question: to what extent is the owner-managers' fear of loss of intellectual property rights inhibiting the collaborative and subsequent innovation process?

Conclusions and a research agenda

The literatures on small firms, intellectual property and innovation management are vast and span a variety of disciplines. Yet the absence of any serious attempt to bridge the literatures represents a fundamental weakness in our understanding of small firms' management of intellectual property and innovation. A number of questions emerge from this overview to form the basis for a research agenda. What are owner-managers' understanding of the intellectual property system? How useful do they perceive this to be in their day-to-day activities? What are their experiences of using formal systems of protection? Do business owners recognise intellectual property assets? Do owner-managers make links between innovation and formal intellectual property rights? Do business owners perceive threats to their intellectual property? How do they seek to protect their intellectual property? What are the inter-industry differences in the relevance and practices of intellectual property management in small firms? What special intellectual property issues are raised in collaborative ventures? What are the barriers to further engagement in the formal intellectual property system? Is exhortation to engage with formal rights desirable?

Whilst the answers to these questions cannot be covered in a single volume, the following chapters make a major contribution to answering some of them. Policy-makers should pay attention to them if they are to raise the efficacy of formal intellectual property systems for SMEs. For researchers, this book is a starting point. Much of the material proffered in the book is empirical because of the dearth of evidence. In this light, it has provided a foundation for subsequent research and theorising to help our understanding of intellectual property management in small firms.

Notes

1 For example, ACID has around 900 member companies including textile designers and manufacturers, jewellers, furniture manufacturers, fashion designers and so on. The organisation seeks to educate and change attitudes in design-led companies in order to combat design theft (see ACID, 2001).

2 See the Patent Office for more information. There are also a number of specialist intellectual property groups, including the Oxford Intellectual Property Research Centre (www.oiprc.ox.ac.uk).

3 The argument that firms innovate, in part, to secure monopoly power also has important ramifications for relationships between the developed and developing world. For example, Primo Braga (1990) argues that enforcement costs for strong intellectual property protection can be high, and since foreigners hold the bulk of patents in developing countries, these costs may simply lead to increased royalty gains for foreigners and greater royalty expenses for nationals in developed economies.

References

ACID (2001) 'Commission It Don't Copy It', *ACID News*, 10, May, Anti Copying in Design, London.

ACOST (1990) *Developments in Biotechnology*, Report of Advisory Council on Science and Technology, HMSO, London.

Amendola, G., Guerrieri, P. and Padoan, P. (1992) 'International Patterns of Technological Accumulation and Trade', *Journal of International Comparative Economics*, 1, 173–97.

Bainbridge, D. I. (1996) *Intellectual Property*, Pitman, London.

Barnett, E. and Storey, J. (2000) 'Managers' Accounts of Innovation Processes in Small and Medium-Sized Enterprise', *Journal of Small Business and Enterprise Development*, 7 (4), 315–24.

Biemans, W. G. (1992) *Managing Innovation Within Networks*, Routledge, London.

Budd, A. and Hobbis, S. (1989) *Co-integration, Technology and Long-Run Production Function*, discussion paper 10, Centre for Economic Forecasting, London Business School.

Cobbenhagen, J. (2000) *Successful Innovation Towards a New Theory for the Management of Small and Medium-Sized Enterprises*, Edward Elgar, Cheltenham.

Coleman, J. S. (1989) 'Social Capital in the Creation of Human Capital', *American Journal of Sociology*, 94, Supplement, 95–120.

Competitiveness White Paper (1998) *Our Competitive Future*, cmnd 4176, Department of Trade and Industry, London.

Derwent Information (2001) 'The Patenting Process; For SMEs Does Size Really Matter?', *IP Matters Derwent Information*, July (www.derwent.com/ipmatters/research/smes2.html).

Dickson, K. (1996) 'How Informal Can You Be? Trust and Reciprocity Within Co-operative and Collaborative Relationships', *International Journal of Technology Management*, 11, 129–39.

European Patent Office (2001) *The European Patent Organisations, The World of Patents, Latest Figures 2000*, European Patent Office, Munich.

Freeman, C. and Soete, L. (1997) *The Economics of Industrial Innovation*, Pinter, London.

GEM (2002) *Global Entrepreneurship Monitor*, 2001 Executive Report, Kauffman Center for Entrepreneurial Leadership at the Ewing Marion Kauffman Foundation, Kansas.

Gibb, A. A. (2000) 'SME Policy, Academic Research and the Growth of Ignorance: Mythical Concepts, Myths, Assumptions, Rituals and Confusions', *International Small Business Journal*, 18 (3), 36–50.

Granstrand, O. (1999) *The Economics and Managements of Intellectual Property*, Edward Elgar, Cheltenham.

Greenhalgh, C. and Longland, M. (2002) 'Running to Stand Still? – Intellectual Property and Value Added in Innovatory Firms', *Oxford Intellectual Property Research Centre*, St Peters College, Oxford.

Gilbert, R. J. and Newbery, D. (1982) 'Pre-emptive Patenting and the Persistence of Monopoly', *American Economic Review*, 72, 514–26.

Griffiths, J. (1999) 'Holding Back the Tide – A Review of Recent Developments in Copyright Law in the United Kingdom', *International Review of Law, Computers and Technology*, 33 (3), 283–301.

HM Treasury (1998) *Innovating for the Future: Investing in R&D*, HM Treasury/DTI, London.

Hofinger, S. (1996) 'Determinants of an Active Patent Policy – An Empirical Study', *European Patent Convention Information*, 3, 91–8.

Hull, R. and Kaghan, W. N. (2000) 'Innovation – But For Whose Benefit, For What Purpose?', *Technology Analysis and Strategic Management*, 12 (3), 317–25.

ICIP (1995) *Use and Exploitation of Intellectual Property by Small Firms*, HMSO, London.

Johannisson, B. (2000) 'Networking and Entrepreneurial Growth', in D. L. Sexton and H. Landström (eds) *The Blackwell Handbook of Entrepreneurship*, Blackwell, Oxford.

Mansfield, E. (1986) 'Patents and Innovation: An Empirical Study', *Management Science*, February, 173–81.

Moore, B. (1996) 'Sources of Innovation, Technology Transfer and Diffusion' in A. Cosh and A. Hughes (eds) *The Changing State of British Enterprise*, ESRC Centre for Business Research, Cambridge University, Cambridge.

Nicholson Report (1983) *Intellectual Property and Innovation*, HMSO, London.

Oakey, R., During, W. and Kipling, M. (2000) *New Technology Based Firms at the Turn of the Century*, Elsevier Science, Amsterdam.

Patent Office (2002) What Is Intellectual Property or IP? (Patent Office website: http://www.intellectual-property.gov.uk).

Phillips, J. (1986) *Introduction to Intellectual Property Law*, 3rd edn, Butterworth, London.

Primo Braga, C. A. (1990) 'The Developing Country Case For and Against Intellectual Property Protection', in W. E. Siebeck (ed.) *Intellectual Property Rights: Global Consensus, Global Conflict?*, Westview Press, Boulder, CO, 69–87.

Rothwell, R. (1983) 'Innovation and Firm Size: A Case of Dynamic Complementarity', *Journal of General Management*, 8 (3).

Rothwell, R. (1986) 'The Role of Small Firms in Technological Innovation', in J. Curran, J. Stanworth and D. Watkins (eds) *The Survival of the Small Firms*, vol. 2, Gower, Aldershot.

Rothwell, R. and Zegveld, W. (1982) *Innovation and the Small and Medium-Sized Firm*, Frances Pinter, London.

Schumpeter, J. A. (1934) *Theory of Economic Development*, Harvard University Press, Cambridge, MA.

Schwander, P. (2000) 'Is European Innovation Really Lagging Its Competitors?', (www.derwent.com/ipmatters/statistics/00113-Lies.html).

Small Business Service (2001) *Think Small First*, Small Business Service, Sheffield.

Small Business Service (2002) *Small and Medium Enterprise (SME) Statistics for the UK, 2000*, Small Business Service, Sheffield.

Stanworth, M. J. K. and Curran, J. (1973) *Management Motivation in the Smaller Business*, Gower, Epping.

Storey. D. J. (1994) *Understanding the Small Business Sector*, Routledge, London.

Vaver, D. (1999a) 'Recent Copyright Developments in Europe', notes for a session at the International Conference on 'The Commodification of Information', Faculty of Law, Haifa University, May.

Vaver, D. (1999b) 'Intellectual Property: Where's the World Going?', seminar paper 19 January, *Oxford Intellectual Property Research Centre*, St Peters College, Oxford (www.oiprc.ox.ac.uk/Seminar0199.html).

Vossen, R. W. (1998) 'Relative Strengths and Weaknesses of Small Firms in Innovation', *International Small Business Journal*, 16 (3), 88–94.

Walker, W. (1991) *From Leader to Follower: Britain's Dwindling Technological Aspirations*, SPRU mimeo, University of Sussex, Brighton.

Williamson, O. E. (1985) *The Economic Institutions of Capitalism: Firms, Markets, Relational Contracting*, Free Press, New York.

2 Innovation, intellectual property and informality

Evidence from a study of small enterprises and some implications for policy[1]

John Kitching and Robert A. Blackburn

Introduction

Despite a good deal of evidence indicating the need to understand intellectual property management in small firms, little is known about how SME owners attempt to protect their knowledge assets using intellectual property rights. Small businesses, it is argued, face problems of cost, complexity, time, the need for secrecy and difficulty in enforcing intellectual property rights (ACOST, 1990; ICIP, 1995; CBI, 1997; HM Treasury/DTI, 1998) and, as a consequence, do not protect or exploit their knowledge assets and innovations fully (Cabinet Office, 1983; DTI, 1986; ICIP, 1995). Instead, small business owners tend to protect their innovations through non-legal means, such as maintaining a lead time advantage over competitors (Moore, 1996) and developing high-trust relations in business transactions (Dickson, 1996).

Recent reforms to the legal framework were also expected to benefit small businesses and encourage them to engage more actively in the legal system. Reforms include: the reduction in patent, registered design and trademark fees implemented in October 1998; the provision of free internet access to the UK patent, designs and trademarks registers and recent European and Patent Co-operation Treaty applications; and changes introduced in December 1999 aimed at simplifying and speeding up legal protection applications and dispute procedures.

Intellectual capital, innovation and intellectual property

In order to contribute to an understanding of intellectual property rights in the small firm, it is important initially to undertake some definitional and conceptual ground clearing. Intellectual capital comprises the knowledge, skills and other intangible assets which businesses can convert into usable resources to generate a competitive advantage (Albert and Bradley, 1996; Teece, 2000). This is embedded in the firm's products, services, working routines and branding. Innovation can be defined as the commercial exploitation of intellectual capital. Intellectual property can be defined as those legal rights, existing under national and international law, which can be asserted in respect of intellectual capital and its products and which entail legal sanctions for their infringement. Such rights might require formal registration with the relevant national or international authorities, arise automatically without registration, be created through contractual relations with others or exist under common law. Some forms of intellectual capital can be protected as intellectual property: for example, design images, engineering drawings, software code, confidential technical, market or customer information, and trademarks indicating the origin of goods and services. But not all intellectual capital and the products or working practices within which it is embedded can be protected by law. Knowledge which is in the public domain, for example, cannot be protected as intellectual property, yet it may be of considerable economic value to businesses. Clearly, the types of intellectual capital, and its products, will vary depending on business owners' particular products and processes.

Business owners need not, however, attempt to protect their innovations using the intellectual property rights framework. There are several reasons why innovations may not be protected using intellectual property rights, each with distinct implications for policy-makers wanting to promote greater use of such rights among small business owners. First, business owners may not be aware that particular innovations can be protected using intellectual property rights. The policy implication here is to raise business owners' awareness of intellectual property issues and the rights potentially available to them. A second reason might be that many innovations cannot be protected by intellectual property rights because they do not fall within the scope of intellectual property law.[2] For example, it might not be possible to obtain a patent for a particular product because it does not meet the statutory criteria of being new, involving an inventive step and of being capable of industrial application. In this situation policy-makers might consider extending the range of intellectual property rights, though of course any such extension would have to be tempered by a concern not to restrict competition. Third, business owners may be aware of the rights framework but decide not to protect innovations as intellectual property. This approach may be adopted for a number of reasons. They may, for example, prefer to keep innovations secret rather than attempting to protect them with patents, as this would require disclosure, the formula for the Coca-Cola drink perhaps being a famous example. Alternatively, business owners may feel that the benefits of intellectual property rights do not outweigh the costs and risks associated with their acquisition and enforcement. These business owners may prefer instead to allocate their limited resources to the development and commercial exploitation of innovations rather than their protection. Here, policy-makers could reduce the costs associated with the acquisition and enforcement of intellectual property rights to affect owner-managers' calculations concerning take-up of the rights. Fourth, business owners might sell their intellectual property rights to others rather than retain them. This seems likely where the economic value of the right is limited, perhaps because products and services are unique to a single customer. For instance, designers may assign copyright over images to clients because replication for others is either impossible or undesirable.

The purpose of this chapter is to examine the relationship between innovation and intellectual property in SMEs and to draw out some implications for policy. The chapter addresses the following questions. How, if at all, do SME owners attempt to exploit and protect their innovations? Are owners of innovative enterprises more likely to use legal methods to protect their innovations than less innovative business owners? Does the legal framework of intellectual property rights encourage or hinder innovation in small businesses? Do owners of innovative enterprises have different views of the legal framework compared with less innovative business owners?

Research methodology and sample construction

To address these research questions, a study was carried out of small businesses in four sectors, in which a variety of intellectual property issues might be expected to arise: *computer software* (Standard Industrial Classification (SIC) 1992: class 72); *design* (SIC: codes 74.20, 74.40 and 74.84); *electronics* (SIC: classes 30–3); *mechanical engineering* (SIC: classes 28–9).

Data were obtained from a two-stage research design:

1 a telephone survey of 389 SME owner-managers in the four sectors (the telephone survey); and
2 subsequent face-to-face interviews with 99 of these owner-managers (the interview survey).[3]

To carry out the telephone survey, a sampling frame was constructed using a Dun and Bradstreet commercial database, Yellow Pages and other business directories, to avoid the bias inherent in using a single source. The enterprises studied were legally independent, employing less than 250 full-time employees or their equivalents (FTEs),[4] and divided between the four sectors. A response rate of 71.5 per cent was achieved. The telephone survey elicited quantitative data on the perceived threats to SME owner-managers' specialist and confidential knowledge, the methods used to protect that knowledge, the factors limiting the use of formal methods, the incidence and character of any legal action taken to protect the firm's knowledge, and on owner-managers' perceptions of the influence of the legal framework on product development. The interview survey generated qualitative data on the extent to which intellectual property issues were a major concern for owner-managers, their motivations for using particular practices to protect their knowledge, and their perceptions of the legal framework. Interview sample respondents were selected from among those indicating that their firm's products depended on specialist or confidential knowledge and hence were potential users of intellectual property rights.

Both the telephone and interview samples were heavily skewed towards the smaller end of the size spectrum, as is the UK enterprise population (DTI, 2002a). Over half of the telephone sample respondents owned enterprises employing less than ten FTEs, and their average (mean) size was 18.3 FTEs (Table 2.1).

Table 2.1 Size distribution of telephone sample enterprises by sector and enterprise size (%)

Size category (FTEs)	*Design*	*Electronics*	*Mechanical engineering*	*Software*	*ALL*
Micro (0 < 10)	47.7	54.2	60.2	54.4	54.4
Small (10 < 50)	47.7	30.2	35.0	37.9	37.4
Medium (50 < 250)	4.7	15.6	4.9	7.8	8.2
All	100.0	100.0	100.0	100.0	100.0
Mean size (FTEs)	16.9	21.6	14.0	20.8	18.3
N	86	96	104	103	387

Source: Telephone survey.

Note

Employment figures include owners and employees. Part-time workers are treated as half a full-time equivalent. Some columns do not sum to 100 per cent due to rounding. Precise employment data is missing for two enterprises; hence mean size data is for 95 electronics and 103 mechanical engineering enterprises.

Threats to knowledge

In the telephone survey, 72 per cent of respondents reported that their products, services or methods of working were dependent upon specialist or confidential knowledge. These respondents were asked about the threats to this knowledge, their use of intellectual property rights and other informal practices to protect this knowledge. Respondents were questioned about whether they perceived various parties as potential threats to their specialist or confidential knowledge (Table 2.2). The vast majority of respondents (92 per cent) reported at least one threat to their knowledge. Loss of knowledge via the departure of key personnel was the most commonly reported threat: 68 per cent reported it as a threat and 43 per cent reported it as the most important threat. Six in ten cited competitor copying as a threat. Threats from collaborators, customers and suppliers were less frequently reported.

The interview data demonstrated that owner-managers valued their specialist and confidential knowledge as their most significant asset, without which the business would not exist. But, surprisingly, in spite of the importance business owners attached to their knowledge, most were not particularly concerned about the potential for its loss, imitation or unauthorised use by others. Evidence from other sources suggests that counterfeiting and piracy are widespread. The Alliance Against Counterfeiting and Piracy estimates that counterfeiting costs the UK economy over £8.5bn a year (DTI, 2002).

Respondents' experience of knowledge loss was, in most cases, limited and, as a result, they perceived the risk of future loss as low. Many business owners acknowledged that copying, theft and unauthorised use occurred, but treated the continued survival of the enterprise as evidence that such losses were not critical. Moreover, several respondents anticipated positive consequences arising out of intellectual property loss. For example, it could be used as a means of marketing the firm's products. Frequently there was a recognition among business owners that the

Table 2.2 Perceived threats to specialist and confidential knowledge

	% of sample reporting as a reason	*% reporting as 'most important' reason*
Any threat	92.1	–
Departure of key staff	68.2	43.3
Competitor copying	62.8	22.4
Collaborator firms	40.1	5.4
Customers	36.5	10.5
Suppliers	20.9	0.4
Other threat	9.0	4.3
No main threat	n/a	10.8
No data	n/a	2.9
N	277	277

Source: Telephone survey.

diffusion of knowledge within the industry could be beneficial and that they were often able to take advantage of *others'* knowledge loss.

A framework for understanding knowledge protection practices

Businesses can adopt a variety of practices to exploit and protect their knowledge; these can be represented along a continuum categorising different practices according to their legal formality (Figure 2.1). At the left pole of the continuum is the *do nothing* approach where business owners do not consciously implement *any* practices specifically to protect their innovations, a position unlikely ever to occur in practice. *Informal* practices are extremely varied. Examples include: building specialist know-how into products to restrict the possibility of reverse engineering; regulating access to information or, alternatively, disseminating knowledge within the business to avoid dependence on particular individuals; or, joining or using an organisation whose purpose is to protect the interests of intellectual property owners, such as the Federation Against Software Theft. What these informal practices have in common is that they do not directly entail the creation of legal rights. Instead, the management of intellectual property is embedded in other activities, including human resource management practices. This does not, however, mean legal sanctions are irrelevant to the use of informal practices. Trade secrets, for example, may enjoy protection under the law of breach of confidence. *Formal* practices entail the deliberate creation of legal rights. This category can be sub-divided into two: those rights requiring registration (patents, registered designs, registered trade and service marks), and those rights created through other means such as contract or which arise automatically (such as copyright). Clearly, these types of practice are not mutually exclusive. Business owners can, and do, use a mix of informal practices and legal rights to protect their knowledge and the innovations it generates. An adequate explanation must account for how and why small business owners attempt to protect their intellectual property in the ways they do.

Type of practice	*'Do nothing'*	*'Informal protection practices'*	*'Non-registrable legal rights'*	*'Registrable intellectual property rights'*
Examples	No conscious strategy to protect intellectual property	Develop high-trust relations with customers, suppliers and employees Maintain lead time advantage over competitors Build specialist know-how into products Member/user of an organisation which seeks to protect intellectual property	Confidentiality clauses and restrictive covenants in customer, supplier and employment contracts Prominent copyright notices Licensing Restricted publication Unregistered design/ design right	Patents Registered design Registered trade and service marks
		Increasing legal formality ——→		

Figure 2.1 A continuum of intellectual property protection practices.

The preference for informal protection practices and the selective adoption of intellectual property rights

The study highlighted a number of key findings. First, small business owners adopt a wide range of practices to protect their innovations. Telephone survey respondents reported using a wide range of informal practices and legal methods for protecting their specialist or confidential knowledge (Tables 2.3 and 2.4). Respondents were asked whether various types of practice were used to protect specialist and confidential information. Nearly all respondents reporting that their products relied on specialist or confidential knowledge (98 per cent) reported at least one informal practice for protecting knowledge, and 87 per cent reported at least one legal method. Only four respondents reported no protection practices at all – the 'do nothing' approach. Most respondents (86 per cent) used both legal and informal methods.

Second, the interview data showed that informal protection practices were preferred to formal, legal methods. Specifically, practices such as creating high-trust relations with customers and suppliers, maintaining a lead time advantage over competitors in bringing products to market, and operating in niche markets were perceived by most respondents to be of greater importance. Such practices were not used purely to protect knowledge but also to exploit it. Indeed, these practices constituted a key component of SME owners' broader competitive strategies. By using informal knowledge protection practices, SME owners saw themselves as less vulnerable to its loss or unauthorised use and, consequently, they perceived formal rights as offering fewer benefits. These informal practices were embedded within the businesses' customary working routines, and served a variety of purposes; business

Table 2.3 Use of informal intellectual property protection practices by level of 'innovativeness' (%)

	'Non-innovative'	*'Moderately innovative'*	*'Highly innovative'*	*All*
Trust relationships that ensure specialist knowledge is not stolen	77.8	78.0	81.7	79.1
Maintaining a lead time advantage over competitors	48.1	60.7	70.7	62.5
Building in specialist know-how	25.9	57.7	68.3	57.8
Occupying a market niche	25.9	53.6	72.0	56.3
Copy protection[1]	75.0	45.8	62.5	53.2
Spread information across staff	29.6	51.8	58.5	51.6
Limited key information to selected staff	33.3	38.1	48.8	40.8
Membership of an association	11.1	23.2	20.7	21.3
Threat of bad publicity	14.8	20.8	18.3	19.5
Dongles[1]	25.0	11.6	17.6	15.4
DACS[2]	40.0	10.4	13.6	13.0
Other informal method	7.4	7.7	17.1	10.5
N	27	168	82	277

Source: Telephone survey.

Notes

Respondents were asked, 'Do you use any of the following to minimise threats to the specialist knowledge or confidential knowledge that your business has?', and they were then offered a list of practices. Includes only those respondents reporting that their products, services or methods of working were dependent on specialist or confidential knowledge.

Column percentages do not sum to 100 due to multiple responses.

1 'Copy protection' and 'dongles' only prompted for electronics and software respondents.

2 'DACS' only prompted for design respondents.

owners perceived them as familiar and not requiring additional resources. The limited number of known cases of loss or unauthorised use of the firm's knowledge buttressed owner-managers' confidence in the efficacy of informal practices.

Third, small business owners were extremely selective in the adoption of intellectual property rights. Although a large majority of business owners reported the use of legal methods to protect their knowledge, and 53 per cent reported registrable rights (patents, registered design, trade or service marks) (Table 2.4), the interview data clearly demonstrated the relative *un*importance of legal rights. Most commonly, respondents reported the use of contract to protect their knowledge. At first sight, these data may appear to suggest that intellectual property rights were important to business owners, but these figures merely relate to the percentage of business owners who *ever* use a particular method. They are not very sensitive indicators of the *importance* of the particular method in any particular business. On the contrary, the interview data suggests that SME owners were extremely selective in their adoption of intellectual property rights requiring registration. Most tended to obtain such rights only under very specific conditions: where they anticipated high commercial benefits from the exploitation of innovations; where they believed that formal intellectual property rights offered superior protection to informal methods; and where they possessed the necessary resources to acquire formal rights.

Table 2.4 Adoption of formal intellectual property rights by level of 'innovativeness' (%)

	'Non-innovative'	*'Moderately innovative'*	*'Highly innovative'*	*All*
ANY FORMAL RIGHT	59.3	85.7	97.6	86.6
ANY REGISTRABLE RIGHT	25.9	50.0	67.1	52.7
Trade or service mark	17.4	38.8	57.7	42.5
Registered design	4.5	22.2	37.2	25.2
Patent	17.4	21.5	38.2	26.1
ANY NON-REGISTRABLE RIGHT	59.3	82.7	95.1	84.1
Confidentiality clauses in customer and supplier contracts	29.6	63.7	67.1	61.4
Confidentiality clauses in employment contracts	37.0	55.4	74.4	59.2
Prominent copyright notices	30.4	56.1	66.2	56.8
Licensing	39.1	34.0	53.8	40.4
Restricted publication	21.7	34.4	44.7	36.3
Unregistered design/design right	13.0	28.1	33.8	28.5
Other formal method	0	1.7	5.9	2.9
N	27	168	82	277

Source: Telephone survey.

Note

Respondents were asked, 'Which of the following strategies do you use to protect your specialist and confidential knowledge?' and they were then offered a list of strategies. Includes only those respondents reporting that their products, services or methods of working were dependent on specialist or confidential knowledge.

Column percentages do not sum to 100 due to multiple responses.

Business owners sought to adopt registrable rights where they perceived the potential benefits as outweighing the potential costs. The benefits of such rights depended on there being a big enough market to protect. Where the business served a small, niche market, respondents often had little incentive to invest resources such as time, money and effort in obtaining registrable rights.

> We regard putting a patent on anything as a total waste of time. If you have got an idea get it made, market it and our marketplace is too small anyway for the big boys to be too worried about. It is not as though we are selling to the general public, that's a different issue. We did try. About 10 years ago we had an idea and did all the things like not telling anybody and keeping it to ourselves and got involved with a patent agent but he more or less said: 'There is no point in doing it. It is a waste of time' . . . Because there [were] no patentable items in the design as far as he was concerned. It just cost a lot of money and [was a] waste of time. We could have got in and got the product sold. That was what it was all about . . . We just carried on making the damn thing and if people copy it they copy it. There is not an awful lot you can do, not in such a small marketplace. If you are talking about a major product which is going to go to the domestic marketplace that is an entirely different matter as far as we can see . . . If the world is your customer then you want to protect your ideas to make sure you get the

> maximum return from it. But if the customer is a very limited number of people then it is not worth all the hassle. Just get on and do it.
>
> (J29: owner-manager, mechanical engineering, 15 workers)

> We've been very selective about what we have applied for patents for in the past because the sheer cost of maintaining these which rises steeply over [the] years. We knew we couldn't afford to patent absolutely everything that we felt needed defending. So we would select the prominent ones and even while we were doing that we were mindful that we just didn't want to give away details of certain items. We would take the risk of not patenting it, using prior knowledge as defence, as a protection . . . I think we've got a policy that any other means of protection other than patent first. Patent is a waste of time . . . It's only worth investing in a patent if you can afford to fight it. It may do some good in other terms, of frightening people off to see a patent number on it, but the man that's really going to run with it, to take it is the guy that's going to look at you. He's going to get the D&B [Dun & Bradstreet database] out, which tells you everything about the company . . . So they look in there and they say, 'Oh yes, we can squash this one out. They won't be able to find the resources'. And truly they can't.
>
> (J9: owner-manager, electronics, 49 workers)

The costs of obtaining, maintaining and enforcing registrable rights in terms of money, time and effort were often perceived by business owners as prohibitively high. Such costs might include not only application and renewal fees but also the services of a patent agent to conduct a patent search and prepare an application. Registration costs were perceived as particularly high where the business required protection in more than one country.

> Taking protection is quite time consuming and costly. Possibly [being] time consuming is rather more important than the cost in that regard. In our instance, one of the difficulties in taking protection – and patents are the obvious one that comes to light – is the nature of our business, in that it is worldwide. And once you get that far, the cost and the complexity of taking out worldwide patents is very questionable . . . In our case, the obvious place to take a patent is the UK but actually it's the smallest of our markets so, in our case, I am not sure the government can do very much. What I would have said is that if there were such a thing as a worldwide patent then, yes, that would be a big advantage, but I am not sure that that is a realistic thing for me to say.
>
> (W40: owner-manager, mechanical engineering, 96 workers)

But the key factors in the decision *not* to adopt registrable rights concerned the financial cost of enforcement and the risk of failure. Many respondents, even those in 'highly innovative' enterprises, felt that without sufficient resources to pursue lengthy litigation, probably against larger, much wealthier organisations, the value of registrable rights was limited. Owner-managers also reported doubts about whether registrable rights could provide effective protection. Concern about financial costs combined with the risk of failed litigation persuaded many respondents to be wary of the supposed benefits of registration.

> Obviously, it is prejudiced against the small company because of costs involved. Costs of a patent are much higher for a small company. I think one of the reasons we are not very keen on patents is they are expensive to service initially and certainly on an annual basis, renewal fees. And if someone infringes it then you have got to have quite a substantial funding behind you to be able to defend it. If a big company goes after it and it goes to the High Court, you could be looking at a £50,000, £100,000 bill and to offset that you have got to weigh up the risks of whether or not you are going to win and who is going to pick up the costs. Patents are OK but unless you have the funding to defend it then you have got to be slightly cautious about whether or not it is worth it.
>
> (WP17: owner-manager, electronics, seven workers)

A further factor militating against the adoption of intellectual property rights was the requirement to disclose the technical details of innovations to obtain patents. Clearly, there is a risk that others will appropriate the knowledge embedded in the disclosed product in spite of the protection afforded by the law. This raises the issue of how small business owners should respond when they feel their intellectual property rights have been infringed. The following director of a 'highly innovative' electronics company considers the range of issues relevant to taking out a patent.

> The process of actually going and applying for a patent actually then puts your particular design into the public domain because you've then got to do a patent search to see if somebody else has done it. So you go to the patent office and say, 'well, here's a design which we're about to put into manufacture' and having done so, everybody else can then look at it. And if they're particularly unscrupulous, they might decide they're going to do it anyway on the basis of 'well, they won't be able to sue me will they? It will take them time to find out'. So it's questionable really. You have to be pretty convinced that what you've got is first of all special, secondly patentable, and thirdly that if you patent it you are prepared if somebody copies it to take legal action. And if you're not prepared to take legal action and you're not prepared to go and pursue anybody who copies it, then don't bother to waste your time. So it's then got to be something that is, if you've gone down that route then you must have made a decision that that particular invention or whatever that you've got is actually capable of making you a lot of money. It's no good patenting something that wouldn't make you a lot of money because there's no point in patenting it.
>
> (J16: owner-manager, electronics, 91 workers)

SME owners' reluctance to become embroiled in the law was also evident in their responses to perceived losses of specialist or confidential knowledge. There were limits to respondents' capacity and/or willingness to litigate against reputed infringers. Only 6 per cent of owner-managers reported actual litigation although a further 8 per cent reported out-of-court settlements. The costs associated with undertaking legal action – money, time, difficulty of establishing infringement, risk to commercial reputation – in relation to any benefits were, in most cases, felt to prohibit litigation. Once theft or copying had occurred, for most SMEs, there was usually no serious question of litigation to obtain a remedy. Instead, formal rights were treated primarily as *deterrents* rather than as potential means of seeking legal redress for infringement. Respondents adopted formal rights primarily to deter misuse or theft, or to be able to threaten litigation. The use of prominent copyright notices, trade, patent and registered design marks were used by business owners to indicate to others the proprietary character of their products to deter copying or theft. Deterrence was a key objective even among 'highly innovative' business owners as the following remarks indicate:

> In many instances I will apply for a patent, even knowing that maybe there is some aspect that will stop me from getting one, because it gives me breathing space for a couple of years. I had an instance in America fairly recently where we had made an application for a patent which was a little bit possibly dicey as to whether we would actually get it, and one of our American customers who was using our product showed us a product [of] which one of his friends in the Far East had produced a copy. We told him that we had a patent application in America and that was enough for him to drop that particular idea of using a copy of our product because he knew that if we got that patent then we would be after damages from him for loss of business going back from the time he started to use another person's product. I understand the way that this thing works and you can get retrospective damages as well. That actually has some teeth but, of course, you have got to have the patent in the long term. Whether you get it or not is another matter. Getting a patent is not that easy. You have got to have something that is sufficiently innovative and you have got to be able to have the ability to protect the particular bits that you consider important. You can't always get that.
>
> (W35: owner-manager, electronics, 27 workers)

While there are potential benefits of registrable rights, business owners were selective about their adoption. The apparent contradiction between the quantitative telephone sample data and the qualitative interview data can be accounted for in terms of the importance attached to registrable rights and not just the frequency of their adoption. Though many SME owners reported the use of registrable rights to protect products and processes, many had strong reservations about the costs and effectiveness of such methods. Even owners of 'highly innovative' enterprises were critical of rights requiring registration and, consequently, very judicious in the adoption of such rights. For most business owners, the adoption of formal IPR was to deter rather than punish infringement.

Innovativeness and knowledge protection

Businesses differ in the extent to which they can be described as 'innovative'. Wood (1997), for example, distinguished six types of innovative SME on the basis of the existence and novelty of innovations introduced, and the proportion of business sales comprised by new or upgraded products.[5] A similar procedure has been adopted here to create an 'innovativeness' index, the aim being to examine whether there is a relationship between level of 'innovativeness' and the use of various practices to protect specialist or confidential knowledge. Telephone sample respondents were distinguished according to their responses to questions concerning the uniqueness of their products/services and methods of working, and the introduction during the previous two years of any new or significantly modified products/services or methods of working. Three sub-groups were differentiated:

1. *highly innovative* businesses – reported the introduction of new or significantly modified products/services *and* the introduction of new or significantly modified methods of working during the previous two years; and, *either* reported unique products/services *or* unique methods of working ($n = 89$, 23 per cent of telephone sample).
2. *moderately innovative* businesses – reported either the introduction of new or significantly modified products/services *or* the introduction of new or significantly modified methods of working during the previous two years *or* that they had unique products/services or methods of working ($n = 235$, 60 per cent of telephone sample).
3. *non-innovative* businesses – did not report unique products/services or methods of working *and* had not introduced new or significantly modified products/services *and* had not introduced new or significantly modified methods of working during the previous two years ($n = 65$, 17 per cent of telephone sample).

There was considerable sectoral variation in the level of 'innovativeness'. Over a third (36 per cent) of mechanical engineering businesses were categorised as 'non-innovative' compared with between 8–10 per cent of businesses in the other three sectors. Many mechanical engineering businesses manufactured products to customer drawings, the copyright residing with clients, *not* the sample firm.

'Highly innovative' businesses were more likely to report the use of all of the formal intellectual property rights and more of the informal practices than 'non-innovative' firms (Tables 2.3 and 2.4). For instance, 71 per cent of 'highly innovative' business owners reported maintaining a lead time advantage over competitors in introducing new products, compared with only 48 per cent of 'non-innovative' owners. Such practices enable the firm to exploit knowledge commercially before it becomes widely circulated in the public domain and are particularly appropriate in conditions of rapid market and technological change. The following designer and manufacturer of electronic control instrumentation emphasised the importance of introducing new products, while at the same time highlighting the problems with formal rights, in particular the financial cost of litigation to enforce rights:

> What we tend to do now is to say: 'Let's not waste any time or money on registering design or getting patents raised. Let's get products out there, get them in the market, be first, hit the market and get on with the next one'. We have found that that works quite well for us. We don't feel that we get sufficient protection from patents and registered designs. There's really no point in us going in for them . . . Probably about 2 or 3 years ago, we were working on a product which was our own funded development and we looked at patenting it and we were into £5,000 or £6,000 and we felt that although it was useful to have that patent it wasn't really going to be of any value to us and the best thing to do was to get out into the market. If you have got a patent and somebody breaches your patent you have then got to go after them and you have got legal costs and all the rest of it and it is not worth it. It really isn't worth it. The cost of doing that is enormous and the time that it involves . . . It takes energy out of selling the product or developing new products and we felt that we didn't want to put energy in that area. We wanted to put the energy into getting the products out and developing them.
>
> (J11: owner-manager, electronics, five workers)

'Highly innovative' businesses were more likely to use formal rights than 'non-innovative' firms (Table 2.4). Not surprisingly, adoption of registrable intellectual property rights was positively associated with 'innovativeness'. 'Highly innovative' firms were more likely to encounter the conditions under which business owners choose to adopt formal rights, particularly regarding expectations of commercially exploitable innovations. This argument should not, however, be pushed too far. Like their less innovative counterparts, owner-managers of 'highly innovative' firms preferred informal protection methods too.

'Highly innovative' enterprises tended to be larger in employment terms, which was also associated positively with adoption of formal rights (Kitching and Blackburn, 1998), and therefore they were more likely to encounter the conditions under which formal protection seemed more effective. Furthermore, both software and electronics firms were more likely to be 'highly innovative' and to be larger in employment terms. In software, licensing arrangements, under which software copyright owners permit clients to use software, have become an industry standard and even very small businesses adopt the practice. Thus the relationship between the adoption of formal intellectual property rights does vary according to size of enterprise but this relationship is not universal, as it is compounded by the sector in which the enterprise operates.

Innovation and owners' perceptions of the legal framework: some implications for policy

A key concern for policy-makers is whether the intellectual property rights framework facilitates or hinders innovation by SMEs. Too little protection may prohibit innovation; too much protection may restrict the diffusion of innovation and stifle competition. Where it is believed that the legal framework provides insufficient protection, an argument can be made for policy to intervene to offer greater protection to innovators. Where the legal framework is thought to suffice, then it is harder to support a case for intervention. Scarce public resources may be better allocated to achieve policy objectives by other means, or to achieve other policy objectives.

The results presented here demonstrate that most owner-managers perceived the law as largely irrelevant to their innovation. Only 16 per cent of telephone sample respondents whose products were dependent on specialist or confidential knowledge reported that the law encouraged product development; nearly three-quarters (72 per cent) reported that the law had no effect on their product development. Nor were 'highly innovative' business owners more likely to view the impact of the legal framework in a more positive light; business owners classified as 'moderately innovative' were the most likely to do so (Table 2.5).

Data from the telephone survey indicated that those respondents using legal means to protect their specialist and confidential knowledge were only marginally less likely than others to believe that the legal framework had no effect on product development. Among those using registrable rights, 71 per cent reported the legal framework had no effect, compared with 73 per cent of those without registrable rights. A similar picture emerged of non-registrable rights: 72 per cent of users of these rights and 77 per cent of non-users felt the legal framework had no effect on their product development. It should be noted, however, that the proportion of respondents claiming that the legal framework encouraged product development was higher among adopters/users of legal rights than non-adopters/users. For instance, 20 per cent of adopters of registrable rights reported that the legal framework encouraged product development whereas only 11 per cent of non-adopters did so. Users of non-registrable rights were more likely to claim the legal framework encouraged product development than non-users by a margin of 17 per cent to 7 per cent. Though policy-makers may take encouragement from these figures, the overwhelming message is one of owner-managers' indifference to the

Table 2.5 Effect of legal protection on product development by level of 'innovativeness' (%)

	'Non-innovative'	*'Moderately innovative'*	*'Highly innovative'*	*All firms*
No effect	70.4	69.0	79.3	72.2
Encourages innovation	7.4	19.0	11.0	15.5
Discourages innovation	11.1	7.1	7.3	7.6
Don't know/no answer	11.1	4.8	2.4	4.7
N	27	168	82	277

Source: Telephone survey.

Note

Respondents were asked, 'Overall, do you feel that legal protection encourages, discourages or has no effect on the development of new products, services or methods of working in your firm?' Includes only those respondents whose products or services depended upon specialist or confidential knowledge.

legal framework. Most business owners feel it neither supports nor hinders their innovative efforts.

When the link between the legal framework and innovation was probed in more depth in face-to-face interviews, even those respondents who had earlier reported the positive impact of the legal framework on their product development became equivocal about its influence. Though some respondents in the software sector argued that without the legal framework their industry would not exist, the majority of business owners perceived the law to be an irrelevance. While such views reflect the taken-for-granted character of intellectual property law, founded in part on business owners' limited contact with it, they also demonstrate that legal concerns were not paramount in decisions to create, develop and exploit new products and processes. Moreover, many business owners reported that legal rights could not provide effective protection from the unauthorised use, imitation or theft of intellectual property.

Overall, the data suggest there is no major gap or only a minor deficiency in the intellectual property rights framework for small business owners. The limited use and significance of intellectual property rights requiring registration has not had an adverse impact upon innovation in small enterprises. Asked if the legal framework encouraged, discouraged or had no effect on product development, the following owner of a 'highly innovative' software business reported:

> It certainly doesn't encourage it. I would say it generally has no effect. If anything it would tend to discourage because for most people there is no protection. If you had an idea and wanted some software and you put an idea out in the market, a new IT idea, it is very difficult to protect, very difficult, and most people feel that. And I feel that our idea could be ripped off any day and we would have almost no protection. Somebody could do almost exactly what we are doing and one suspects that when the thing came to court, if you took them to court, they might win because they were different in one tiny aspect. And, at the end of the day, it is who pays most to lawyers as to who wins the case, so I would say that in most people's opinion the law gives you no protection whatever and doesn't necessarily have any effect.
>
> (J32: owner-manager, computer software, four workers)

For most firms, product development work is undertaken without legal protection though in some instances respondents reported they would not pursue a project without legal protection. In such cases, the legal framework can be seen as enabling certain kinds of innovation which would not have occurred otherwise. Such cases were rarely expressed. Factors other than the legal framework were perceived by business owners as having a greater influence on innovation. Respondents felt that the major constraint on their product development arose from a lack of other resources, notably finance for investment or expansion.

> The very fact that I am pausing must mean that it [the legal framework] has no effect because I don't perceive a great effect. I certainly don't think it

> encourages. I wish there was something to encourage. If you ask us why we are not developing more new products, the primary answer, of course, is lack of resources for investment. But then probably the next answer after that is that you just wonder how worthwhile it would be and might there be easier ways of making a living . . . I guess it discourages. That is not to say I have any good ideas about how you could make a better one.
>
> (J8: owner-manager, computer software, nine workers)

> It [growth of the firm] has not been limited by lack of protection for ideas. It has been limited by lack of funds for development. It is very difficult in this country to get money for smaller developments. If you have a wonderful thing that is going to make millions then it may be a different matter. There are people who have money to put into wonderful ideas that are going to turn into a large business and make lots of money. The usual problem with those is that they want a large slice of the action for doing it. However, if you have a smaller idea that needs some funding, say a few tens of thousands, then it is much more difficult to get that funding. It is partly a size problem because if the amount of money is relatively small then very few people are willing to expend the effort to evaluate the ideas.
>
> (W37: owner-manager, electronics, two workers)

Instead of acquiring and enforcing intellectual property rights to protect *existing* products, SME owners preferred to allocate resources to the development of new product and process innovations. They viewed acquiring formal registrable rights as an inferior use of the firm's limited resources.

> We tend to be very focused on supplying good value product to a customer, getting it there on time or getting the development done quickly so that they can get to market on time. I think that that is the biggest issue, is being there, doing it and the bureaucracy doesn't add to the sale of the product. It doesn't add to the value. It just diverts you from going out there and selling it or developing it or whatever. Leave the bureaucrats to sit there and push paper about. We will put together products and put them out to the market and sell them.
>
> (J11: owner-manager, electronics, five workers)

Contrary to the opinions of policy-makers, there is little evidence overall that the level of take-up of registrable rights has had an adverse impact upon innovation in small enterprises. The vast majority of business owners, even those of 'highly innovative' enterprises, reported that the rights framework had *not* restricted their product development. Most considered the legal intellectual property rights framework to be of limited relevance to the conduct of their business and few suggested how the law could be reformed to serve their interests better. Though any policy which reduces the money, time and other costs associated with obtaining registrable rights would benefit some SME owner-managers, because few would undertake litigation to enforce their rights owing to the perceived risks, such reforms are unlikely to increase take-up of formal rights significantly. Initiatives aimed at making enforcement simpler, cheaper and more likely to result in success are likely to be more attractive to small business owners.

Factors other than the legal framework were seen as greater influences on the firm's capacity to innovate, most notably the availability of resources for investment. Consequently, policy-makers may be better advised to target scarce public resources at encouraging the creation and exploitation of new products and processes, rather than at the protection of erstwhile innovations. Indeed, the Smart programme aims to do just that. However, given the large number of small businesses in the UK economy, such a programme is unlikely to be able to reach more than a very small proportion of innovating enterprises.

Conclusions

SMEs are often at the forefront of product and process innovations. But business owners may not attempt to protect their innovations using formal intellectual property rights. Business owners may be unaware that innovations can be protected; specific innovations may not fall within the scope of legal protection; or, alternatively, business owners may choose not to use legal methods to protect their intellectual property. SME owners are able to protect some innovations using legal mechanisms, both through contract and through rights requiring registration. In general, however, owner-managers preferred informal protection methods. Such practices were cheaper, embedded in the firm's everyday routines and, for the most part, perceived as successful. In contrast, legal rights, particularly those requiring registration, were generally viewed by owner-managers as costly to acquire and enforce in terms of money, time and risk to commercial reputation, and frequently perceived to be of limited efficacy. The primary function of intellectual property rights was to act as a deterrent to infringement rather than as a means of seeking compensation or boosting innovation. Small business owners have exhibited similar attitudes towards other government initiatives aimed at formalising what are perceived by government as informal and sub-optimal practices: for example, regarding the quality standard ISO 9002 (North *et al.*, 1998).

'Highly innovative' firms, though more likely to use legal methods to protect intellectual property than 'non-innovative' business owners, were not markedly more enthusiastic regarding their adoption. A higher proportion of these owners acquired registrable rights, as they were more likely to develop new products and processes. They were, however, very critical of the cost of enforcing such rights and were doubtful about the possibility of successful litigation against suspected infringement. Even 'highly innovative' business owners were selective, and to some extent reluctant, adopters of registrable rights.

The evidence suggests that access to and use of intellectual property law is not widely regarded as an impediment to innovation by SME owners. While there may be some instances where a business owner decides not to innovate without some form of legal protection – usually those projects perceived as riskier or more expensive – these examples seem to be few and of limited significance. Even in these cases, contractual mechanisms in the form of non-disclosure agreements, licensing arrangements and, to a lesser extent, restrictive covenants in employment contracts, were preferred to rights requiring registration. For most business owners, developing and exploiting new products and processes took place without too great a concern for the legal framework.

For policy-makers, the implications are mixed. Policies to help overcome the barriers to using registrable rights, real and perceived, would have only a limited impact on take-up by SMEs. It will take a great deal of effort on the part of policy-makers, and a dramatic decline in the efficacy of informal methods, to encourage owner-managers to move away from their present reliance on informal practices to protect their specialist and confidential knowledge towards legal protection mechanisms. Yet policy-makers should not be too concerned that what *they* may perceive as a low level of adoption is restricting the development of new products and processes. Most small business owners did not view it in this way. The limited impact of suspected loss, imitation or unauthorised use of knowledge served to restrict business owners' desire to obtain registrable rights. Policy-makers may do better to allocate resources to support new innovations rather than to protect existing innovations.

Notes

1 The authors would like to thank the Economic and Social Research Council for funding this study (Grant No. L325253004).
2 Conversely, some business owners may enjoy the protection of the law for some of their products and processes, yet not define themselves as particularly innovative. For example, in design and software businesses where new design images and new or upgraded software products are created frequently, these products may enjoy copyright protection even though such business owners do not view these activities as particularly innovative.
3 The research findings reported were part of a broader research programme. Face-to-face interviews with 18 'collaborators' with the interview sample respondents were also conducted; these are not reported here.
4 Part-time workers are counted as half a full-time equivalent worker.
5 The six types were: 'product and process originators'; 'product originators'; 'process originators'; 'product and process imitators'; 'incremental product and process imitators'; and 'occasional imitators'.

References

Advisory Council on Science and Technology (ACOST) (1990) *The Enterprise Challenge: Overcoming Barriers to Growth in Small Firms, Report of Advisory Council on Science and Technology*, HMSO, London.

Albert, S. and Bradley, K. (1996) *Intellectual Capital as the Foundation for New Conditions Relating to Organizations and Management Practices*, Open University Business School Research, Working Paper Series 96/15.

Cabinet Office (1983) *Intellectual Property Rights and Innovation*, cmnd 9117, HMSO, London.

Confederation of British Industry (CBI) (1997) *Tech Stars*, CBI, London.

Department of Trade and Industry (DTI) (1986) *Intellectual Property and Innovation*, cmnd 9712, HMSO, London.

Department of Trade and Industry (DTI) (2001a) *Small and Medium Enterprise (SME) Statistics for the UK* (available at www.sbs.gov.uk/statistics).

Department of Trade and Industry (DTI) (2002b) 'Don't be Duped by the Counterfeit Cheats', DTI press release, 17 December 2002, available at (http://www.gnn.gov.uk/gnn/national.nsf/TI/FCE931A84618D52B80256C920038DBD0?opendocument).

Dickson, K. (1996) 'How Informal Can You Be? Trust and Reciprocity Within Co-operative and Collaborative Relationships', *International Journal of Technology Management*, 11, 129–39.

Hayward, P. A. and Greenhalgh, C. A. (1994) *Intellectual Property Research Relevant to Science and Technology Policy*, ESRC, Swindon.

HM Treasury/DTI (1998) *Innovating for the Future: Investing in R&D*, HM Treasury/DTI, London.

Kitching, J. and Blackburn, R. (1998) 'Intellectual Property Management in the Small and Medium Enterprise (SME)', *Journal of Small Business and Enterprise Development*, 5 (4), 327–35.

Inter-departmental Committee on Intellectual Property (ICIP) (1995) *Use and Exploitation of Intellectual Property by Small Firms*, HMSO, London.

Moore, B. (1996) 'Sources of Innovation, Technology Transfer, and Diffusion', in A. Cosh and A. Hughes (eds) *The Changing State of British Enterprise*, ESRC Centre for Business Research, Cambridge.

North, J., Blackburn, R. and Curran, J. (1998) *The Quality Business*, Routledge, London.

Rothwell, R. (1983) 'Innovation and Firm Size: A Case for Dynamic Complementarity', *Journal of General Management*, 8 (3).

Rothwell, R. and Zegweld, W. (1982) *Innovation and the Small and Medium Sized Firm*, Frances Pinter, London.

Teece, D. (2000) *Managing Intellectual Capital*, Oxford University Press, Oxford.

Wood, E. (1997) *SME Innovator Types and Their Determinants*, working paper 72, ESRC Centre for Business Research, University of Cambridge.

3 A strategic approach to managing intellectual property

Duncan Matthews, John Pickering and John Kirkland

Introduction

The extent to which competitive, technology-based companies invest in research and development has assumed increased policy significance in recent years. To ensure continued investment in research and development, firms need the incentive of sufficient commercial returns in order to make future investment worthwhile (for a wider discussion see Taylor and Silberston, 1973; Mansfield, Schwartz and Wagner, 1981; Levin, Klevorick, Nelson and Winter, 1987). As part of a strategy of bringing sophisticated technology-based products to market ahead of competitors and ensuring significant commercial returns, intellectual property plays an important role in corporate planning (see, for instance, Nevens, Summe and Uttal, 1990). When successfully used, an intellectual property strategy will ensure that competitor firms will encounter barriers as they attempt to enter a pioneering firm's markets (see Tran, 1995). The barrier created by a corporate intellectual property strategy means that competitors lose valuable time in being able to launch their own products, allowing the innovative firm a temporary market share so as to recoup its investment in research and development and achieve a profit margin significant enough to encourage future investment.

A corporate strategic plan is likely to address four aspects of a company's intellectual property: patents, trademarks, copyright and trade secrets. Although these four strands of intellectual property have common characteristics, the balance of their importance to individual companies will vary. They also differ from each other in that patents protect functional and design inventions, trademarks commercial indications of origin and identity, copyright creative expression, and trade secrets the protection of ideas, know-how and the property interests of the firm.

This chapter reports on a study conceived at the National Institute of Economic and Social Research in London to identify the main determinants of intellectual property strategy in research-intensive companies based in the United Kingdom (for a full description of the research, see Pickering, Matthews, Wilson and Kirkland, 1998). The study set out to gather evidence from individual companies by undertaking a programme of face-to-face interviews to identify the similarities and differences in the management of corporate intellectual property and test whether intended best practice is borne out by actual strategies adopted by managers within firms.

Between June 1996 and July 1997, the research team interviewed 56 managers who held a variety of posts in the 18 large research-intensive companies. These included research and development staff, commercial managers, patent agents, marketing managers and external collaborations managers. Since the companies were selected to identify the most effective mechanisms used to manage intellectual property, the sample particularly focused on large, research-intensive firms with an established record of managing intellectual property. The sample of companies was compiled after consulting the industrial liaison officers of five UK universities, each of whom had considerable experience in negotiating collaborative research agreements with the private sector, and they provided advice on the profiles of large research-intensive firms (see Pickering, Matthews, Wilson and Kirkland, 1999).

This chapter reports the results of the research, identifying the factors that lead to the formulation of corporate intellectual property strategies; the common characteristics of intellectual property strategy in large UK companies; the way that companies learn and adapt in relation to intellectual property; and the messages that the study provides for research-intensive small- and medium-sized enterprises (SMEs).

This chapter focuses on one particular aspect of intellectual property that is of particular concern to research-intensive companies: patents. There are three essential statutory requirements that must be met if an invention is to be patentable: novelty, utility and non-obviousness of the subject matter over prior art. Patents seek to provide sufficient incentives for invention, while at the same time providing for widespread diffusion of benefits by conferring a temporary monopoly (normally 20 years) in return for a public disclosure intended to ensure access to the benefits (for a more detailed discussion of the role of patents, see Levin, Klevorick, Nelson and Winter, 1987).

In particular, we take the view that the factors which determine corporate intellectual property strategies are 'people' issues – the corporate view will be the sum of its employees' perceptions of what the priorities should be. Various types of employee will have views on the value of legal protection, competitor strategies, etc. and the company as a whole will respond with a strategy based on its interpretation of the information and views supplied by the various individuals involved.

How a company interprets information and takes decisions on intellectual property strategy is itself a complex issue. Personnel with different responsibilities in a company will have different viewpoints on the role and importance of intellectual property. These views may all need to be taken into account – company strategy on intellectual property is, in this sense, the result of a series of prior decision outcomes taken within the organisation.

By acknowledging the importance of different types of individuals within a company, we will identify who the 'key actors' are within large UK companies. We will then examine how these actors determine an organisation's strategy on intellectual property through a process of interaction and decision making by staff who hold different responsibilities within a firm.

The chapter will then illustrate what type of corporate strategies typically emerge from these internal decision-making processes, identifying how large research-intensive UK companies are currently behaving in terms of managing intellectual property.

As well as giving something of a 'snapshot' in time as regards identifying intellectual property strategy in UK companies, we have sought to go rather further than a simple description of current practice. We have sought to do this because corporate intellectual property strategy is not static. It is constantly changing and evolving as companies respond to new threats, opportunities and experiences, reappraising how effective its approach has been and observing how other organisations have responded differently in the same circumstances. This is what we have termed a process of 'corporate learning'. The chapter will therefore examine how companies learn (and relearn) to manage intellectual property as part of a dynamic process of revision and refinement. Our argument is based on the premise that companies are always willing to learn from past experience and improve on existing company practice. How this process of learning is undertaken by a company is often of key importance in determining what corporate intellectual property strategy will actually emerge.

Identifying intellectual property

The first task in the development of a corporate intellectual property strategy is that of identifying what the firm's intellectual property actually is. This may be either an on-going or a one-off activity. Since all the firms surveyed operate in research-intensive industries, they tended to stress that identifying new intellectual property was an on-going process that all company personnel were engaged in. These companies felt that their employees, particularly research and development (R&D) staff, had a good understanding of the value of intellectual property to the organisation and were aware of the importance of alerting their line managers when the circumstances arose. Intellectual property was seen as being so crucial to their core business activities and profitability that these firms felt awareness of intellectual property was an integral part of the corporate culture and not a separate activity to be dealt with only by staff with direct responsibility for intellectual property management.

An alternative approach to the on-going monitoring of intellectual property opportunities might involve regular formal audits of an organisation's intellectual property portfolio, either on a one-off or on a regular basis. Audits allow companies to find out what they own, what licensing agreements exist, how much maintaining their intellectual property portfolio costs and whether these assets are being used effectively.

The advantage of conducting an intellectual property audit is that it requires firms to think rationally about whether they are best utilising the intellectual property that they hold. This is particularly true of patent portfolios, where renewal fees can be paid without serious consideration of whether a particular patent is being used in products on the market, is likely to used in the future, could be a source of income if licensed out, or is simply useful as a way of preventing competitors from gaining market access. By reviewing the value of intellectual property portfolios, audits can help firms reduce costs and maximise the potential of their existing intellectual property.

Few of the firms surveyed, however, claimed to have ever considered an audit of intellectual property and only one of the firms said that it had actually undertaken an audit in the past. Even that firm had not repeated the exercise again in later years.

The generally held view is that audits are only carried out when they are triggered by irregular events, such as merger or acquisition (see, for instance, Spelman and Moss, 1994), seems to be borne out by these findings.

In large part, the reason why intellectual property audits are often absent from the strategies of companies is precisely because the process of reviewing and assessing the potential of intellectual property is on-going, an integral part of the day-to-day management of the organisation rather than a separate task carried out only infrequently.

Formulating a corporate intellectual property strategy

Formulating a strategy depends on how different company employees view the importance of intellectual property, how those individuals interact with one another, what outcomes emerge from those interactions and ultimately where the overall responsibility for intellectual property strategy lies. Our view is that the task of identifying the various categories of people, and the various interests they represent within a company, is crucial to understanding how corporate strategy on intellectual property actually works in practice. From our interviews with R&D staff, commercial managers, patent attorneys, legal advisers and academic liaison officers it was clear that each of these groups of people often had different perceptions about the role and importance of intellectual property, even when we were talking to members of staff within the same organisation. As they described to us their own involvement in the corporate management structure and their own views on the importance of intellectual property, it also became clear that each category contributed to the type of decisions that were ultimately being taken.

R&D staff

Our survey looked particularly at firms with a recognised strength in research and development. It is perhaps not surprising, then, that personnel involved in taking the inventive step and taking the lead in subsequent development work were generally well aware of the importance of patent protection and considered it an indication that their work was eliciting successful innovation outcomes. Since research and development were central to core business activities, R&D staff seemed well aware of the importance of the legal protection of intellectual property, not only as a measure of their own performance, but for company performance in a wider sense. So, for example, the importance of keeping well-documented laboratory notebooks, so as to comply with the 'first to invent worldwide' provisions of US patent law, was widely known, if not always adhered to.

On the face of it, companies had few problems in convincing their R&D staff to be aware of the importance of intellectual property. Staff induction and training programmes often contained an 'IP awareness' element which bolstered the corporate culture of attaching importance to intellectual property. Staff were particularly aware of the sensitivity of pre-patented information which could be commercially sensitive and appreciated the importance of confidentiality in these circumstances. They did not, however, receive financial remuneration to supplement the provisions of the UK statutory scheme, since they were generally seen as being employed to produce inventions.

Where companies did differ from one another was in the extent to which R&D staff were either passive recipients of the company's strategy on intellectual property or actively involved in day-to-day decisions on corporate intellectual property strategy. In none of the cases were R&D staff solely responsible for decisions on issues such as when to file for patent, whether to renew patents or when to launch and market products reliant on new patents. Rather, these decisions relating to patenting strategy were the prime responsibility of the company's patent attorneys who would, to varying degrees, act on the advice of R&D staff (and commercial managers).

In most cases their R&D expertise played an integral part in the company's process of managing intellectual property and the value of scientists and engineers to the company was well appreciated. Despite not always playing a formal role in intellectual property decision making, the technical expertise of R&D staff was nonetheless needed on a practical level to help in drafting the patent application. In many respects, R&D staff were particularly enthusiastic in advocating that patenting should take place, especially where the number of patents applications on which a member of the R&D staff is a named inventor, was taken into account in staff appraisal and career progression.

Commercial managers

'Commercial managers' is a generic term used to describe a broad category of generalist managers that we interviewed in large UK companies. They possessed a variety of job titles and were located in various departments within the organisation. Yet they had in common the fact that they normally took primary responsibility for assessing the potential commercial value of the invention and advising whether the patent application being proposed by the R&D staff was actually worth investing in. After the initial application for a patent has been filed, it was the commercial managers who were likely to take primary responsibility for strategic decisions on the geographical coverage of patent protection, patent renewal and enforcement actions. These decisions were often taken in consultation with the company's patent attorneys and legal advisers.

It was the commercial managers who also took the lead on decisions about the exploitation of intellectual property, particularly when to launch products containing new patents, when to consider the life of earlier patented products to be at an end and how this strategy relates to competitor companies and key geographical markets.

Patent managers

Most large research-intensive UK companies have dedicated patent departments in-house (sometimes these departments also undertake trademark and copyright work and are known as 'intellectual property departments' to reflect their wider responsibilities). Patent departments are generally staffed by qualified UK patent agents and European patent attorneys. They take the lead in formulating the company's strategy on intellectual property and ensuring that new inventions identified by R&D staff and considered significant by commercial managers receive adequate legal protection.

Patent managers are normally qualified patent agents or attorneys who are also involved in enforcement litigation when patent infringement occurs. Patent attorneys (and company lawyers) tend to take a more pessimistic view than commercial managers about the viability of engaging in enforcement litigation, particularly in overseas jurisdictions but, while most companies attempt to avoid litigation due to the costs involved, the generally held view is that court action should be used as a last resort when defending patents. This is necessary to maintain the credibility of the organisation in the eyes of its competitors.

Patent staff also have the important task of building up and maintaining a high level of awareness about the importance of intellectual property amongst R&D and commercial staff. Most patent/intellectual property departments host IP awareness seminars and produce guidance notes for researchers and managers. This work is in addition to the on-going contacts that patent staff maintain with researchers and managers to ensure that inventions of significance receive adequate protection. However, attempts to raise intellectual property awareness through guidance notes and training sessions are not always successful. Publishing a manual with advice for employees is all very well but, in practical terms, it will only be useful if it is actually read.

The role of patent managers in liaising with other company personnel is often crucial in getting this message across. In many ways, the patent manager is reliant on the researcher responsible for the invention for technical expertise during the patent filing stage. In some companies there is a relationship of co-existence between R&D staff and patent managers which is emphasised by the fact that the latter are assigned to a particular research group so as to become familiar with their area of technical specialisation, and they develop a good working relationship with the research staff involved.

Integrating patent managers fully in the inventive and patenting processes also ensures a greater degree of continuity for long-term patenting strategy. Researchers may easily leave the organisation and take their intimate knowledge of the patented invention with them. Ensuring that a wider range of company personnel have detailed knowledge of the patent specification helps to ensure that a safety net is provided so that detailed technical knowledge can be readily available if patent infringement or patent renewal decisions arise in the future.

In recent years, there has been a trend for companies to relocate patent managers away from the research environment, bringing them closer to the legal department in the sense that both are now treated as a corporate function, to be drawn on as a central resource. While this may make perfect sense in terms of management structures, financial accountability and communication routes, it also carries with it the danger that patent managers may not be sufficiently close to corporate R&D staff to ensure a good working relationship. The implications for future patenting strategies will be interesting to observe. Locating patent managers further away from the research environment may also have implications for the role of cost allocation in patenting strategy. This issue is discussed in a separate section later in this chapter.

Legal advisers

Corporate legal departments, often augmented by independent legal advisers bought in by the company on a case-by-case basis, play a greater role in the implementation of intellectual property strategy than in its formulation. They do so in two respects: (i) in enforcement actions and dialogue with a view to seeking dispute settlement terms (such as cross-licensing agreements) with other firms when patent infringement has been detected; and (ii) in the conduct of contractual negotiations leading to research being placed with universities or other organisations. Many firms, however, acknowledge that corporate lawyers may not be best placed to deal with intellectual property. While corporate lawyers interface with commercial and patent managers on litigation decisions, and are involved in general contractual negotiations on behalf of the company, few lawyers have detailed knowledge of intellectual property law and even fewer have first-hand experience of patent litigation or the issues arising when negotiating collaborative research agreements with other organisations. Seeking the expertise of barristers with specialist knowledge of patent infringement cases is often advisable where company lawyers have little or no direct practical experience of intellectual property cases.

External collaborations managers

Managers responsible for a company's external collaborative research, undertaken in partnership with other firms or academic institutions, become involved with intellectual property strategy to the extent that collaborative research agreements normally include contractual arrangements on who would own intellectual property resulting from the work. With regard to the role of academic liaison officers responsible for managing a company's collaborative research with universities, the key relationships are those between the academic liaison officer and the company scientist, on the one hand, and between the academic liaison officer and the commercial manager on the other. The role of external collaborations managers in managing corporate intellectual property is discussed in detail by the authors elsewhere (Pickering, Matthews, Wilson and Kirkland, 1998; Kirkland, Matthews, Pickering and Wilson, 1998). This chapter will now focus instead on the internal organisational aspects of intellectual property management.

Internal organisation for intellectual property management

Budgetary arrangements and the role of cost in intellectual property strategy

The recent trend for the services of patent/intellectual property departments to be treated as a corporate function has meant that intellectual property services may then be used by operating groups or cost centres within the company as and when the need for expertise arises, either by purchasing the services from head office, or by using it as a free resource. Even when in-house intellectual property expertise must be purchased from the centre, these costs are normally provided at a lower cost than from commercial patent agents. Company patent specialists also have the advantage over private firms of patent agents that they have a detailed knowledge of the operating group's overall intellectual property strategy to ensure a better 'fit' between the requirements of the recipient firm and the services it provides.

Most company patent departments are not, however, profit centres in their own right, and are either funded from the overall R&D budget or are centrally funded as a corporate function. When patent search and filing costs and patent renewal fees are borne by research and development or commercial cost centres, there are considerable pressures to discard (potentially valuable) intellectual property in the interests of prudent financial control. The existence of devolved budgets therefore has important implications for company decisions on intellectual property, although corporate funding is often provided for litigation arising from patent infringement.

Appropriate financial arrangements need to be made by companies, either in the form of a specific budget allocated for intellectual property and held by a central patent department, or clear provision for intellectual property protection in the overall budgets of R&D departments or operating companies.

It is common in large companies to reappraise the value of particular intellectual property assets, in particular patents, as part of a wider financial review of corporate performance, either on a quarterly or an annual basis. Budgets for R&D and patent departments are generally reviewed at the end of each financial year. In the months preceding the end of the financial year, the department responsible for paying patent renewal costs (normally either R&D and or the patent department) will engage in a detailed process of reviewing whether particular patents are still useful to the organisation and whether they are worthy of continued expenditure.

If the patents held are not supporting products already on the market, that review process is taken one stage further with research and commercial managers contacted to ask whether or not they would object to a patent being abandoned in order to reduce the overall budget for renewal costs. Companies use different procedures to ascertain whether or not it is worthwhile to continue paying: for example, renewal fees on a particular patent. These range from quite sophisticated intranet-based procedures whereby early warning of the intention to abandon a patent is given to the appropriate R&D and commercial managers on a worldwide basis, through paper-based systems where forms must be countersigned by the appropriate research and commercial managers before the patent department will take the decision to abandon a patent, to relatively informal procedures where a patent manager within the firm will simply discuss with the appropriate R&D staff and commercial managers whether or not they consider a particular patent to be worthwhile.

Despite a wide range of review procedures used by the companies included in our sample, each company shared the belief that patents should on no account be abandoned if there was any degree of uncertainty as to whether it might be useful to the company in some form. This was often particularly difficult to ascertain when the company operated as a group with several businesses in separate, but related, industry sectors. In such cases it was particularly important that patents held by one business were made available to others in an operating group of trading companies before they were abandoned in order to make a saving in renewal fees. This requires a high degree of co-ordination at group level by a central patent department with the strategic overview and understanding of the individual trading companies.

The firms surveyed for this research stressed that patents would rarely be abandoned simply to reduce costs. Where any element of doubt remained about whether a patent should be abandoned or not (for example, if certain sections of the business had failed to indicate that the patent was no longer useful to them), all the companies said that they would err on the side of caution, continuing to pay patent renewal fees until a categorical decision had been made that the patent was no longer required. This particularly applies to defensive patenting, where the payment of renewal fees is made in preference to letting the patent lapse, with the danger that the out-of-patent invention may subsequently be taken up and exploited by a rival firm.

On occasion, a company chairman or CEO may query a perceived high level of corporate expenditure on patent renewal fees for intellectual property not being used in any of the products that a company has on the market. We learnt of one such case where a board-level enquiry had led to research and commercial managers considering the abandonment of potentially valuable patents as a cost-saving exercise. In the event, however, the patent department of the company concerned was able to justify the expenditure in terms of the range of medium-term strategic opportunities that a patent portfolio could offer the firm. The chairman of that company was subsequently satisfied that a patent-rich portfolio was in the wider interests of the firm and became convinced that patents should not be abandoned simply as part of a cost-cutting exercise to achieve short-term financial gain.

Putting in place an effective system of safeguards to ensure that patents are not unnecessarily abandoned has often been motivated by past mistakes. Several companies we spoke to recalled instances where they had ceased payment of patent renewal fees, only to then see a competitor firm file their own patent and launch a profitable new product as a result. Mistakes made in the past had subsequently provided a powerful stimulus for the company to consider the value of its patent portfolio very seriously, not only in terms of its own commercial strategy, but also taking into account that of its competitors. In particular, for many firms this has led to an integrated approach to patent renewal decisions, taking into account not only the views of research and commercial managers involved in the development and launch of new products, but also managers with a broad overview of how product ranges are likely to develop, the activities and interests of its competitors and the different approaches that need to be taken in geographical markets worldwide.

Protecting intellectual property

The UK-based companies that we spoke to in our survey generally followed a strategy of filing a patent application as early as possible after the date of invention. None of the companies said that they delayed patenting, for example while undertaking development work in secret (for example, in order to prolong the period of market exclusivity of 20 years under UK patent law). The legal certainty that patent protection had been afforded was always the primary goal. In the very rare instances where companies considered that patenting an invention was not commercially viable, they would consider putting information in the public domain, not least in order to ensure that other companies did not profit from patents based on their research.

Once an invention has been legally protected through a patent, a company may find that its intellectual property rights have been breached and that a competitor firm has infringed the patent. The patent-holding firm must then consider seriously whether to enter into litigation to enforce its rights. Litigation is generally only used as a last resort. The cost of entering into litigation is likely to be prohibitively high, particularly where the alleged infringement has occurred in a foreign jurisdiction, requiring the case to be heard before a local court in that country. In addition to the direct costs of entering into litigation and hiring attorneys to represent the company in court, contingency must be made for the prospect that the case may be lost, introducing financial uncertainty for the whole organisation, possibly for several years, until the case is resolved. One large UK-based multinational in our survey reported a case whereby, for several years, a large proportion of its financial reserves were committed to a contingency fund necessary to cover the likely costs of losing an infringement case that it brought in a foreign court. That company said that it would be deterred from bringing an infringement action again in a foreign court since, although it eventually won the case, it had now learnt that legal uncertainty can bring with it financial implications that far outweigh the benefits of winning an infringement case.

Due to the high cost of litigation and the financial uncertainties that persist while a legal case is pending, all the companies surveyed for this research indicated a marked reluctance to enter into litigation to enforce their intellectual property rights. Patent litigation insurance was not considered a cost-effective option for any of the companies that we spoke to due to the high premiums charged. In the final instance, however, the companies expressed a willingness to be prepared to go to court where this was deemed necessary to ensure the credibility of the company and show that the threat of litigation was real as a deterrent to potential infringers.

All the companies surveyed tended to prefer negotiation and compromise to litigation if at all possible. Either the infringing company simply has to stop using the intellectual property owned by another firm, or a compromise must be found through licensing or cross-licensing arrangements. Cross-licensing is often considered an effective solution (see also Nevens, Summe and Uttal, 1990). On occasion, companies allegedly infringing other firms' intellectual property rights (often unintentionally) are able to obtain a licence to use those rights legitimately in return for a fee and subsequent royalties. For firms competing in the same market, it also appears not uncommon for cross-licensing arrangements to be set up. Under the terms of a cross-licensing arrangement, each company licenses to the other intellectual property rights under a mutually beneficial arrangement that allows each access to innovation owned by the other. The competitive relationship between two companies thus takes on an (entirely legal) collusive character, allowing wider diffusion of the disputed intellectual property rights with the presumption that it will then be more widely available in the market.

On occasion, a firm may decide not to exploit the intellectual property that it owns. It may choose to explore licensing strategies to generate income. A policy based on royalty maximisation would result in the owner of intellectual property assets selectively licensing a patent (or indeed a trademark) that it holds to non-threatening firms in other industries (i.e. defining the use of intellectual property by field of use) or in other geographical markets.

Exploiting intellectual property

The primary benefit of patent protection is the market power it conveys when it is exploited. This is reflected in sales volume (for a product patent) or in higher levels of productivity (in the case of process patents). There are also a number of other strategic uses for patents.

Licensing out patents to other firms would be one viable option. However, for the companies we spoke to, generating revenue through licensing was generally a secondary objective pursued only when the opportunity happened to arise. It did not normally form part of the overall strategy when a patent application was being made.

One approach open to a company is to patent defensively. Once a promising technology has been disclosed through a patent application, the company will patent around the new invention. The company establishes a portfolio of patents with numerous variations of the basic technology in such a manner as to minimise the risks of a competitor firm entering the market with a variation of its invention (Tran, 1995). Large firms often develop patent portfolios as part of their overall intellectual property strategy, increasing the overall protection that a single patent accords by 'fencing' or 'creating a maze' of patents that will make it more difficult for competitors to patent a rival invention without breach of existing rights.

Key elements of an intellectual property strategy

Integrating intellectual property strategy throughout the organisation

In the light of what has been said above about the role of different types of individual in the formulation of intellectual property strategies, it will come as little surprise that the idea of integrating intellectual property strategy throughout the organisation was a recurring theme in the companies included in our survey. Companies readily acknowledged that it is not sufficient for patent managers alone to deal with intellectual property. It was widely acknowledged by large companies that research staff, commercial managers, lawyers and managers responsible for negotiating external collaborative research contracts all need to be involved in decisions about what the corporate intellectual property strategy should be and how it should then be integrated into day-to-day company operations. Nevens, Summe and Uttal (1990) insist that competitive success will increasingly depend on the co-ordinated efforts of researchers, manufacturing staff and managers. All the companies included in our survey agreed with this integrated approach in principle. However, they differed from one another in the steps they took to ensure this was achieved in practice.

Setting up written policies and procedures

Strategic management decisions relating to intellectual property are often codified in corporate policy documents that explain to personnel involved in various aspects of research and management exactly what procedures should be followed when potentially valuable intellectual property is identified and setting out where responsibilities for intellectual property actually lie, together with details of how to contact the relevant personnel for advice and assistance.

Codified policy documents on intellectual property may also have a more general strategic role, reflecting overall priorities for the company: for example, setting out the circumstances in which the company would normally seek to patent, as well as establishing an overall position on the importance of intellectual property to the organisation as a whole in the form of a 'mission statement'.

Developing appropriate management structures

Creating a management structure capable of providing clear lines of responsibility for intellectual property decisions is often important for firms. Many companies set up a formal intellectual property committee, or equivalent body, with overall responsibility for intellectual property. Staff represented on this type of a committee tend to represent the legal, commercial, research and financial interests of the company, although the precise role of intellectual property committees varies from company to company. In some instances these committees take decisions on intellectual property protection such as patent filing and patent renewals and decide when to instigate litigation for infringement or when to enter into licensing agreements, as well as determining the overall budget for intellectual property. In other cases, the role of an intellectual property committee is confined to a strategic overview of company policy when committee meetings are convened on a six-monthly or annual basis. Other companies have dispensed with regular meetings altogether and use intranet services for virtual conferences and to alert colleagues of planned patent filing and patent renewal decisions as and when they arise.

Raising awareness of intellectual property through training initiatives

Once a corporate strategy on intellectual property has been put in place, the task of disseminating that information to company employees can be undertaken. Many companies appreciate that it is not sufficient for a company to distribute copies of its written policies on intellectual property if no-one actually reads them – indeed, we saw one or two instances where staff used weighty volumes on intellectual property as 'door stops' and patent staff had subsequently issued more manageable summary documents in a readable form which were less off-putting to already busy company employees.

To put this another way, if an intellectual property strategy is to have any meaningful impact on the company, it must be internalised and acted upon by staff, not merely encapsulated in a written document and then put to one side. For many companies, holding training sessions for employees is an effective way of ensuring that intellectual property strategy transcends formal corporate documentation and has a meaningful impact on the day-to-day operations of firms by encouraging staff to 'think intellectual property' as an integral part of day-to-day company activities. Staff not directly involved in the innovation process are a particularly important target audience. Marketing departments, for instance, regularly encounter trademark and copyright issues, but are not always aware of the implications of infringing intellectual property rights.

Establishing innovation 'gates'

The principle that managers should ask questions about the intellectual property implications of their work throughout the research and development cycle is widely acknowledged (see Nevens, Summe and Uttal, 1990). As part of this process of integrating intellectual property into new product development, several companies that we surveyed had adopted a variation on the idea of innovation 'gates' within a research and development 'funnel' (see Pickering and Matthews, 2000), whereby the decision on whether development work on an invention should be funded and an assessment of the feasibility of those ideas must be accompanied by company approval to support progression to the next stage of the innovation process. Within this appraisal system, intellectual property considerations, such as patentability of the invention and the existence of competitor patents in the same field, are then taken into account as part of the overall process of assessing the viability of continued company commitment to fund the invention. This is perhaps the clearest example that we found of integrating intellectual property strategy into wider management considerations in a coherent and structured manner.

Learning to manage intellectual property

These key elements of a company's strategy on intellectual property will be the result of a series of prior decision outcomes within the corporate organisational structure. This, in turn, will reflect the history of past mistakes, prior experiences, observations and continual revision and review within a company.

Learning from past mistakes

The process of learning may be experienced, albeit painfully, by a company making its own mistakes – for example, by failing to renew a patent which subsequently proved lucrative for one of its competitors.

Learning from the experience of other personnel within the same organisation

The dissemination of an intellectual property strategy within an organisation conventionally works 'top-down', as patent staff disseminate information on the importance of intellectual property to research staff or commercial managers (see also Nevens, Summe and Uttal, 1990). However, this transfer of knowledge is a two-way process. It also operates 'bottom-up' as patent staff learn from the experiences of their colleagues who are managing research and commercial considerations on a day-to-day basis and are well placed to take a more holistic view of the role of intellectual property in the wider scheme of corporate strategy. The way that a company develops its knowledge of intellectual property is thus a two-way learning process, the result of individual employees in a company constantly bringing their own experiences of best (and worst) practice to the organisation and, in doing so, giving corporate intellectual property strategy a dynamic of its own.

Learning from observing other organisations

Observing other companies' strategies for dealing with intellectual property may also be an effective means of observing how not to do business. In this sense, the process of developing a corporate intellectual property strategy includes a measure of learning from others' past mistakes.

Companies may seek to act alone, gaining competitive advantage through first mover strategies, or may seek to replicate the behaviour of other organisations. In our survey of large firms we have seen instances where managers have brought with them, from their previous employers, expertise on the management of intellectual property and introduced an approach to managing intellectual property that is derived from the strategies used successfully by others.

Learning as a continual process of revision and refinement

In this sense, corporate intellectual property strategy is often derived from that of others as part of a process of observing and learning from others. Some of those experiences will be positive – for example, observing best practice in other companies – while some will be negative – for example, failing to file for a potentially valuable patent which is then taken up by one of its competitors. Above all, company policy on intellectual property will be constantly changing and undergoing a process of adaptation in order to take account of the firm's most recent learning experiences.

Corporate intellectual property strategy is therefore something that is formulated as the result of a dynamic process of change: of knowledge transferred between different types of people within the firm which can help to explain why companies adopt particular approaches towards intellectual property, while observed behaviour external to the firm may also be important if a particular company is to learn from the experiences of others.

Bargaining

By disentangling the various components of decision-making processes within a company, we then start to see a complex web of corporate interests internal to that firm which determine why particular organisations behave as they do towards intellectual property. We would suggest that a consensus will be built up within the company and a policy approach constructed to determine how best to deal with intellectual property.

Is it simply the case that managerial hierarchies are so strong in UK companies that renegade behaviour (such as company research staff announcing pre-patented research findings at conferences in order to receive peer group recognition) simply does not occur in the same way as it does amongst the academic community? We would suggest that this is a key difference between corporate structure, where managerial hierarchies are strong, and academic institutions, where intellectual property also arises from R&D initiatives but where research staff have much more autonomy. If it is actually the case that strong management is important, this would support our view that structures and procedures for managing the people involved in decisions are the crucial determinants of intellectual property strategy in UK companies.

Implications for SMEs

Our study focused primarily on the activities of large companies. Given that the management structures and level of investment available to large firms are unlikely to be found in SMEs, there is a need for caution in applying our results to the small-firm sector. Nevertheless, our findings do have some implications for SMEs. It is clear, for instance, that a significant degree of contact exists between large and small companies on intellectual property issues. The view of large companies engaged in collaborative or contract research with SMEs thus offers an interesting perspective on intellectual property management.

Inter-relationships between large and small firms

Our survey revealed four types of contact between large and small firms that inform intellectual property strategies. These are: supply chain relationships; joint ventures; dissemination of best practice; and exploiting intellectual property developed by another firm.

The supply chain offers a clear route for influencing SME behaviour, particularly by increasing awareness of intellectual property issues. Where a small firm is a supplier, a large company purchasing goods or ideas with an innovative content will normally require some assurance that the supplier's intellectual property position is secure. As more companies come to view supply chains as a partnership rather than a seller–purchaser relationship, the potential exists for a much wider sharing of experience. In this type of relationship, SMEs take effective steps to protect their intellectual property, not least because purchasing companies so often demand it.

Joint ventures arise when two or more firms agree to develop, manufacture or market a product containing intellectual property that one party owns. Large companies might be expected to welcome approaches from SMEs that have potentially valuable intellectual property. In practice, however, they often have reservations. A particular concern is that the ideas being promoted by an SME overlap with those being developed within the larger firm. In some circumstances, informal discussions between companies can lead to disputes over ownership of intellectual property and, because of this, many larger companies are extremely cautious when approached by an SME. One large company told us that their policy was only to engage is discussions with an SME when a patent application had already been filed, since this offered protection and a clear legal means for resolving any dispute. Where no clear policy currently exists, companies would be well advised to think through their mechanisms for disseminating and receiving new ideas.

Some large firms take the view that sharing good practice on intellectual property management should be undertaken as a matter of goodwill, even when the direct benefits are difficult to quantify. Dissemination of best practice might involve links with local agencies established to promote innovation and help small business, such as Regional Technology Centres and Business Links. Other large firms are of the opinion that, when negotiating major collaborative contracts, for example under the EU Framework Programme or UK government LINK schemes, they have a duty to protect the interests of SME partners, who may have less experience of negotiating on intellectual property issues. Care should be taken, however, not to inadvertently promote inappropriate strategies. Intellectual property strategies appropriate for SMEs may be very different from those that are best for large firms. In one collaborative agreement that we observed, the partners had devised a contract that, on the face of it, appeared fair on grounds of equity but, in practice, favoured the larger company because each partner was required to pay equal amounts towards the cost of any patent filing or litigation costs necessary to protect intellectual property rights resulting from the collaboration, without consideration being given to the ability of the SME partner to pay the sums involved.

Finally, in some cases larger companies license out intellectual property where this is not directly relevant to their businesses. Licensing can be mutually beneficial to both large and small companies. When the R&D departments of large firms produce more exploitable innovation than can be effectively marketed by the company, SMEs are often well placed to take on a licence and develop a new product in their own field of expertise. Licensing out intellectual property to small firms is, however, a relatively marginal activity for most large companies, particularly since R&D strategies normally focus on technologies that relate to core business activities and can be fully exploited in-house.

To summarise, there are circumstances where interactions between large and small companies are mutually beneficial for each party. Such arrangements, however, need to recognise the different aspirations and resources of each party. It will be helpful now to review the extent to which the intellectual property strategies of large firms are relevant to SMEs.

Managing intellectual property in SMEs

The significance of intellectual property for SMEs has been widely acknowledged. Mansfield *et al.* (1982) noted that many economists seemed to believe that patent protection is more important in smaller firms than in larger ones. However, there is also contradictory evidence that few SMEs actually choose to protect their intellectual property through the existing patent system (see, for example, *Innovation and Technology Transfer*, 1997). The most commonly cited reasons for this are the cost constraints. Preparing a patent application and paying subsequent patent renewal fees may not in themselves present a significant cost burden but, unlike large firms, SMEs are unlikely to have a qualified patent agent working in-house. Since the services of a patent agent are normally considered essential in order to conduct patent searches and prepare a good application, costs are likely to far exceed those payable to the Patent Office for actual filing and renewal costs.

Once an SME has obtained a patent, the protection it accords becomes reliant on the willingness of the small firm to enter into lengthy and expensive litigation to defend its intellectual property rights. If a competitor infringes an SME's patent, the small firm may not have the financial resources to go to court to defend its rights. So although, in theory, patents provide protection to small, innovative companies, in practice this protection is worthless if the rights it accords cannot be enforced. SMEs simply do not have the financial resources available to large firms when it comes to litigation costs.

One possible option is for an SME to take out litigation insurance to pay for court costs in the event of an alleged infringement of its patents. However, there is no evidence that SMEs consider this a realistic option. Even large firms surveyed for this research found the premiums for litigation insurance too high to be worthwhile.

Alternatively, SMEs may choose not to file for patent when they are in possession of patentable inventions at all. Instead SMEs may be better advised to rely on trade secrets (see Mansfield, 1986) and their ability to adapt and innovate faster than competitor firms. In many cases, technology is progressing so rapidly that it would be obsolete before a patent is issued in any case. Moreover, even where a patent could provide legal protection it is often difficult for a small firm to enforce its patent rights before a court in proceedings where the alleged infringer is a larger, more economically powerful and, in many cases, foreign company that could only be brought before a court in another country.

As we noted above, from the perspective of interactions between large and small firms, a further option is for the SME to consider licensing or selling its intellectual property rights. Licensing or selling intellectual property rights to a larger firm may be attractive to an SME since the larger company will subsequently have an interest in helping prevent rights being infringed by a competitor (see Tran, 1995). This strategy is particularly attractive when an SME lacks the financial resources or manufacturing capability to exploit its intellectual property fully. Under this arrangement, the larger firm purchasing an SME's intellectual property would also pay licensing fees and royalties on subsequent sales. The potential financial benefits of forming alliances with larger firms are clear to SMEs.

Where it is not possible to form alliances with larger firms and given the drawbacks of patent filing, renewal and enforcement costs, many SMEs choose not to patent at all, preferring instead to stay ahead of their competitors by 'out-inventing' or 'out-researching' them (Elliott, 1992). In some sectors, computer software for example, relying on their own ability to be consistently innovative and staying one step ahead of competitors to gain market share makes good commercial sense because the market life of the product is relatively short. The flexibility of SMEs to be innovative and get products to market quicker than larger firms can thus be used to gain competitive advantage and reduce the need for legally enforceable intellectual property protection.

There are, of course, many significant differences between large firms and SMEs which hinder the adoption of large-company 'best practice' on intellectual property management by small firms. Small firms are unlikely to have the luxury of in-house intellectual property expertise, partly due to smaller financial reserves, but also because SMEs may well encounter the need for intellectual property expertise less frequently than their larger counterparts. It may also be the case that the divisions between the types of personnel with intellectual property interests in large firms simply do not exist in SMEs: quite often the financial manager, commercial manager and research and development specialist may actually be the same person in a small firm, while whole departments are dedicated to the same tasks in larger organisations. In a small firm intellectual property strategy may, in fact, be handled by the managing director personally, with recourse to outside advice from lawyers and patent agents when and where appropriate.

The nature of the technology involved may, however, make the size of the company irrelevant in relation to the need for intellectual property protection. Fast-moving and innovative sectors such as computer software and biotechnology are frequently the domain of small, specialist firms, for whom intellectual property is the key to business success. Particularly in innovative sectors, it may well be that SMEs are as adept in formulating a coherent intellectual property strategy as their larger counterparts, if not more so.

Concluding remarks

While the development of a coherent intellectual property strategy may be particularly difficult for SMEs due to cost constraints, lack of specialist personnel in-house or lack of familiarity with intellectual property issues which mean that they often rely on the advice of external lawyers and patent agents, SMEs have the great advantage that their size allows a flexible approach to be taken to changing needs. Above all, SMEs should be encouraged to treat intellectual property as one of their greatest corporate assets. They should be made aware that it is crucial to involve all company personnel in intellectual property management and to 'think intellectual property' at all stages of the research and development process.

To summarise, the message for SMEs on intellectual property is that they should be encouraged to:

- *organise* their operations to make staff aware of intellectual property and to engender a commitment to intellectual property rights as part of everyday management operations;
- *protect* company intellectual property assets, either by formal protection (such as patenting) or by using trade secrecy to gain competitive advantage over rival firms;
- *exploit* corporate intellectual property, either by bringing to market new products containing their inventions, or by being aware of the potential value of licensing or cross-licensing of intellectual property assets that it owns but does not market in products; and
- *adapt* to changing circumstances, constantly updating and revising corporate intellectual property strategy in response to changing market conditions. Companies that manage intellectual property well are those which are always willing to learn from past experience and improve on their past performance.

These are the basic steps that any SME should take as they plan their intellectual property strategies. The evidence, however, indicates that they are not steps that are widely followed. In 1995 the UK government published an inter-departmental report on intellectual property. It found that many small firms do not see patenting as an integral part of their marketing strategies, often approach patent agents with a view to filing for a patent only after public disclosure of a new invention, and that even when SMEs seek advice at an early stage, they lack familiarity with intellectual property issues, which prevents them from protecting and exploiting their intellectual property assets in the most cost-effective manner. The results of this government report are alarming. We hope that this chapter will help small firms to learn from their larger counterparts in UK business and go some way towards highlighting the value of intellectual property to SMEs in the future.

Acknowledgements

This chapter reports the results of a research project based at the National Institute of Economic and Social Research in London. Caroline Wilson acted as Research Officer on the project and assisted with many of the company interviews on which this chapter is based. The authors are grateful for financial support given by the Economic and Social Research Council, the Department of Trade and Industry, and the Intellectual Property Institute within the Intellectual Property Research Programme (award no. L325253023). This study was made possible by the co-operation of the following UK-based research-intensive companies: BT; Chiroscience; EKA Chemicals; GEC; GPT; Glaxo Wellcome; Hewlett Packard; ICI; Lucas Varity; Pfizer; Philips; Reckitt and Colman; Shell; SmithKleinBeecham; Smith and Nephew; Symbionics; Unilever; Zeneca. Assurances were given to these companies that published results would not identify individual companies and these assurances have been honoured. Any errors remain the sole responsibility of the authors.

References

Elliott, C. (1992) 'Crucial Issues in IP Commercialisation', *Managing Intellectual Property*, November, 13–16.

Innovation and Technology Transfer (1997), vol. 4, 13–18.

Kirkland, J., Matthews, D., Pickering, J. F. and Wilson, C. (1998) 'University-Industry Research Contracts. Symbols of Co-operation or Unexploded Bombs?', *Industry and Higher Education*, 12 (2), 101–6.

Levin, R. C., Klevorick, A. K., Nelson, R. R. and Winter, S. G. (1987) 'Appropriating the Returns from Industrial Research and Development', *Brookings Papers in Economic Activity*, 3, 783–820.

Mansfield, E. (1986) 'Patents and Innovation: An Empirical Study', *Management Science*, 32 (2), 173–81.

Mansfield, E., Schwartz, M. and Wagner, S. (1981) 'Imitation Costs and Patents. An Empirical Study', *Economic Journal*, 91, 907–18.

Mansfield, E., Romeo, A., Schwartz, M., Teece, D., Wagner, S. and Brach, P. (1982) *Technology Transfer, Productivity and Economic Policy*, W. W. Norton, New York.

Nevens, M. T., Summe, G. L. and Uttal, B. (1990) 'Commercializing Technology: What the Best Companies Do', *Harvard Business Review*, May–June: 154–63.

Pickering, J. F. and Matthews, D. (2000) 'Managing Patents for Competitive Advantage', *Journal of General Management*, 25 (3), 15–32.

Pickering, J. F., Matthews, D., Wilson, C. and Kirkland, J. (1998) 'The Strategic Management of Intellectual Property: Review of the Interview Programme', *National Institute of Economic and Social Research Discussion Paper* No. 129, NIESR, London.

Pickering, J. F., Matthews, D., Wilson, C. and Kirkland, J. (1999) 'The University-Industry Interface in the Generation of Intellectual Property', *Higher Education Quarterly*, 53, 6–28.

Spelman, K. C. and Moss, J. (1994) 'The Intellectual Property Inventory: Why Do It?', *Computer Law and Security Report*, 10, 22–4.

Taylor, C. T. and Silberston, Z. A. (1973) *The Economic Impact of the Patent System: A Study of the British Experience*, Cambridge: Cambridge University Press.

Tran, B. (1995) 'IP Law Aspects in Strategic Planning', *Managing Intellectual Property*, March, 31–4.

4 Copyright protection strategies by small textiles firms

Anne-Marie Coles, Keith Dickson and Adrian Woods

Introduction

This chapter reports on a study that investigated a global problem concerning the illegal copying of textile designs in furnishings fabrics. One objective was to assess the impact of firm-based knowledge of both national and international copyright law on design protection practices. Other aims concerned the identification of factors that influence the probability that a firm will suffer from design infringement, such as firm size or type, its organisational strategies, and its position in international markets. In addition, it was intended to provide a comparative perspective between the UK industry and the industry in two other countries, Italy and the United States, as well as assessing the impact of changing production technology, including the increasing use, worldwide, of computer-aided design. Finally, a range of copyright protection strategies were identified, with particular relevance to small firms in the industry.

Methodology

The study was carried out in two parts. Interviews with firms in the three countries were undertaken in order to develop an understanding of issues faced by firms working within three different legislative systems. In addition, a statistical survey was carried out in the United Kingdom in order to investigate the scope of the problem on a wider domestic scale. The variety of the interviews that took place in the United Kingdom reflected the complex nature of the industry. Face-to-face interviews with relevant organisations were undertaken, including fabric suppliers, which included representatives working at all levels of the market. A range of firms was chosen, specialising in both prints and weaves and in modern and traditional designs. Some of the firms were directly involved in retail, while others supplied fabrics and curtains to all sections of the trade. The interviews helped to ascertain the general background to the issue of design infringement in this sector. Further information on the role of design was provided from design educators, independent design firms and freelance designers. Guidance on the application of the law was gathered from interviews with lawyers practising in this field, while information on the governmental role in this area was supplied by information from the Department of Trade and Industry and the Designs Registry.

The general, industry-wide issues concerning copyright infringement were investigated through a survey of firms based in the United Kingdom. A telephone questionnaire was used to interview a mixture of design firms and fabric suppliers. Although this latter group was quite heterogeneous, all firms were commercially affected by design infringement. The dominance of SMEs in this sector was clear, as 78 per cent of the sample had less than 100 employees. The questionnaire provided an estimate of the extent of design copying faced by UK firms, both in the domestic market and overseas. Firms' individual responses to copying were also investigated, including identification of factors which influence decisions to turn to legal protection. In addition, the questionnaire provided information on the trade in fabric designs in the United Kingdom, giving an estimate of the amount of bought-in designs being used and the type of inter-firm interactions that predominate.

Comparative data was gathered from interviews with firms in Italy and the United States. Como was chosen as the main Italian destination, as it is a centre for Italian textile design, which has developed due to its proximity to the major silk-weaving area. The Italian organisations interviewed comprised mainly SMEs representing a range of fabric manufacturers, independent designers, design converters and trade associations. The firms covered all sectors of the market and were all involved in export mainly to other European destinations and to the United States, although countries in the Far East were also mentioned as actual or potential markets. Many of the firms were small, family-run businesses that had been established for more than 20 years. The design studios ranged from small operations employing not more than three full-time designers, working by hand in a traditional manner, almost exclusively relying on commissions, to a much larger studio employing 15 full-time designers, and using up-to-date computer-aided design technology. The Italian trade associations are involved in the problem of design infringement and many are active in the control of design copying. In the United States, interviews took place with small fabric suppliers, independent designers and copyright lawyers, one of whom is a major legal representative for the Textile Producers and Suppliers Association (TPSA), an industry-supported organisation which becomes involved in overseas infringement disputes for the industry as a whole.

Industry structure

Small and medium-sized enterprises (SMEs) dominate the UK sector, both in terms of fabric supply and design, which is often an external function of the manufacturing process. Fabric manufacturers are a diverse group in the United Kingdom, ranging from very small, exclusive concerns through to firms which supply not only middle-ranking department stores but also the largest high-street chains. Many firms have a mixture of both modern and traditional designs, and the majority of independent designers offer both types of design, representing the preferences of the UK market. Another group are very high-profile firms, which trade on their own distinctive style, and in many cases rely on their established name and associated reputation for business. Some of these firms have their own retail outlets while others rent 'space' from major retailers.

SMEs also dominate this industry in Europe and the United States, both as fabric suppliers and as independent designers. Externalisation of the design function in both these countries is a major reason for the existence of many very small enterprises dedicated to selling designs and often employing less than ten people. The findings of this study are biased heavily towards the point of view of SMEs, and in the analysis their particular concerns are identified. It is worth pointing out, however, that one aspect of the UK statistical survey was the homogeneous nature of the responses, indicating an apparent agreement between firms of all sizes and types over the nature of design infringement and design protection in this sector. This chapter will first consider characteristics of the furnishing fabric industry and the problem of design copying in the three countries under study. It concludes with an outline of the type of strategies SMEs employ to protect themselves against infringement. The implementation of such protection is identified as a design management issue affecting all sections of the trade.

Copyright protection in the United Kingdom

In the United Kingdom, the textile industry is still of major importance to the economy despite long-term concern over its decline (National Institute of Economic and Social Research, 1958). In general, economic reviews focus on specific fabric types (for example, Morris, 1991; Roche, 1995), rather than drawing a line between furnishings and other type of textiles. In marketing terms, a separate furnishings sector has been identified (Keynote, 1993), which is, however, still very general, including bedding and household linen. Interior design trade fairs attract firms which are primarily producing fabric for upholstery and curtains and it is the protection of these fabric designs that has been the primary focus of this study.

The relevance and scope of copyright protection cannot be understood without some appreciation of the concept of copyright in UK law. The current legislation in this area is the Copyright Designs and Patents Act, 1988. Copyright covers form and appearance and therefore fabric designs are covered, along with other designs for surface decoration. Designs on furnishing fabrics are protected by copyright as artistic works industrially produced, with automatic copyright protection for 25 years from the date of first marketing. To secure copyright protection it is necessary to keep documentary records of the design process as it is evolving to prove originality (Pearson and Miller, 1990). Designs represented in document form, but which have been produced by independent designers who are not employees, are treated slightly differently. They are automatically protected by copyright as artistic works for the life of the author plus 70 years. Such designers will also have moral rights to their work, distinct from copyright. Whereas copyright can be assigned to the purchaser of the design, moral rights cannot be assigned, but can be, and for practical commercial reasons often are, waived by the designer. A change that came into force with the 1988 Act is that copyright of commissioned designs is no longer automatically owned by the commissioning body (Jacob and Alexander, 1995). In addition to the protection afforded by copyright, design registration before launch is available for new designs. Such protection can last for up to a maximum of 25 years, but there is a set charge for each design registered. Design registration, however, gives exclusive rights to the use of the design in the United Kingdom to the registered proprietor (Johnson, 1995; Pearson and Miller, 1990).

To prove that an infringement has occurred, the law states that a substantial part of the design must have been copied (Jacob and Alexander, 1995), although specific details such as ideas and layout are not protected by copyright and neither is colour. This opens up a grey area in the present law. In cases where there may be many similar versions of a particular design it is not always easy to identify which designs are strictly illegal. There is also an area of debate over common designs such as checks and stripes as to whether copyright can be enforced. Another problem area is related to the status of retail under the present law. Although, in some cases, copied fabrics have been discovered in retail outlets, retailers in the United Kingdom are considered secondary infringers and cannot be prosecuted. It is possible, however, to obtain an injunction to remove the infringing fabric from the point of sale. Information is available to the trade, which attempts to elucidate these points (Catterall, 1995; Hurn, 1996; Wilson, 1994).

The problem of design copying for UK firms is not confined to the domestic market, and some firms have discovered that the UK position with regard to design infringement has been overshadowed more recently by the problem of copies overseas (Fabrics and Furnishings International, 1995). Some designs are being copied and produced more cheaply overseas and imported back into the United Kingdom to compete with the original fabric. When such imports are discovered, UK law allows for the fabric to be removed from the point of sale even if the source of the fabric cannot be traced. Much more of a problem occurs when fabrics are found on sale in another country, with the necessity of taking expensive legal advice based in the country concerned. Major problems can arise from international differences in copyright law, and the desire expressed by some firms for EC harmonisation in this area is a recurrent theme. Small firms are particularly vulnerable in terms of gaining access and implementing their rights under the law, and prosecution does not tend to be an important means of protection for small firms in this industry (Dickson and Coles, 1998).

The United Kingdom industry and design copying

The United Kingdom furnishings industry is estimated to be worth in excess of £5 billion, and textiles is the largest section after floor coverings (*Carpets and Furnishings*, 1988). The market is quite highly stratified, with a number of firms at the top end being generally recognised as design leaders, while large firms tend to supply the mass market through high-street chains. Both traditional, classical styles and very modern, fashionable designs sell well in the United Kingdom. Although a certain amount of furnishing fabric is supplied to the trade, much fabric is still supplied direct to consumers through small, independent high-street shops, and through department stores. This is a situation in flux, however, as high streets are continually being challenged by out-of-town shopping complexes. Other methods of commerce are also becoming more important, with a growth in mail-order catalogues and television-based shopping, and computer-based outlets are also emerging in terms of both catalogues stored on compact disc and new internet links. As the UK population is also ageing, the customer base is changing and becoming wealthier, with more sophisticated tastes, which is a factor leading to changes in retail and product positioning (Godbold, 1996). Such realignments point to a situation in which copyright infringement is in a process of change.

Many of the respondents in the UK interviews remarked on the changing nature of the industry, particularly over the past 30 years, in terms of the increasingly dominant role that fashion fabrics now hold over more traditional, slower-changing classical designs. The dictates of fashion entered the furnishings sector during the post-war period, but it was the increasing popularity of co-ordinated designs over the past two decades which reinforced this trend and introduced issues such as design leadership, design obsolescence and design competition into this sector (Davis Cooper, 1993). A number of interviewees expressed the view that design lifetimes have become shorter over this period, from around eight to ten years to the current two years. It is also recognised that new styles are continually imitated and diffuse through the market from the top, which is a spur to continual investment and change in design. The view was also expressed that increased copying has been an outcome of the changing industry. Whereas direct infringement was relatively rare 20 years ago, it is now blatant, with the contract market, such as hotels, being a particular problem area.

The top end of the market can be considered to be design-led; the middle market is a mixture of design- and market-led. The bottom of the market, dominated by high-street outlets and ready-made items, is based on popular, cheap fashion fabrics. One problem that exists in the United Kingdom is that these bases may overlap. Customers can turn to fabrics in a cheaper price bracket if the designs look similar, and this is a major problem if good-quality designs are copied more cheaply. Firms at the top end of the market can be particularly affected, and their heavy investment in design can be threatened by copies which are both cheaper and of lower quality. Design infringement particularly threatens the reputation of firms which have a high profile, are design leaders, but produce very popular designs. Firms at the lower end of the market rely on selling a large quality of fabric at a cheaper price, but depend on large volume sales. They may also face problems when popular design is copied, because copiers can circumvent the process of 'picking a winner' in terms of design by waiting to copy those that prove popular. The experience of copying is very wide from the top of the market right through to the lower end and it affects all types of designs, both traditional and modern and prints and weaves. Design infringement appears to be a particular problem for firms with a high profile and a distinctive and popular style.

Many firms emphasised the importance of good relationships throughout the process of fabric production. Reputations are important in the UK industry and much information passes informally between firms (Bain, 1994). Firms that are primarily market followers also have to tread the fine line between taking inspiration from a popular design and imitation of a design belonging to another firm. While all firms, reluctantly or otherwise, accept the legitimacy of similar yet altered designs in the market, they are united against the immorality of direct copying. The aim of the copier is to gain financial advantage by cheaply reproducing an original. This is achieved both by saving on the investment and risk of producing a new, untested design, and by reducing production costs: for example, by reducing the number of colours in the design. The finished copy thus appears as an inferior version of the original fabric. Copies now seem to be reaching the market much more quickly after a design has been launched: two to three months was often quoted. This leaves the firm little time to make a return on its investment, as sales can peak at about 12 to 18 months after launch.

Design protection practice

Both the process of discovering copies, and of taking advice on how to proceed after they are found, relies on the good relationships between firms throughout the United Kingdom (Coles *et al.*, 1997). Some firms rely on their reputation for prosecuting every case to deter infringers. While this policy may be successful in the domestic market, it is difficult to enforce for firms which are copied widely all over the world, and it is especially difficult for SMEs to follow this strategy. On the other hand, SMEs also view design registration as an expensive option, which duplicates the protection offered by copyright. Small firms which rely on bought-in designs often feel there is a problem with freelancer designers, as they have no control over whether the same designs will be sold on to other firms. A common means of attempting to control the situation is to request that similar designs be removed from the freelance portfolio. Another practice is to alter bought-in designs to minimise the chance of someone else having exactly the same design.

Small firms often do nothing about copies, especially if these are found overseas, because of a lack of resources to invest in protection strategies. Firms that are often copied also face a resource problem in terms of restricting the number of cases that can be pursued, and retaliation may be restricted to those copies posing the greatest commercial threat. Most firms want to develop a reputation for design protection but have limited time and money available. Firms copied widely in Europe favour EC harmonisation of the law, because they fear that domestic laws favour domestic firms. In the United Kingdom more recently, trade associations have become involved in measures to control the problem of design copying. The British Interior Textiles Association (BITA) has been involved in setting up a voluntary European Code of Conduct against copying, recognised at the major annual trade exhibition Heimtex, where proven copiers are now excluded. On the design side, a new association, Action on Copying in Design (ACID) offers legal advice to members. Other tactics that were reported include: flooding the market with copyrighted pattern books; constantly changing designs; offering competitive price and quality; and developing complex designs. These latter two tactics attempt to make copying commercially unattractive.

Statistical survey of UK design infringement

Responses to the UK telephone survey supported the general perception in the trade that copying is widespread. Nearly 40 per cent of the total sample had found a copy in the United Kingdom over the past three years, with an average of one copy per year. Some firms were finding an average of two or more copies each year, indicating that design copying might be a particular problem for a small number of firms. The pattern for finding overseas copies was similar, with 34 per cent of the sample discovering a copy in the past three years. Five firms had found more than twelve, which amounts to an average of one every three months. Firms copied extensively overseas were a mixture of large well-established firms and smaller more specialised ones. In the United Kingdom, the results indicated that, while firms were more likely to discover a copy themselves, either in the high street or at a trade exhibition, information from other firms in the industry was just as important in finding overseas copies. When questioned about the worst problem areas for discovering copies, the United Kingdom and Europe topped the list, although the Middle East was also named as a problem area.

Responses suggested that after a design had been verified as a copy (the most usual method was to compare samples of the two fabrics), about half the firms sought advice. In both the United Kingdom and overseas the majority of these firms turned to a solicitor for advice, but in both cases about half the firms (43 per cent overseas) did not take the matter any further. Court cases appear to be involved in the outcome of a copyright dispute in about 12 per cent of all cases in the United Kingdom, while settling the matter amicably, either with or without the use of solicitors was the most likely outcome. Court cases were a more likely outcome for cases of copying overseas, possibly due to language barriers and the desire to obtain publicity for a successful case to deter others in the future.

Large firms were more likely to look for copies than small firms and also more likely to find them. It appeared that modern designs were more likely to be copied than traditional ones, indicating the availability of out-of-copyright archives as a legal source of ideas for traditional designs. The survey showed that the vast majority of firms protect themselves in terms of keeping a record of design documentation and ensuring they own the copyright to any design. On the other hand nearly 57 per cent of the designers reported that they had been asked to imitate a design, indicating that a large section of the market is looking for similarity in design. Half of the firms that bought designs from freelance designers reported that they frequently asked designers to remove similar designs from their portfolios. This represents an attempt to control the tendency for similar designs to appear on the market at the same time. Overall there was a high degree of coherence between both large and small firms in the sample about the threat posed by design infringement and appropriate responses to it. Although copying overseas emerged as a large and possibly intractable problem, it is also apparent that copying in the United Kingdom remains a major source of loss for domestic firms. There is a factor related to firm size involved, with small firms unable to contemplate recourse to the law to settle their disputes. One strong outcome was the respondents' belief that better training on copyright matters is necessary in the United Kingdom (Woods *et al.*, 1999).

Italy and Europe

Textiles and clothing are major industries in Italy, representing around 14 per cent of total manufacturing. Italy is also a major exporter to the rest of Europe, with important markets in West Germany, France and the United Kingdom. Textile production is concentrated in the north of Italy, particularly in Lombardy and Tuscany, with 80 per cent of all silk production in Como. Small units are dominant and represent around two-thirds of the total number of firms in this sector (Lewis, 1988a). Large integrated firms in the textile and garment trade are few, which means that much of the production process is sub-contracted out and the industry is quite flexible. There is some evidence to suggest a decline in international competitiveness over a number of years, as the Italian industry suffers from competition provided by firms situated in the Far East, where production costs are cheaper, as well as from other European firms (Lewis, 1988b).

Italy is a market for very traditional designs, and weaves are particularly important here. The Italian industry differs from the United Kingdom in a number of ways. Copyright as a legal concept is seen to be narrower than in the United Kingdom, applying only to identical copies of a design that are competing in the same market. Design is very competitive – there are around 200 design studios in Como alone – and related to this is the fact that new designs are seen as being relatively cheap compared to the price of design in the United Kingdom. Another factor is new technology. Some traditional designers felt that studios using computer-aided design were turning out too many low-quality designs which were seen as pushing down the price. In this way large design studios may threaten the existence of small ones. Overseas firms are seen as becoming more competitive in design terms, as well as having much lower production costs, and this is another factor in the concern of Italian designers and suppliers that the long-term viability of the industry could be under threat.

In Italy there appeared to be little trust between firms. There are many small firms, specialising both in design and weaving, often family-owned, and as a consequence firms do not seem to be widely known by their reputation. If a copy is found, designers particularly felt that they came under suspicion, although the source could be from anywhere in the production chain: designer, converter, mill, printer or even customer. It was also felt that the strict labour laws in Italy encouraged fragmentation in the industry, by making it difficult to retain freelancers on a casual basis. This keeps design as an external function of the manufacturing process, but mitigates against the development of long-term trusting relationships.

The application of Italian law is seen as limited because it works slowly and is expensive. In general it was felt that imitation of a design could go very close to the original and still be legal. An average case takes three years and one firm had been through a legal battle that was only successfully resolved after nine years. In addition many firms rejected the possibility of design registration as too expensive. In addition, ownership of copyright by Italian firms has not generally been seen as important, compared to the value placed on ownership by firms based in the United States and the United Kingdom, which routinely require formal copyright assignment. As the same designs can be used in non-competing markets presumably the design firm is used to retaining rights to its use, although some felt that there is a growing trend to exclusivity and copyright agreements.

Speed of copies reaching the market and the trend to follow popular fashion are also issues for Italian firms. Copying is seen as part of a European problem, for which harmonisation of EC law could be useful in tackling. At least it would ensure the same standards in every country. In Italy it was felt that as design is relatively cheaper and very little design alteration is necessary to comply with the law, most companies would rely on design substitution rather than blatant copying. Italian trade associations have stepped in to fill the gap, and many are in the process of setting up formal arbitration systems for cases of alleged copying. There are limitations, in that agreements only apply to association members, all of whom must agree to abide by the scheme. There might be limited success in dealing with overseas firms, although the one system in place at the moment successfully resolved a dispute between an Italian and a Greek firm. The associations also run a design depository, where designs are kept in sealed envelopes before the first date of marketing, as an alternative to formal registration. Other informal methods of protection mentioned included: dropping designs from the firm's collection if a copy is found; adding colours to a print design; developing complex weaves to make it more difficult to copy effectively; and improving co-operation and communication between firms.

A number of design firms sampled from other European countries felt their domestic laws were quite strong. For example, in France it is accepted that a design must differ by at least 30 per cent not to be an infringement. In the Netherlands the industry is small, promoting close long-term relationships between firms, which decreases the opportunities for domestic copying. In Spain the law is based on design registration, and was felt to be adequate by the design firm interviewed. In Austria the domestic market for designs is particularly small, forcing designers to become very export-oriented.

Copyright protection and the United States

In the United States, home textile sales were estimated to be worth around $7 billion in 1994 (a total for all sheets, towels, curtains, blankets and upholstery). The market is almost totally supplied by domestically produced fabric and imports account for less than 5 per cent of total sales in this area. Fabric production is heavily automated, and the industry is quite fragmented, although it is dominated by some large integrated firms. Many small firms are working in niche markets, from design through to production and finishing, and no single company is dominant. New fabric designs are estimated to cost between $50,000 and $120,000 to develop and piracy of home furnishing fabric designs represents an estimated annual loss of $50 million (USA Industry Survey, 1996).

Consumer trends are towards purchasing more custom-made items in home furnishings and away from off-the-shelf merchandise. Retailers are therefore under pressure to continually offer new lines which are unique and exclusive. There have been changes in the retail sector, with traditional department stores losing out to discount stores at the lower end, and to national chains and speciality stores, while mail-order catalogues are becoming a significant outlet for sales of home furnishings. Such trends indicate an increasingly sophisticated consumer base. Fabric design at the top end of the market is dominated by classical designs based on antique documents. Many firms buy old documents or pieces of fabric as sources of design ideas, and not only are there potential copyright problems with this, but designers also fear the possibility of a rival firm obtaining the same design. Although this has been known to occur, it is fairly rare. Many of the firms at this level of the market are small and mainly concerned with domestic sales. The domestic market is itself not homogeneous and there are quite different regional tastes in design. There appears to be much larger differences between different markets in the United States than in the United Kingdom, and not so much overlap. One consequence of this is that firms appear to be more willing to accept that cheaper copies exist, and often allow the copy to remain in the market in return for a royalty, rather than having the whole stock destroyed. The existence of a cheaper fabric is not so readily damaging either to the reputation of established firms or to the volume of sales of the original fabric.

At the top end of the market, a successful design can have a long lifetime and remain in a collection for many years. As very high-quality fabric is used, customers may return after many years looking for the same colour and pattern. Most firms emphasise that this mode of operation is in contrast to the lower end of the market, which is driven by costs, rapidly changing fashions, and lower-quality fabric with design lifetimes of around 18 months. One significant factor at the top end is that business is done with the trade rather than the general public, either with furniture manufacturers or interior designers. This is in contrast to equivalent firms in the United Kingdom where much of the business is directly through retail to the final customer. Interior designers, in particular, tend to develop close links with firms. They know the designers involved and they like the particular collection, which they recommend to their own customers. In this way fabric companies develop close links with their customer base whose requirements are well understood. Good-quality fabric is bought by interior designers when they have a contract for furnishing a home. In the United States there is more of a tradition that interior design is carried out by professionals rather than home-owners. Therefore there is a professional group with detailed knowledge of different company designs, who recognise a copy and are not inclined to purchase inferior fabric or design.

Copyright law in the United States is regarded as generally one of the strongest in the world. It gives a firm power to prevent the sale of a copy, also implicating the retailer as a disincentive to conceal the source of the copied fabric. The expense of a court case, however, is something that many firms want to avoid, and design leaders were divided over whether they felt design registration was important. Although some firms are meticulous in registering all their designs and maintaining documents relating to design development, others do not worry particularly about copies that are made and sold outside 'their' level of the market. The approach to copyright infringement and copying is an internal design management matter specific to the firms involved, and depends partly on the past experience of copying and perceived ability to prevent it happening. The strength of the law appears to give firms confidence in being able to tackle cases of copying even if they do not register designs and would not be prepared to go to court. An on-going problem is copies found overseas: the numbers have increased dramatically during the past ten years, as overseas markets have grown and firms have moved their production to cheaper areas. As this has affected some of the largest companies, there has been much publicity in the trade press which had alerted others to potential problems. Response from the industry has been on a more co-operative level with the formation of a pressure group, the Textile Producers and Suppliers Association (TPSA) in 1991, with the specific aim of fighting copyright infringements worldwide. There is no doubt that the TPSA, which represents a wide range of firms including SMEs, has taken a high-profile position, being active in countries with weak copyright laws. To date it has helped firms to challenge infringements in countries such as Mexico, Indonesia and Korea.

Discussion

Copyright infringement in this industry is a large and complex problem. Many factors affect both whether a copy will be found and the action a firm can take to challenge it. Small firms have a major role to play within the industry and are universally important in Europe and the United States, but it must be recognised that these are the firms which lose most in terms of design copying. At the moment there are also widespread and far-reaching changes affecting the industry in general. Emerging worldwide competition, and widespread adoption of computer-aided design and other communications technologies, are affecting the speed and quality of design copying as well as the location of production. The implications of new information technologies for challenging existing copyright laws are very pertinent to this industry as well as being of more general concern (Barton, 1995; Dillon Weston, 1997). Over the next decade new information technologies, including computer-aided design, will continue to have an impact on textile design practice, and may improve the ability of firms to copy designs in terms of speed and accuracy (Dickson and Coles, 2000). These trends, together with the speed of design change due to increasing pressure of fashion in the market, means that certain types of firms will be victims of design copying much more frequently than others. Thus, although in the United Kingdom at least firms are in general good at maintaining documentation and obtaining copyright assignments, there are wider issues at stake in terms of design protection policies.

Although copyright law applies to all companies in the furnishing fabric sector, there are a variety of responses that individual firms can make to the discovery of a copy, which depends as much on the design management strategy within the firm as it does on strict interpretation of the law. Much of the design management literature has focused on the role of design in product development and commercial success (Moody, 1980; Walsh *et al.*, 1988; Lorrenz, 1993; McLeod, 1988; Roy and Potter, 1993, etc), and some consideration has been given to the relationship between design suppliers and their clients (Bruce and Docherty, 1993; Davies, 1993). The findings of this project should contribute to the understanding of the role of design management and design innovation, and further elucidate the issue of inter-firm relationships (Dickson, 1996; Coles *et al.*, 1997).

Although there are cultural differences between the industry in the three countries studied, the increasing threat of copying from overseas and the dominance of small firms has resulted in identifiable moves towards industry associations attempting to aid and control the problem. Small firms face common problems due to their size and relative difficulties in gaining access to their respective legal systems. They all face situations which are rapidly changing in response to wider changes in the industry worldwide. Changes in technology, in the scope and demand for fashion fabrics, and the globalisation of the market, in terms both of the international basis of fabric production and its consumption, have resulted in an infringement problem affected by the speed, location and frequency of copies found. Small fabric suppliers, as well as small design firms, are now more export-oriented and are affected by such factors as variations in copyright law, lack of trust between firms in different countries and a weak inter-firm network. In all three countries discovery of an infringement is part of design management function, as is management of inter-firm relationships, although these concepts are not well understood in terms of the management literature (Coles *et al.*, 1997).

In terms of SMEs that are fabric producers, a number of protection strategies can be identified that are already implemented by many firms. Although protection can mean taking persistent infringers to court, the UK survey indicates that this is a fairly rare occurrence. Common strategies that are used include settling disputes informally or through legal representatives out of court, pursuing frequent changes in design, competitive pricing to discourage potential infringements, and increasing the technical complexity of the design to make copying difficult. Other protection strategies include joining an active trade association, buying and commissioning designs only from trusted, known sources and buying designs from a wide range of sources to gain access to many new designs and not become dependent on a limited number of suppliers. In many cases bought-in designs are specifically altered by the fabric manufacturer. In conclusion, fabric suppliers need to balance their resources between defensive and offensive methods of protection against design infringement.

References

Bain, N. C. (1994) 'Changing Relationships', *Textile Horizons*, June, 5.

Barton, J. H. (1995) 'Adapting the Intellectual Property System to New Technologies', *International Journal of Technology Management*, 10 (2/3), 151–72.

Bruce, M. and Docherty, C. (1993) 'It's All in a Relationship: A Comparative Study of Client–Design Consultant Relationships', *Design Studies*, 14 (4), 404–22.

Carpets and Furnishings (1988) *Editorial*, 30.

Catterall, T. (1995) 'Design Protection in Home Furnishing Textiles', *Cabinet Maker*, 6 October, 3.

Coles, A.-M., Dickson, K. and Woods, A. (1997) *Not Designed Here? Decision Making over Design Sources for United Kingdom Textile Firms*, paper presented at the British Academy of Management Conference, London, September.

Copyright Designs and Patents Act (1989), HMSO, London, Chapter 48.

Davies, H. (1993) 'The Impact of Competitive Structures and Technological Environment on Design Management: A Case Study of the United Kingdom Touring Caravan Industry', *Design Studies*, 14 (4), 365–78.

Davis Cooper, R. (1993) 'Investigating British and European Retail Buyer Attitudes and Perceptions of British Design', *Design Studies*, 14 (2), 194–209.

Dickson, K. (1996) 'How Informal Can You Be? Trust and Reciprocity with Co-operative and Collaborative Relationships', *International Journal of Technology Management*, 11, 129–39.

Dickson, K. and Coles, A.-M. (1998) 'Inspiration or Infringement? Design Protection and Copyright Issues for Small Textile Firms', *Design Studies*, 19, 203–15.

Dickson, K. and Coles, A.-M. (2000) 'Textile Design Protection: Copyright, CAD and Competition', *Technovation*, 20, 47–53.

Dillon Weston, M. (1997) 'Consideration of the Impact of Modern Technology on Copying Designs and International Counterfeiting', paper presented at 'Textiles and the Information Society', 78th World Conference of the Textile Institute, Thessalonika, May.

Fabrics and Furnishings International (1995) *Stop The Copies*! Winter, 110–14.

Godbold, B. (1996) 'The Designer and the Retail Industry', presented at 'What Next?', seminar, Winchester School of Art, March.

Hurn, E. (1996) 'International Copyright Infringement: Thoughts From Abroad', *Textile Horizons*, Feb/Mar, 51.

Jacob, R. and Alexander, D. (1995) *A Guidebook to Intellectual Property: Patents, Trade Marks, Copyright and Designs*, Sweet and Maxwell, London.

Johnson, D. (1995) *Design and Protection: A Practical Guide to the Law on Plagiarism for Manufacturers and Designers*, The Design Council/Gower, London.

Keynote (1993) *Home Furnishings: A Market Sector Overview*, Keynote Publications, Hampton.

Lewis, M. (1988a) 'Profile of the Italian Textile Industry', *Textile Outlook International*, July, 43.

Lewis, M. (1988b) 'Profile of Italian Textile and Clothing Companies', *Textile Outlook International*, November, 19.

Lorrenz, C. (1993) *The Design Dimension: Product Strategy and the Challenge of Global Marketing*, Blackwell, Oxford.

McLeod, T. (1988) *The Management of Research, Development and Design in Industry*, Gower, Aldershot.

Moody, S. (1980) 'The Role of Design in Technological Innovation', *Design Studies*, 1 (6).

Morris, D. (1991) *Cotton to 1996, Pressing a Natural Advantage*, London Economics Intelligence Unit, London.

National Institute of Economic and Social Research (1958) *Structure of British Industry*, Cambridge University Press, Cambridge.

Pearson, H. and Miller, C. (1990) *Commercial Exploitation of Intellectual Property*, Blackstone Press, London.

Roche, J. (1995) *The International Wool Trade*, Woodhead, Cambridge.

Roy, R. and Potter, S. (1993) 'The Commercial Impact of Investment in Design', *Design Studies*, 14, 171–93.

Walsh, V., Roy, R. and Bruce, M. (1988) 'Competitive by Design', *Journal of Marketing Management*, 4 (2), 201–16.

Wilson, J. (1994) 'Intellectual Property: Protecting Your Most Valuable Assets', *Textile Horizons*, August, 46.

Woods, A., Coles, A.-M. and Dickson, K. (1999) 'Copyright Awareness and Training for Textile Design Protection', *Journal of European Industrial Training*, 23 (6), 329–34.

United States Industrial Survey (1996) 28 September, 78–84.

5 Intellectual property in biotechnology firms

Sandra Thomas

Introduction

Biotechnology is opening up new routes to novel products, processes and services in a wide range of industries. Applications in pharmaceuticals, chemicals, agriculture and food are being widely pursued by established large companies and new biotechnology SMEs. These companies need strong intellectual property (IP) protection because, in principle, many biotechnology inventions, once published, are easily copied. IP issues in biotechnology have focused on the legal difficulties of distinguishing molecules and defining categories of organisms as well as the ethics of ownership (Dworkin, 1997; McTaggert, 1996). Although patent law now covers a wide variety of rDNA molecules, processes and organisms in industrialised countries, the immaturity of the biotechnology industry and the complex and sometimes controversial legal decisions taken to protect its inventions, coupled with diverse national patent systems, suggest that this is likely to continue. Within biotechnology, a rapidly expanding range of technologies continues to pose challenges to existing patent systems.

Within the biotechnology industry, much of the innovative activity in creating new technologies and products has taken place in the small firm. The biotechnology SME has been essentially a US phenomenon although the sector has shown recent growth in Europe. These SMEs have consistently led in the development of new areas of technology in biotechnology, including genomics, gene therapy, antisense and combinatorial chemistry (Ernst and Young, 1997). The US firms have generally been very successful in filing for key biotechnology patents, several of which have been granted. How the European SME, which has been disadvantaged in several respects in terms of IP regimes, lack of venture capital and lack of experienced managers, copes with the ever increasing importance of IP is uncertain. As biotechnology becomes ever more knowledge- and capital-intensive, so the role of IP is emphasised.

This chapter describes recent research in this under-examined area of IP and biotechnology SMEs. The study had three main aims. These were, first, to compare the experiences of UK SMEs in the biotechnology industry in their management of intellectual property; second, to assess the barriers to the development and use of intellectual property faced by UK SMEs in the biotechnology industry in entering and maintaining a presence in their respective industries; and, third, to examine the extent to which UK SMEs in the industry take advantage of existing patenting systems in the United Kingdom. The importance to SMEs of licensing to raise revenues and access technologies in this sector was also considered. Finally, the study aimed to assess the implications of the findings for UK policy and for the innovative and competitive position of UK-based biotechnology SMEs.

The UK biotechnology industry

Biotechnology is best viewed as an expanding series of enabling technologies. For the purposes for this research, biotechnology was broadly defined using the OECD (1982) definition: 'the application of scientific and engineering principles to the processing of materials by biological agents' (OECD, 1982). However, because the term biotechnology has been so loosely applied over the last 15 years, this definition alone is too generalised to describe an industrial sector. For the purposes of this study, therefore, the principal technologies falling within biotechnology were deemed to be:

gene amplification
DNA sequencing
DNA synthesis
diagnostics kits
DNA probes
protein synthesis
protein sequencing
monoclonal antibodies
cell/tissue culture and engineering
purification/separation
electrophoresis
transgenic plants and animals
transgenic plants and animals
gene therapy
gene antisense technology
biotransformation
enzyme engineering.

Three different types of biotechnology SMEs can be recognised: 'developers', fully integrated SMEs and 'supplier' SMEs. 'Developers' are those companies which take ownership of an idea and convert it into a commercially valuable product or service. Fully integrated biotech companies are those which have invested in research, development, manufacturing, sales and marketing. There are relatively few such companies because of significant barriers to forward integration where product approval is a relatively slow process. In the United Kingdom, there is also a growing supplier sector, i.e. companies which supply equipment, materials or service either to specialist biotechnology concerns or to user industries. Only those supplier companies which were specialists in biotechnology were included in the study described here. A total of 120 biotechnology companies from across the United Kingdom were incorporated into an ACCESS database. All were undertaking activities relevant to the list of technologies given above.

A sample of 33 biotechnology companies was selected for intensive analysis. These represented a broad range of sectors including biopharmaceuticals, vaccines, gene therapy, genomics, diagnostics, transgenic animals, microbiology, environmental diagnostics, biotechnology reagents and instrumentation and plant biotechnology.[1] The sectoral focus of the companies interviewed is illustrated in Table 5.1.

All except one recently acquired firm were independent. Detailed financial information was only available from those firms (about 40 per cent) which were publicly owned. The majority of these firms were from the biopharmaceutical sector and had been started with venture capital before being floated on the London Stock Exchange.[2] Less than a quarter of the companies surveyed had significant sales of developed products. None of these were from the biopharmaceutical sector. Although some of the other companies undertook small amounts of contract research or had income from licensing, these activities were relatively small-scale and certainly not enough to offset the losses incurred through R&D expenditure.

The firms were interviewed using a structured questionnaire to facilitate data collection. The questions covered the following:

- the size, age and financial background of the firm;
- the firm's knowledge of existing IP legislation, the effectiveness of IP legislation and its impact on innovation;
- the means for developing IP, including the number of personnel involved;
- the strategies for protecting and exploiting the firm's IP;
- the limitations of using patents;
- the problems encountered in entering and staying in the market.

A range of industry organisations were consulted to gather information on the effectiveness of current and pending IP regimes for biotechnology, particularly in relation to the European Directive for the Protection of Biotechnological Inventions and its implications for the protection of intellectual property by European SMEs.[3]

Table 5.1 Sectoral focus of 33 UK biotechnology SMEs

Sectoral focus	*No. of firms*
Animal biotechnology	2
Biopharmaceuticals	16
Diagnostics	4
Other	3
Gene therapy	2
Plant biotechnology	0
Technical	5
Vaccines	1

Types of intellectual property protection

For most UK biotechnology SMEs, protection of their biotechnology inventions is fundamental for the viability of the enterprise. This is especially so for SMEs in the biopharmaceutical sector. Although patents and trade secrets are the most important methods of IP protection in the biotechnology industry, lead time, rapid technology development and effective marketing can also be effective in protecting products in the marketplace. In the study, all of the companies using patents rated the effectiveness of patents to protect imitation highly. The majority of these firms also viewed patents as a highly effective means of securing royalty income. This result suggests that although licensing out (see below) was occurring at a fairly low level, most companies saw this activity as having important economic potential. The same companies using patents consistently viewed trade secrets as an ineffective means of protecting their products.

Lead time was seen as a reasonably effective means of protection by most companies. Rapid technology development was viewed as particularly unimportant by those companies having long product development pipelines, namely those from the biopharmaceutical sector. The exceptions here were the gene therapy and animal biotechnology companies which are at a relatively early stage and where rapid developments in technology may be critically important but unpatentable. Companies from the diagnostics, vaccines and technical sectors emphasised the importance of rapid technology development as a means of protecting their products. A steady stream of incremental improvements was seen as essential to retaining market share.

The protection of IP through patents

About half of the companies interviewed use patents as their principal means of intellectual property protection. All these firms file early on in the research and development process in order to secure priority in their patent applications. Patents are used extensively by all firms in the biopharmaceutical, gene therapy, medical device and animal biotechnology sectors and those SMEs marketing environmental devices. Firms which are not using patents directly to protect their products and processes include those developing and marketing diagnostic kits, biotechnology reagents including antibodies, cell lines and other similar products, and those developing and marketing microbe-related products.

In general, when biotechnology companies use patents, they will aim to protect the invention of a process or a product at the earliest possible stage when potential value is indicated. Such patenting activities generally precede the arrival of a potential product or process in the market by several years. This is particularly so in biopharmaceuticals. In this sector, all 16 firms emphasised the importance of patents for potential new drugs. This is unsurprising given the long development time and high capital expenditure on research and development required within the pharmaceutical industry and the added uncertainty of new technologies. Strong intellectual property protection on new inventions was seen as essential and all respondents engaged in this sector indicated that the viability of R&D programmes was necessarily dependent on strong IP protection. Compounds with useful therapeutic activity but poor IP protection potential were not pursued. For example, British Biotechnology did not take the candidate drug IGF II (insulin-like growth factor) into pre-clinical and clinical development because of the compound's weak IP position. This decision was made despite its potential in the treatment of osteoporosis.

As expected, all firms associated with the biopharmaceutical sector[4] were high users of patents, which were used to protect between 90 and 100 per cent of their inventions. Most used trade secrets at a very low level and about eight claimed not to use them at all. In the other sectors, there was generally much less emphasis on the importance of patents as a means of protecting a company's inventions. This was particularly so for those companies producing biological reagents such as novel antibodies, enzymes and cell lines. Here, reliance on trade secrets was often 100 per cent, as these inventions were generally viewed as unpatentable. A similar situation existed for one veterinary pharmaceutical company and a microbiology company. In the experience of these companies, trade secrets were felt to be an important and effective means of protecting in-house expertise and products. However, two firms producing devices, one medical, one diagnostic, relied on patenting their products wherever possible.

Using the patent system

How do UK biotechnology SMEs use the various patent systems? The majority endorsed the widely held view that uncertainty about what is and is not patentable in biotechnology is a fundamental problem of engaging with current IP regimes. There was general agreement that the diversity of national patent systems and policies complicates the process of obtaining intellectual property protection. Nearly all of those using patents used the PCT (Patent Convention Treaty) application system rather than filing directly at national or regional offices such as the European Patent Office (EPO). Using the PCT route was viewed as the most cost-effective and efficient method. The PCT application is made direct to WIPO (World Intellectual Property Organisation) in Geneva which undertakes the initial searches. All companies using patents in the survey used the UK national office to file patents to establish priority and the European Patent Office at a later stage of the PCT application. The time taken for such applications to be processed varies. Three years was frequently cited as a common period between filing and granting at the national offices. Significantly, about a quarter of those companies who used patents also filed in the United States Patent and Trade Mark Office as well as using the PCT route. This was viewed as a faster route to achieving US priority than by proceeding along the PCT route alone. US and European patent offices were both viewed as very important while the UK office was valued mainly for its use as a cost-effective means of filing a patent application to secure priority. This application was frequently allowed to lapse once a PCT application was in process. Most companies surveyed did file applications at the Japanese Patent Office, but this office was thought considerably less important than the others. The most important determinant of patent office preference was market size. The initial and maintenance costs of various offices was not an important criterion for its use nor was time to approval or likelihood of grant.

All the companies using patents viewed this means of IP protection as essential to the operation of their business. Despite the considerable costs involved in both filing and maintaining patents, only one company viewed these expenses as an entry barrier to commercialisation. The majority viewed patents as a necessary expense and were inclined to patent a process or potential product when advised to do so. Although there was agreement that many early patents awarded in biotechnology were excessively broad, most companies aimed to obtain the most extensive scope possible for their own inventions. Most of the firms regularly reviewed their patent portfolios so that those inventions which no longer met the criteria for commercial potential are allowed to lapse. In this way, flexibility in IP protection and the costs incurred can be retained. Why do these UK biotechnology SMEs use patents? Improvement of the company's negotiating position with other companies was viewed as very important by virtually all the biopharmaceutical companies within the sample. Obtaining access to foreign markets was viewed as a significant use of patents, as was the prevention of imitation, although the uncertainty of securing a monopoly for particular inventions was generally acknowledged.

In contrast to a report earlier in 1997 that UK biotechnology SMEs are failing to implement procedures to establish priority for US interference proceedings,[5] this study showed that nearly all SMEs using patents were fully aware of the need to comply with these requirements. Research staff regularly kept detailed laboratory notebooks which were signed and dated each day and witnessed once a week.

The extent of patent ownership

Analyses of patent ownership can provide a range of insights into corporate strategy. However, there are important limitations. The actual strength of a patent is unknown unless it is challenged in court. There is, moreover, wide variation in the period between the filing, granting and publication of patents at different patent offices, leading to limitations in the interpretation of patent data. Patent analyses are best viewed as 'snapshots' of broad, longer- term trends.

In this study, the patent family data[6] shown in Table 5.2 confirmed the importance of patents to those firms in biopharmaceuticals, gene therapy and animal biotechnology. In these areas, patents are used extensively to protect new technologies and potential products. Despite the fact that both animal biotechnology and gene therapy are at an early stage of development (the latter being, as yet, clinically unproven), their perceived potential has resulted in intensive patenting activity characterised, on the one hand, by some very broad patents (for example, Genetics Institute's *ex vivo* gene therapy patent) and, on the other, patents of relatively narrow scope. The numbers of patent families in the diagnostics companies was much lower, reflecting the short product cycle and rapid market entry of the diagnostic products market. This is not to say that patents are unimportant to diagnostic companies. As the rate of

Table 5.2 Total number of patent families in 33 UK biotechnology SMEs

Sector	*No. of companies*	*Total no. of patent families*	*Mean no. of patent families*
Animal biotechnology	2	26	13.00
Biopharmaceutical	16	331	23.64
Diagnostics	5	22	4.40
Gene therapy	2	45	22.50
Other	2	0	0.00
Technical	5	3	0.60
Vaccines	1	0	0.00

identification of human genes increases over the next five years, opportunities for licensing may be limited. Potentially important disease genes may be beyond the budgets of the small firm (personal communication, 1997).

IP and research collaboration

Research collaboration has become almost de rigueur for much of biotechnology research in both the public and the private sectors. This mode of working became established early on, as biotechnology developed, mainly in the United States in the 1970s. The early spin-off of biotechnology SMEs from the US academic science base provided the foundations for the continuing process which has been unmatched in Europe (Ballantine *et al.*, 1997). The majority of biotechnology SMEs, both in the United States, Europe and elsewhere, have been dependent on collaboration with larger firms for research, development and marketing. Although biotechnology SMEs have demonstrated their ability to attain venture capital funding and successful public flotations, there has been and continues to be a need for collaboration with large firms, mostly multinationals, to sustain existing research programmes and develop new ones. This mode of operation developed during the first half of the 1980s when multinationals in the pharmaceutical and agrochemical industries were reluctant to invest in their own in-house biotechnology programmes and instead formed a series of alliances with the emerging biotechnology industry, many of which were pursuing research programmes focused on recombinant therapeutic proteins and monoclonal antibodies.

Today this pattern has continued and extended into a 'second wave' of biotechnology SMEs. These companies are specialising in new technologies such as gene therapy, genomics, antisense, DNA chip technology and combinatorial chemistry, and many are dependent on major alliances with pharmaceutical multinationals (Ballantine *et al.*, 1997). Indeed, major alliances between pharmaceutical and biotechnology companies increased by more than 32 per cent in 1997.[7]

In the study described here, all the firms surveyed aimed to capture as much intellectual property as possible from research collaborations. Indeed, obtaining IP from collaborations was, in many ways, a primary goal and 'our life-blood' as one firm put it. The primary drivers behind this objective were the importance of a substantive IP portfolio to attract private sector collaborators, venture capital and shareholders. The view that some start-up firms overvalue their intellectual property was endorsed by several of those interviewed. At least two-thirds of the firms using patents in biopharmaceutical-related areas had significant collaboration with other companies, mainly multinationals. Many biotechnology SMEs are highly dependent on research funds and research investment by larger companies. Multinationals and other companies investing in these biotechnology SMEs, however, will only do so if the area is backed by a strong IP protection. Similarly, all the companies using patents attracted venture capital at the start of their operations, showing a strong association between patents and the availability of finance. Collaboration between SMEs in the United Kingdom was virtually non-existent. Where it did occur, the SME was usually US-owned.

Despite their commitment to patents, those companies using them were aware of their limitations. Nevertheless they were generally optimistic about the patentability of their inventions. They were also consistently confident about the validity of those patents. The fact that other companies do not always enforce patents and that such competitors can legally invent around patents were not seen as important limitations. Rather they were seen as effects of the patent system that companies, in the words of one research and development director, 'have to live with'. The limitation that 'the technology development renders patents obsolete' was not perceived as important by firms producing new therapeutics. On the other hand, those companies involved in genomics, diagnostics, reagents and biological materials such as antibodies viewed this factor as a more significant limitation.

Companies varied in how much they were disadvantaged by disclosure. A small number of firms disliked the extent of disclosure but the majority viewed it as simply part of a system that worked reasonably well for them. The fact that firms participate in cross-licensing agreements with others was seen almost unanimously as an advantage rather than a disadvantage of the patent system. There was one exception when one sales and marketing director had the view that cross-licensing between large firms made it very difficult for small firms to compete in the same product area (thermophilic enzymes). Those firms not using patents viewed the principal limitations of the system as being that patents become obsolete in the short term and that competitors would legally invent around patents. They also viewed their inventions as potentially unpatentable and unlikely to be valid if challenged.

Licensing

Licensing patents for products or new technologies is an important objective of IP strategy for many biotechnology SMEs. By licensing out a technology, for example, which is sought by others, a start-up company can quickly secure a stream of income. However, the cost of doing this may be high in the long term. Licensing out key enabling technologies may allow a company's competitors to develop high-value products and reduce the company's own chances of success in the market. There is as yet little analysis of licensing strategies in the biotechnology industry. The confidential nature of some licensing deals can make research difficult. In the study described here, relatively few of the companies were significantly active in either licensing in or licensing out technology or products.

Licensing in

Although not all firms were willing to disclose detailed information, the majority indicated that licensing in technology or specific products was generally not a major component of their intellectual property strategy. For example, in one of the largest biopharmaceutical companies, less than ten patents were licensed in, these being for both products and processes. Most firms across the various sectors were licensing in, in some form: small amounts of technology or products from the private and public sectors. Details about the nature of licensed-in technology was generally considered confidential, though it was apparent that this was happening on a relatively small scale. At least 50 licenses for products and technology were being 'licensed in' by a group of 23 companies. A small number of these were licenses for patents on technology or products owned by founders of the company. Of the few companies who were not licensing in patents at all, only one was a biopharmaceutical company and all had been established within the last seven years.

Licensing out

However, the majority of those companies actively patenting their inventions indicated that licensing out their intellectual property was an important objective of their corporate strategy. Nevertheless, amongst the biopharmaceutical SMEs, few actually appeared to be licensing out their potential products or technologies at a significant level. This was even the case for relatively well-established companies. Celltech was the exception, where 80 per cent of the company's patents were licensed out. About half of the companies issued at least 96 licenses for products (56) and technology (40), mostly to the private sector, while the other half were not licensing out any technology. What kind of companies were not licensing out their technology and why? Those companies engaged in the highly competitive, capital-intensive but relatively immature areas of gene therapy and animal biotechnology were in this group. For these firms, patenting is the main means of protecting intellectual property. The strategy of not licensing out means that the intellectual property is developed in-house, maximising the comparative advantage and limiting external competition. Three other biopharmaceutical companies avoid licensing out for much the same reasons. However, the latter are likely to offer product licences in future marketing deals with large companies. The remainder were either non-patent-users or recently established genomics companies which may license out in the future.

There was a general consensus that licensing income played a potentially important role in supplementing other forms of income. However, the more established companies indicated that they expected the importance of licensing income to diminish as the company brought its own products to market. Only in the truly research-based company which has no ambitions towards vertical integration does licensing income appear an on-going objective.

Other methods of intellectual property protection

The companies not using patents relied heavily on trade secrets as a means of protecting their products. Rapid technology development and efficient marketing are also seen as important means of protecting their intellectual property. These firms generally produce products and/or technology with rapid development times and market entry, such as antibodies, cell lines, reagents, diagnostics and enzymes.

Lead time was seen as particularly important for those firms that were pre-eminent in their field and without market competition in the United Kingdom and Europe. These firms used frequent technical improvements to their inventions. Being first on the market was also seen as extremely important. In general these firms, which did not include the biopharmaceutical group, were relatively inactive in research collaboration. Most of their research was undertaken in-house with up to three collaborations which were usually in the public sector. The collaborations generally take the form of specific pieces of contract research rather than research collaboration, to develop a basic/strategic research area which is not being pursued in-house. Intellectual property agreements were not important per se in these collaborations and confidentiality was achieved through the imposition of contract conditions. These firms were characterised by a lack of venture capital or public shareholders and therefore the existence of an IP portfolio in this respect was unimportant.

Companies not using patents limited their intellectual property commitments. This was generally confined to the drawing up of licensing agreements for licensing out technology or products. Monitoring systems were not employed to keep abreast of potential infringement, and informal networks and awareness tended to be the most useful method of avoiding potential problems. Three companies commented that the way in which they usually learn that they are infringing another inventor's patents was by receiving notification from the holder's lawyers. As such firms were not in a position to defend their alleged infringement, such matters are usually resolved by withdrawing the allegedly infringing product from the market.

Most of the SMEs who were filing patents used their own know-how to draft patent applications. The majority used external patent agents to file and process patent applications. About a quarter used patent databases to assist their decision-making relating to patent filing and only two used consultants to advise them about intellectual property protection. The majority of firms were aware of the need to keep ahead of potential infringement although there were five who did not take any steps to do so. The most common method used by two-thirds of the companies was simply the acquisition of information through informal networks. About a third of firms used scientific literature and databases to monitor infringement. Few firms had designated staff to monitor infringement.

It was clear that there was almost no experience of litigation for infringement of patents belonging to other parties. Because most of the companies were at a relatively early stage of their development with the majority not yet having products in the market, experience of patent infringement was extremely limited. How are UK biotechnology SMEs coping with the prospect of defending patents when they are often constrained by funding? A few firms insured themselves against the costs of litigation. This tends to occur in those which have been founded on the basis of specific IP. At least half the companies using patents took the view that they could afford to meet potential infringement costs, while about 25 per cent felt that they could do this through the agency of their multinational collaborations. There were at least nine firms using patents, mainly those outside the biopharmaceutical sector, which were uncertain about their capacity to defend their intellectual property. A further five firms using patents on the margins of or outside the biopharmaceutical sector, had the view that they could *not* defend their intellectual property. Obviously in such cases these SMEs were proceeding with the hope that their patents would not be challenged.

Conclusions

IP protection, along with several other external factors within the business environment, strongly influences the availability of opportunities for new biotechnology companies entering and maintaining a presence in the sector. The distinctive nature of IP in this respect is, however, by no means uniform. UK biotechnology SMEs are broadly divided into two groups on the basis of their IP strategies: those using patents and those using trade secrets. IP in the form of patents is seen as crucial to the survival and potential success of UK biopharmaceutical SMEs in the marketplace. There are also a number of companies in the UK biotechnology sector which do not use patents but which nevertheless have a significant economic impact. These companies are primarily suppliers of biotechnology-related reagents and materials and play a crucial role in providing other biotechnology SMEs and large user firms with essential specialist materials. They recognise the essential nature of protecting their inventions and use trade secrets, frequent technical improvements and lead time as a means of maintaining their position in the marketplace. As the application of biotechnology develops in the marketplace, reliance upon patenting for protection of many biotechnology-related products and processes is necessary to maintain UK competitiveness in Europe and European competitiveness in global markets.

What does the study tell us about intellectual property as a potential barrier to entry and a barrier to maintaining a presence in the industry? What is quite clear is that in the majority of cases where patents are used conventionally as a form of protection for inventions, the lack of patent portfolio will preclude the raising of venture capital or funds from private investors. Thus, for several sectors of the biotechnology industry, namely biopharmaceuticals, gene therapy and medical devices, a patent portfolio owned directly by the firm or indirectly through exclusive licensing is a *prerequisite* to raising financial support. In turn, lack of venture capital, which generally revolves around IP, prohibits the development of companies in the previously mentioned sectors. There are very few examples of biopharmaceutical-related UK SMEs which have not raised venture capital.

IP also provides a critical barrier to maintaining a presence in industry, as multinationals will only collaborate with those SMEs with strong IP portfolios. Virtually all the firms involved in the biopharmaceutical sector had strong formal links with pharmaceutical multinationals. Such collaborations were underpinned by IP either owned or licensed by the biotechnology SMEs. Those SMEs interviewed rated the importance of patents as a means of attracting private sector collaborators very highly. The role of IP in this respect is particularly interesting. On the one hand, the pharmaceutical multinationals, European and US, are accessing products and technology from UK biotechnology SMEs by collaborative agreements underpinned by intellectual property. At the same time, UK biotechnology SMEs are using IP as a means of establishing this essential support. Why do UK biotechnology SMEs attach such importance, particularly in the biopharmaceutical sector, to these collaborations with multinationals? Relatively few firms have the means to become vertically integrated, as there are formidable entry barriers to doing so. Most of the firms interviewed do not have the capacity to undertake the clinical, regulatory and marketing stages of biopharmaceutical product development. These stages require very substantial investment in both personnel and industrial infrastructure and were simply beyond the means of these small companies. The majority intended to use collaborative arrangements with multinationals as a means of bringing their products to market. Pharmaceutical multinationals with their experience and resources are well placed to take SME inventions, particularly drugs, through the crucial and costly development stages (Ansell and Sparkes, 1996). This pattern, whereby UK and non-UK biotechnology companies are essentially research companies, who will bring their products to market through the agency of others, is very common elsewhere.

In the case of those firms which were developing products with long development cycles, there were other formidable barriers but it is argued that these were intricately related to IP. Raising venture capital, successful IPO offerings, multinational collaborations, multinational co-development and so on are all patent entry barriers to such firms. However, the lack of intellectual property in the form of strong patents will prevent small biotechnology firms from moving forward in respect of these further entry barriers.

What is the role of IP in those firms not using patents? Here we are dealing with a group of small firms which have a very different kind of product to those mentioned above. These products are characterised by rapid innovation and short development cycles. Such firms are vertically integrated in that they design *and* produce products in-house and have almost no collaborations with large firms. Because IP is largely concerned with the immediate needs of the company to protect their products in the marketplace, they have less influence on other entry barriers. The use of trade secrets, particularly in relation to know-how, was held to be reasonably effective by this group of firms. The wide use of trade secrets may not, however, be in the public interest because of the lack of disclosure. What is required here is a balance between disclosure through patents and secrecy being maintained in a way which is optimal, both economically and with regard to the public interest (Hayward and Greenhalgh, 1994). These companies, on the whole, do not require venture capital to start up, relying instead on private investors. The R&D expenditure and other costs of firms outside the biopharmaceutical sector tend to be orders of magnitude lower than those in the sector. These companies can therefore be much more independent. The development of reagents, cell lines and antibodies attracts much lower overheads in terms of R&D expenditure and therefore the entry barriers are lower. Indeed the presence of such specialist companies in the biotechnology industry has grown considerably over the last decade. However, while the entry barriers are lower, there are indications that maintaining their presence in the industry is more difficult. The lack of entry barriers has meant that this sector is extremely competitive due to significant numbers of new entrants, and therefore pricing of products and technical advantage have become very important in maintaining market share.

An interesting point that emerged was the companies' attitude towards infringement. Relatively few of the companies sampled had any experience of infringement. Many of these firms are young and their products have yet to come to market. Infringement may turn out to be a more significant barrier to the survival of such firms once these products are in the marketplace. What is surprising is the apparently high level of confidence that virtually all the firms using patents have in the strength of their intellectual property. Almost none of these firms had had any experience of infringement and yet their procedures for monitoring infringement seemed somewhat ad hoc. Very few appeared to have a systematic approach to monitoring infringement. Overall, firms have the expectation that their external patent agents will have this responsibility but it must be said that this prospect seems somewhat unrealistic. Few appear to be hiring patent agents specifically for this service. Almost no firms have substantive in-house monitoring of infringement of their intellectual property. Even in large UK biotechnology firms which have products in phase III clinical trials have only one or two personnel dedicated to IP.

The lack of awareness about the European Directive for the Protection of Biotechnological Inventions was surprising. Most firms considered the directive unimportant for their company and very few individuals knew anything much about it at all. Given that its first reading was in July 1997, this was surprising. There was a general view that the directive was 'somehow important' for the European bio-industry as a whole but such views were extremely vague. In general, this prevalent attitude reflects the fact that many of these small firms have come to grips with the patent system as it is and do not have the time or the interest to keep up with developments unless these explicitly affect them. There were, however, at least five firms who felt that the some proposed amendments to the European directive could influence them negatively. Such firms were relying on trade associations such as the Bioindustry Association (BIA) to advise them accordingly.

The government role in the UK biotechnology industry

None of the firms felt they had benefited significantly from government assistance to help develop their businesses. Other government agencies were viewed in terms of providing minimal support and bureaucratic obstacles. The smaller firms, i.e. those with less than 50 employees, felt they had neither the time nor the manpower to understand or apply for the various schemes available. Most firms did not see government programmes for SMEs as a priority, and in general very few firms displayed much interest in specific initiatives such as those on offer from the DTI.

The general view was that these schemes are actually more trouble than they prove to be worth.[8] Biotechnology businesses, especially in the supplier area, have to work extremely hard to innovate continually.

The smaller firms felt that the most important kind of government assistance would be funding of some kind. Firms in the technical and diagnostic areas generally held the view that assistance in developing a small patent portfolio would be helpful. Suggestions for an improved government role for IP biotechnology included the provision of funds for start-up firms in patenting key inventions; information on current developments and the implication of legislative developments in intellectual property for biotechnology; and better tax breaks for IP costs. Since the study was completed, the new Labour government has in fact introduced new tax incentives for entrepreneurs running research-based enterprises.

Acknowledgements

The author would like to thank all of the many people who gave up their time to be interviewed and Dr Nick Scott-Ram for his advisory role. The author is also very grateful to Modesto Vega, Michael Hopkins and Nicholas Simmonds for their assistance with data collation and analysis and to Caron Crisp for secretarial support. This research was funded by the ESRC/DTI[9] programme on Grant No. L325253032: Managing Intellectual Property: Electronic Publishing[10] and Biotechnology SMEs.

Appendix 1 Biotechnology SMEs interviewed

Advanced Biotechnologies
Aquaculture Vaccines
Antisoma
Axis Genetics Ltd
The Binding Site
Biocompatibles Ltd
Biogenesis Ltd
British Biotech Pharmaceuticals Ltd
Cambridge Life Sciences
Cantab Pharmaceuticals plc
Celltech Therapeutics Ltd
Chiroscience Group plc
Cortecs International
Environmed Ltd
Genetix Ltd
Genpak Ltd
Hexagen plc
Imutran Ltd (acquired)
Microbio Ltd
Mycoplasma Experience

Oxagen
Oxford Biomedica
Oxford Glycosystems
Peptide Therapeutics
PolymasK
PPL
Prolifix Ltd
Scotia
Therexsys
University Diagnostics (since acquired)
Vanguard Medica
Xenova Ltd
Zylepsis

Notes

1 The sample of 33 firms varied in size and geographical location. Small firms were defined as those that employed less than 49 employees, medium-sized firms between 50 and 249 workers and large-sized firms between 250 and 400. The smallest company interviewed had a total workforce of three full-time employees and the largest had 380. The average number of staff was 112 for biopharmaceutical companies and 13 for companies in the technical sector. In terms of size, the companies sampled fell broadly into a number of distinct groups. Those companies with products on the market ranged from very small firms employing three to 12 full-time individuals to those with up to 340 employees. Those companies with products in the pipeline but none as yet on the market had between 50 to 380 employees. Most recent start-ups had less than 20 employees. The oldest company was Celltech, established in 1980 and the newest was Oxagen set up in 1997. The majority of the companies were founded in the late 1990s.

2 Without exception all UK biotechnology companies involved in biopharmaceuticals made a loss in 1995/96. This averaged nearly £6 million in 1996. The two publicly owned companies from other sectors were also making a loss. Private companies were generally from the diagnostics or technical sectors and, with a few exceptions, had little or no venture capital and turnovers of less than $5 million. The three private biopharmaceutical/gene therapy SMEs aimed to achieve public flotation in the short or medium term. By contrast, the private SMEs from the other sectors had much less ambition in this respect.

3 Those organisations consulted included the representatives from DG XII, the European Commission and the Biotechnology Industry Association. The Association of British Pharmaceutical Industries, the UK Patent Office, the Department of Trade and Industry, EuropaBio, the Patent Forum and several individuals from academia.

4 Included here are biopharmaceuticals, gene therapy, genomics and animal biotechnology.

5 See Nabarro Nathanson (1996)

6 If inventors want protection for their inventions in more than one country, or through more than one patenting authority, this will require specifications to be registered with more than one patent office in what is known as a family of patents. A patent family is a patent whose specifications are published by different patent offices for the same invention. Together they form the patent family.

7 http://www.signalsmag.com/signalsmag.nsf. Major alliances are classified as those valued at $20 million or more.

8 However, several of the firms are members of the non-governmental UK Bioindustry Association (BIA) and most felt that this was a worthwhile activity. Relatively few firms, except the larger longer-established firms, had any connection with or knowledge about

EuropaBio, the European Trade Organisation. There were exceptions, but this was often down to the specific activities of one or two nominated individuals within a firm sitting on a committee or similar with the trade association.

9 Economic and Social Research Council/Department of Trade and Industry.

10 The electronic publishing research component was undertaken by Dr Puay Tang, SPRU. See Tang (1998) and Thomas and Tang (1997).

References

Ansell, J. and Sparkes, K. (1996) *US/European Biotechnology Deals 1992–1994: Unequal Division of the Spoils*, Spectrum Pharmaceutical Industry Dynamics, Waltham, MA.

Ballantine, B., Thomas, S. M. and Burke, J. F. (1997) *Benchmarking the Competitiveness of Biotechnology in Europe*, report prepared for EuropaBio, Brussels.

Dworkin, G. (1997) 'Should There be Property Rights in Genes?', *Phil. Trans. Roy. Soc. Lond. Series B-Biological Sciences*, 352 (1357), 1077–86.

Ernst & Young (1997) *Biotech '97 Alignment*, Ernst & Young, Palo Alto, CA.

Hayward, P. A. and Greenhalgh, C. A. (1994) *Intellectual Property Research Relevant to Science and Technology Policy*, ESRC, Swindon.

McTaggert, R. (1996) 'An Historical Development of Patenting Micro-organisms and Genetically Engineered Animals in the USA and Europe, Part 1 Developments in the USA', *Human Reproduction and Genetic Ethics, An International Journal*, 2 (1); 'Part 2', *Human Reproduction and Genetic Ethics, An International Journal*, 2 (2).

Nabarro Nathanson (1996) *The Prepared Mind*, Confederation of British Industry, London.

OECD (1982) *Biotechnology: International Trends and Perspectives*, OECD, Paris.

Tang, P. (1998) *Managing Intellectual Property: Electronic Publishing SMEs*, Science Policy Research Unit, University of Sussex.

Thomas, S. M. and Tang, P. (1997) *Managing Intellectual Property: Electronic Publishing and Biotechnology SMEs*, Science Policy Research Unit, University of Sussex.

6 Management of intellectual property by electronic publishers

Puay Tang

Introduction

Intellectual property issues have been formulated mostly in terms of legal and regulatory aspects. In the case of electronic publishing, as with a number of other technology-based industries, there has been concern on the part of government and international bodies to tighten intellectual property rights (IPRs). Much is written in the legal literature about defending intellectual property and a considerable amount in the economics literature about the efficacy of IPRs. The main concern, however, in this chapter is with *creating* and *managing* intellectual property (IP) in a context where its existence is reputed to be threatened by competition that may be legitimate or may not, notably piracy. When we speak of creating IP, we do not particularly mean its original spark of inspiration (if that ever exists), but taking things from that point up to the stage of commercialisation by the company or industry.[1] The *managing* of IP, which includes the traditional legal and economic issues, has to be considered in the light of how it is first created and commercialised in fast-moving industries.

A second issue in this chapter is the question of the efficacy of IPR protection, which is explored through the activities of the electronic publishing industry. It is worth noting that relatively little research has been undertaken in the matter of IP management in the service industries. Instead, most of the moderate number of empirical studies that currently exist concentrate on manufacturing activities such as pharmaceuticals. This has considerable implications for the two central issues, not just because of the difference in industries. The size distribution and close integration of the bulk of the firms that compose the electronic publishing industry, the nature and speed of technical progress in the area and the looming reality of piracy in a digital environment, all combine to provide the basis for an interesting and significant industry case study. In other words, an overarching concern of this chapter is to examine how electronic publishers are managing their IP in an environment that appears to foster piracy.

The chapter is organised as follows. The next section briefly presents the structure of the UK electronic publishing industry, which is primarily composed of small and medium-sized enterprises (SMEs), and in particular describes the industry in terms of its perceived strengths and weaknesses. This section also focuses on the problems that technology has caused with respect to tightening IPRs and the conditions affecting entry and exit. Electronic publishing is defined in terms of the activities involved in the creation and production of CD-ROMs and off-line and on-line databases that are also available via the internet. CD-ROMs include compilations of text, audio, image and video content.[2] The chapter then briefly scans the policy responses to the perceived threat of piracy that digital technologies have brought about. This paves the way for the introduction of the data that were obtained from a survey of firms in electronic publishing, relating to both creation and management of IP. Following this the conditions affecting entry and exit from the industry are examined, implying a mismatch between firms' needs and governmental policy-making. This section also presents the views of the firms on the reform to the IPR (particularly copyright) regime, and highlights, at the end, the fact that piracy is not a significant factor in 'business calculations'. The next section advances suggestions for government 'intervention' in the electronic publishing industry. It will be shown, however, that firms do not appear to invest too many resources seeking government help. The final section draws conclusions from the evidence. In particular it contends that national and supranational policies for defending IP, aimed at protecting its *management*, have overwhelmingly been directed at matters, particularly piracy, that are secondary to the main concerns of the industry. We find that pressure to tighten IPRs actually worries the bulk of the smaller firms.

Electronic publishing, technology anxieties and IPR

The production of electronic publications in the United Kingdom is, in large part, dominated by small and medium-sized enterprises.[3] The largest firm in our survey has about 200 employees while the smallest has just two. While the SMEs are dependent on linkages to suppliers and users, the industry remains fragmented, with little vertical integration in the usual sense (more of this below). The fragmentation of the market makes it difficult to estimate its size.

Reviewing the industry

Most of the firms in the survey felt that the industry would grow, but were unsure of the direction it would take. It was suggested that although CD-ROMs appear to be the main form of electronic publications, the internet and other forms of on-line delivery, such as through television, could be the preferred medium, as evidenced by the rapid take-up of the internet. According to the surveyed firms, the excessive hype over multimedia and electronic publications as a mass consumer product over the last decade, with the exception of entertainment products, has not materialised in the way that pundits forecast for a number of reasons.

For the consumer market, the relatively lower penetration of home computers in the United Kingdom does not bode well for electronic publishing, when compared to the developments in the United States. The majority of the firms felt that if the computer continues to be the main means of access to electronic publications, the penetration rate must edge towards that of the VCR (more than 80 per cent in the United Kingdom). If, however, television becomes the other main means of delivery and access, as illustrated by current developments in converting the television into a computer (TV/PC and web-based TV), then UK electronic publishing would be likely to flourish significantly. The firms serving niche business markets, however, felt that they would continue to do well, particularly in the business-to-business segment of the market. Most firms claimed that developing niche markets is a main means by which small firms can survive.

On the whole, the firms surveyed were not pessimistic or dubious about the future of UK electronic publishing. Such results confirmed the widely known strengths of the UK publishing industry and there appeared to be an absence of pessimism. More revealing and portentous are the perceived 'knowledge-based' weaknesses, especially of SMEs, such as the lack of marketing skills and the professionalism of firms of this size. The strengths and weaknesses of the UK publishing industry are indicated in Tables 6.1 and 6.2.[4]

However, UK electronic publishing activity compares favourably to that of the United States, despite the US lead in the development of software applications. The United States employs about 20 million people in software programming; the United Kingdom employs roughly 500,000.[5] Considering the size of the US population, one can suggest that British strength in software is considerable. Furthermore, in a study on electronic publishing, it was found that the United Kingdom is second to the United States in the production of CD-ROM titles.[6] In another study on electronic information services and products, it was found that the United Kingdom is the

Table 6.1 Strengths of UK publishing

Long publishing tradition in the UK	32%
English language	16%
Quality of publishing	16%
Lots of creativity	13%
Awareness of technology	10%
UK is an arts centre	3%

Note
$n = 24$

Table 6.2 Weaknesses of UK publishing

SMEs' lack of distribution and marketing skills	13%
Lack of financial support	10%
Conservative attitude and risk-averse	6%
Lack of government support	6%
Lack of professionalism of SMEs	6%
Computer illiteracy and ignorance of the older generation	3%
Lack of technical standards	3%
Price of products	3%
Segmented market	3%

Note
$n = 24$

predominant producer and user of electronic products and applications when compared to the other member states of the European Union.[7] The study showed that among the member states of the European Union, British firms led in several sub-sectors of the multimedia market. The EU is second to the United States in the production of CD-ROM titles, although there are more companies involved in electronic publishing than there are in the United States.

According to a 1997 report by Olivetti Personal Computers, British pupils lead the world in computer access, with the country at the top of the league for computer literacy among pupils. Britain has proportionately more schools with computers than any other nation. Significantly, there has been an increase in the number of children using a computer at home, with one in five computer-owning households connected to the internet.[8] The recent measures announced by government to help make available computers to a wider segment of the population, as well as 'wiring up' all secondary schools to the internet, augur well for British electronic publishing.

Technology anxieties

Digital products and services have brought about a paradox, which is that electronic publishers, who are in the vanguard of electronic trading, are also lamenting the increased prospects of electronic depredation. There are seven main characteristics of digital technology that help to explain this paradox. They are:

- the ability to morph, restructure, write over and manipulate the information, and combine audio, video and textual information into multimedia products;
- speedy, simultaneous and remote access to centralised sources of information;
- the increasing pervasiveness and decreasing prices of fast and powerful home and business computers that permit easy access to, and misappropriation of, copyright material, such as posting such material on bulletin boards;
- the interconnectivity of private computers which facilitates the interactive and joint creation of works, making it difficult to create an authoritative work, as data and information can be manipulated and modified;
- the masking of original authorship through the use of sophisticated software, and the ability to make unlimited 'perfect' copies that threaten the authenticity and integrity of original works;
- the ability to delete copies instantaneously; and
- the increasing storage capacity of the digital media to store information, such as that found in CD-ROMs, DVD-ROMs and DVD-RAMs (digital versatile disks).[9]

In particular, digital technology is making the *identification* of copyright infringement difficult (copyright protects literary works, such as publications, databases and software). Rapid access to sources of information, and easy and instant downloading complicate the tracking by copyright-holders of the movements of their works. Even if the initial distribution of information is lawful, it is extremely difficult or virtually impossible to control its redistribution, onward transmission or reproduction without the implementation of technical applications (more of this below).

The identification problem, in turn, makes *enforcement* of copyright a formidable task as copyright-holders realise that they may increasingly lose control of the ownership of their intellectual property. The increasingly perceptible difficulties of identification of copyright infringement and enforcement of copyright have created a conundrum for law and business. For instance, in November 1996, the popular British rock band U2 discovered that their new but unfinished songs not due for release until the spring of 1997 were being sold on compact disks in street markets, as well as being distributed through the internet. New sites in Brazil, Japan and France replaced a Hungarian-based site that was responsible for transmitting the U2 songs, although it was closed down by national authorities. This incident illustrates the speed and ease with which digital piracy can be conducted, and the difficulty which national authorities encounter in tackling the 'growth industry' of digital piracy.

Still others claim that pirates have expediently exploited the ineptitude of the current law to deal effectively with digital copyright infringement. Furthermore, the strategy of increasing the prices of electronic information products to deter piracy could imply a diminution of revenues from electronic publishing and a suppression of demand. In such a scenario, access to electronic publications will be limited and investment possibly reduced, thereby constraining the envisaged growth of electronic publications. In other words, unless there is stronger and more effective protection and the tracking of authorised use of digitised information, the development of the digital market could be frustrated.[10]

Such an argument presents yet another paradox. On the one hand, a major asset of electronic media is their ability to reduce the cost of access to, and distribution of, information, and thereby increase diffusion. On the other hand, the fear of widespread digital piracy could lead to potential exclusion through a need to impose higher prices. This is likely to limit access to affluent and educated customers and users. Such an outcome would defeat the very purpose of copyright, which is that 'protection should not alter the existing balance of rights and obligations between the right holders and users . . . [and] that protection should not aim to restrict access to the information but rather to exploit the available technologies to maximise the openness and transparency of the (exploding) information markets'.[11] Argued this way, copyright threats and the fear of piracy tend toward the imposition of higher prices and diminished investment, both of which could imperil electronic publishing.

Legal policy responses to the threat of piracy

It is noted that digital technologies have not only helped to foster a flourishing information marketplace, but also a thriving 'piracy industry'. The contribution of digital technologies to the growth of electronic publishing is decidedly Janus-faced. The increasing trend of selling software through the internet may provide an additional boost to piratical activities, and reinforce the concern with digital piracy.

Yet, despite the rampant illegal reproduction and sales of such products, these industries have continued to flourish. Software grew at a rate of 12.5 per cent for the years 1990 to 1996, nearly 2.5 times faster than the overall US economy. Packaged business software, the common target for pirates, grew at an even faster rate of about

14.1 per cent.[12] In short, while piracy may well be rising, it does not appear to have a commensurate effect on the very group of business people who ought to be most concerned with it, according to the survey.

However, the increased amounts of piracy have been regarded as a main effect of digital technologies by the copyright industries, of which the publishing industry is a major player.[13] In the United States and Europe, the copyright industries have vigorously argued that inadequate copyright protection would threaten the basic incentive of copyright and jeopardise investments in creation and innovation of multimedia products and electronic publications.[14] The arguments and threats of the vocal and powerful representatives of the copyright industries imply overwhelmingly that inadequacies in the current copyright regime are to be held responsible for any eventual slowdown or decrease in innovative digital applications and electronic publications. Equally ominous is the view that information and artistic creations would not be made widely accessible if copyright protection were not extended. Such intimations appear to question the very essence of an 'information society'.

Since the early 1990s, governments in the United States and Europe and the World Intellectual Property Organisation have begun to reform their copyright regime to cope with the digital environment. Copyright, for instance, has been extended in the European Union, from the life of the author plus 50 years to plus 70 years. The European Commission will be issuing a Directive on Copyright and Related Rights in the Information Society with the aim of harmonising these rights throughout the Union. This directive was unanimously accepted by member states in March 2001.[15] Another significant legal move has been witnessed in the Directive on the Legal Protection of Databases, which is now being enacted as national legislation by the member states. In addition to copyright protection, this directive provides an additional 15 years of database protection, as a *sui generis* right.

In the United States, the Digital Millennium Copyright and the Copyright Term Extension Acts are now part of US IP law.[16] The former Act explicitly makes it a criminal offence to import, manufacture or distribute any device that serves to remove or interfere with the workings of technical systems of protection. The Extension Act extends copyright protection in a similar way to that stipulated in the European directive on copyright. In a seminal move, WIPO has negotiated with its member signatories two treaties: the Protocol to the Berne Convention for the Protection of Literary and Artistic Works (WIPO Copyright Treaty) and the New Instrument for the Protection of Rights of Performers and Producers of Phonograms. These two treaties also make illegal the circumvention or tampering with technical systems of protection, or manufacturing and distributing systems to tamper or deactivate these systems. The treaties have just been ratified by all their 56 member signatories.

The overall aim and result of these efforts have been a strengthening of IPR, particularly with respect to copyright and databases.[17] However, some industry groups, including representatives of leading US providers of information technology services, the computer and electronic industries, have objected to the various prohibitions on protection-defeating devices on the grounds that they will, among other things, discourage investment in the multimedia and electronic industries. There is similar resistance to database protection, as several database producers and publishers have strongly argued that more protection could compromise innovation and investment in the production of these and other multimedia products.[18] Two leading senior UK judges and experts in intellectual property, Mr Justice Laddie[19] (1999) and Sir Robin Jacob[20] (1997) have also echoed these warnings. In particular, they highlight the potentially damaging effect of expanding and tightening IPRs, arguing that such a move may also discourage innovation. Leading economists such as Hall Varian, and management experts such as Carl Shapiro, also contend that an aim of electronic publishers should be to maximise the *value* of IP, not *protection.*

Against these developments and arguments, the following section examines *if* and *how* these dilemmas affect the activities of electronic publishers. It begins with a description of the sample of electronic publishers who were interviewed. This is followed by a discussion of how they *create* and *manage* their IPR.

Creation and management

The analysis will be drawn from interviews of a sample of 31 small and medium-sized UK-based electronic publishers.[21] The firms were drawn from throughout the United Kingdom. Interviews were based on a semi-structured questionnaire. The categorised responses in the following tables are drawn *verbatim* from those provided by the firms.

The sample of 31 firms included 13 micro firms employing less than 10 employees, six small firms with 10 to 49 employees, and six medium-sized firms with between 50 and 200 workers (there were quite large gaps between these size bands). The sizes of the remaining six companies in terms of employment are not recorded. The average size of the workforce was 25, the median size was eight. Eight companies distributed their products in the United States, in addition to the United Kingdom and Europe; the balance concentrated their sales efforts in the United Kingdom and European markets. A total of 30 managing directors, five technical directors and eight marketing directors were interviewed.

The oldest vintage of the electronic publishers interviewed was 1980 and the newest was 1997. The majority were established in 1993 and 1994, which includes traditional publishers moving into the field. Sales revenues from electronic publications in 1995 ranged from £120,000 to £2.5 million (the average was £230,000). All but one were privately owned; two firms were considering flotation during the period of the project, although this has still not been realised. Thirty firms were British-owned and one financed by foreign (Dutch) capital.[22]

Of the total, 15 were on-line database producers, with five producing *only* on-line databases. Twenty-one companies produced *only* CD-ROMs, with ten producing a combination of on-line databases and CD-ROMs. The average budget for the development and creation of content as a percentage of total revenues from electronic publications was 70 per cent. In addition, most of the proprietors of the firms came from a technological background of computing and multimedia experience.

Creating IP

Table 6.3 reveals how IP creation is undertaken by the firms. IP comprises both the content and the intellectual effort that go into the innovation and the production of electronic publications.

A significant finding is that only about four firms wholly license the content and software used in their products, with the balance creating most of their content in-house. More than 80 per cent generate most of their IP themselves. A particularly high proportion conduct their own *research*, either in-house or sub-contracted on the premises (the one firm recording the outsourcing of research and all except one of the three recording sub-contracting also reported conducting in-house research as well). Other functions were also seen to be predominantly undertaken in-house, which demonstrates a need or preference on the part of smaller firms to integrate 'technologies' (e.g. *research, testing, design* and *graphic design, software development*), some 'production processes' (e.g. *editorial work, formatting*) and 'products' (*marketing and advertising, distribution*). This is partly explained by the lack of financial resources to outsource some of these activities and a simultaneous need for control of the research and production processes. These factors largely account for their 'vertical integration'.

Table 6.3 illustrates that the 'vertical integration' of functions reached down to quite small firms. All of the medium-sized firms (over 50 employees) and all but two of the small ones (10 to 49 employees) recorded in-house research; so did most of the micro firms (under ten) that had six or more employees. The high proportion of firms producing their own IP implies that they wanted to ensure that they could readily appropriate the fruits of their labour and intellectual effort.

Table 6.3 Sources of IP creation

Functions	*In-house*	*Outsource*[1]	*Sub-contract*[2]
Research	17	1	3
Testing	14	0	0
Design	12	1	0
Editorial work	12	0	1
Formatting	12	2	0
Software development	12	0	3
Marketing and advertising	10	0	0
Graphics design	8	0	0
Production	5	4	1
Hardware development	2	0	0
No in-house data reported[3]	9		

Notes

$n = 31$. Number reporting data = 23. Some firms are recorded more than once: for instance if they produced certain types of research in-house but outsourced other research areas.

1 Outsourcing refers to work done outside the firm.

2 Sub-contract applies to work done within the premises of the firm.

3 Includes one firm (with just three employees) reporting that none of the above were undertaken in-house.

Managing and protecting IP

Table 6.4 summarises the methods of protection adopted by the firms. Contrary to the findings of studies of manufacturing industry,[23] every single electronic publisher interviewed, even the smallest, utilised *legal* means of protection of one form or another. Unsurprisingly, legal protection is crucial to this service segment, but should it be further tightened, and what other forms of protection it should take are discussed below. The categories represented in Table 6.4 are explained as follows:

- *Technical* means of protection include encryption, dongles, key diskettes, firewalls and passwords.
- *Non-technical* means specifically refer to unique abbreviations and seednames; the latter are fabricated names that appear, for instance, on copyrighted mailing lists.
- *Non-technical* also refers to the reliance on collecting societies and trading standards officers to undertake surveillance of suspected pirates.
- *Bad publicity* as another way of protecting their intellectual property is exercised through distribution channels to 'promote the infringing activities' of the offending parties, though, as shown, few saw this as important.

Legal protection of innovations is mainly awarded through copyright, patent and trademark. Legal protection for the use of the innovation is exercised through user agreements and licences. None of the firms surveyed patented their innovations; all of them resort to copyright, which is, at any rate, an automatic process upon completion of a 'literary' product, in which software programmes are also included.[24] Interestingly, several firms did not know that software-based applications could be patented; the few that did know did not see any advantage of applying for this form of legal protection, apart from 'enriching some lawyers'. One medium-sized publisher, however, was considering applying for a patent for its innovative process of language instruction.

A slight majority of the firms (52 per cent) rely, at least in part, on *technical systems of protection.* Of the various forms of technical protection that are currently available, the most popular is encryption, which is currently used in several electronic information products such as CD-ROMs and on-line databases.[25] Despite its reputation as the

Table 6.4 Means of protecting intellectual property

Means of protection	*No. of firms*
Legal (copyright, patents)	31
Market niche	16
Technical	16
Pricing	9
Trust	6
Non-technical	5
Bad publicity	3

Note
$n = 31$

most effective (and difficult) method of protection, encryption is still to be widely adopted in electronic publications. Of the firms interviewed, seven encrypted their products, although one of them has since abandoned its use, claiming that it has made the product unnecessarily expensive and the contents difficult to access. Two others admitted to implementing a weak encryption, but at least claimed that it still offered additional protection. With the exception of five firms who upheld that technological protection would deter piracy, the other firms that adopted this form of protection displayed less conviction, and instead adopted more of 'an act of faith' attitude toward its utility.

Most of the firms perceived that experimentation with, and implementation of, protection mechanisms could lead to 'user-unfriendly' products through potentially increasingly complicated procedures and expensive products, and therefore reduce demand. This comes as little surprise because electronic publications are relatively new products, and customer resistance to and uncertainty about the value of these products, particularly by the large consumer market, have to be overcome. Against a fragmented and competitive electronic publishing industry, users tend to regard critically, and (some even suggest) suspiciously, any measure that hints at undue difficulty or increased cost.

Interestingly, many of the smaller companies perceived the push for technical protection as, in the words of one firm, 'a conspiracy by large companies to protect their territories from more innovative and imaginative smaller players'. It was averred that technical systems of protection would require a reliable customer support service in the event of technical difficulties, and, whereas large companies have the resources to provide well-supported customer service facilities, smaller companies often do not have these resources.

Four firms who voiced resistance to the implementation of technical systems argued that the absence of an accepted industry standard is a major reason for their position. Four companies that technologically protect also expressed concern over the lack of a standard, but felt that it was in their interest to adopt some form of technical protection, despite the possibility of it being replaced with another 'standard' in the future. Many of the newer companies thought it was more important to capture the externalities from easily accessible products than to be excessively worried about the security of their products. All companies worried about getting their product to market in the shortest possible time.

A similar number of firms rely, again in part, on *market niche* to protect their products. This in itself is thought-provoking, as the literature on IP protection has hardly addressed this as any form of protection. Yet it would appear that reliance on this form of protection enhances the opportunity for piracy because of the ease with which pirates can steal the material, given the limited size of the market. Yet it was reasoned that the specialised nature of their product and the limited market would make such pirated copies commercially non-viable.

Such an argument, perhaps unwittingly on the part of the firms, echoes the emphasis Teece and colleagues place on 'replicability, imitability and appropriability' for capturing value from knowledge assets. 'Replication involves transferring or redeploying competences from one concrete economic setting to another.'[26]

Replication is not usually a simple matter of transferring information; instead, what is being transferred or redeployed is likely to embody knowledge. This in turn implies that those undertaking the transfer have to understand what and how the elements being 'transferred' originally worked in order to reproduce the product or process. Often this will necessitate a high degree of background competence in the technologies as well as in the products (process). If these conditions hold true for replication, then perhaps the firms interviewed were alluding to the importance of tacit knowledge, which is also vital for imitability. As widely shown in the technology studies literature, much technological knowledge is indeed tacit rather than codified – the very expression 'know-how' implies a notion of tacit competence. Such knowledge may be best embedded in firms themselves, rather than trying to protect the products.[27]

Policy-makers, on the other hand, regard using tough IPRs and technical systems of protection to reinforce appropriability as *the* form of protection, especially with respect to the electronic publishing industry. This could be explained by their perception of the industry as being one susceptible to easy replicability and imitability, although such a perception appears to be questioned by the firms interviewed. It would appear that electronic publishers view appropriability as sufficiently strong without technical protection.

Furthermore, an important issue is not only to deter piracy but also to determine its source. Another respondent explained that the limited size of the market generally lent itself to easier identification of infringers, since most suppliers of niche markets generally know who their clients and competitors are. Again, the size of the market makes such a task more manageable. Moreover, officers from the Office of Trading Standards and collecting societies have been of considerable assistance in either closing down illegal operations or apprehending counterfeiters.

Odd as it may seem, *trust*, was advanced as the third means of protection. Trust, it was claimed, was necessary to sustain a presence in electronic publishing. It was also argued that the absence of trust could lead to the introduction of all kinds of binding contracts, user agreements and protection systems, all of which could contribute to reduced take-up. At a time in which 'cyber-savvy' users are increasingly used to 'Freeserve'™ internet services, or those similar to them, the imposition of additional terms and conditions of use of electronic products can be considered as somewhat onerous.[28] This trust argument supports a finding of the study by Stewart Macauley (1992). In it, he contends that businesspeople often prefer to rely on a 'man's word' or 'common honesty and decency' even where the transaction involved exposure to serious risk. The study went on to show that contractual arrangements 'may create undesirable exchange relationships between business units . . . [and that such a contract] indicates a lack of trust and blunts the demands of friendship, turning a co-operative venture into an antagonistic horse trade'. Several firms also suggested that that if electronic publishers are overly concerned with piracy of their goods, they should not be in the electronic publishing business, whose very nature makes it vulnerable to widespread electronic plundering.

Pricing, as a means of protection, was used through 'competitively low' prices. Although no profit margins were specifically volunteered, it appeared that they were probably between 5 per cent and 15 per cent above total costs of production. Pricing for on-line services was partly done by surveying the pricing structures of a range of commercial on-line information services. It was, however, claimed that low pricing might not serve as a useful means of protection in a mass consumer market, such as the leisure and entertainment sector, in which the volume of sales compensates for the low price. Such characteristics arguably provide an incentive for piracy. Yet low pricing is a major factor for take-up. As one games publisher put it, 'you have to reduce the current price of CD-ROMs to attract the working class and VCR [video cassette recorder] types to be attracted to such interactive products'. Interestingly, there was much concern about pricing themselves out of the market, e.g. through expensive IPRs.

The importance of such relatively unexplored aspects of managing IP such as reliance on *market niche*, *trust* and *competitive pricing* suggests that the capabilities of firms rest in part on competition in the industry. The following section speaks to these issues.

Competitiveness, entry and exit

This section addresses the competitive aspect of the industry, and focuses on assessing the entry barriers and conditions for exit from it. It also examines the role of piracy in either stimulating or discouraging participation in electronic publishing, especially in the light of national and international policy responses to the threat of piracy as discussed earlier.

Entering the industry

The conditions for entry and exit are firstly reflected in the responses on how IP is acquired for electronic publishing activities. The ranking of the types of IP are illustrated in Table 6.5.

'Resources' in Table 6.5 refer to tangible or intangible means or assets required for the production of electronic publications. The preponderant resources required

Table 6.5 Resources required for entry

Resources	*No. of firms*
Innovativeness	11
Financial resources	10
Management	9
Keeping up with technology	7
Distribution channels	5
Good marketing	5
Good service	3
Experience	2
Risk-taking	1

Note
$n = 31$

lie in intangible assets. The results are rather diverse, without the obvious predominance of any single resource. The 'static' resources like finance and good marketing all get some credit, without any majority support. But these findings suggest, not too surprisingly, that knowledge workers and knowledge-based activities are considered to be central to the vitality of UK electronic publishing. In a fast-moving industry, *innovativeness* comes top of the list, but serious attention is also paid to *keeping up with technology*. Conversely, *experience* comes near the bottom. One wonders, despite the fact that most of the electronic publishers have experience in either traditional publishing or a business that involves the use of information technology, if indeed *relevant* business experience in the electronic publishing industry merits serious consideration, either as a condition for entry or exit.

It is also noteworthy that, contrary to the view that service sectors are predominantly market-oriented, and essentially users rather than producers of technology, the 'products' functions are less important – *distribution channels*, *good marketing* and *good service* all get some support but substantially less than the 'technologies' functions. This perhaps implies that in highly competitive and possibly 'unstable' business environments, knowledge-based resources matter just a little more than product-based resources.

The factors seen as limiting entry into the industry, or entry barriers, are shown in Table 6.6. *Keeping up with technology* constitutes the leading impediment, although it was widely acknowledged that the wide and easy availability of reasonably priced computers and software has made it easier for prospective entrants than it would have been otherwise. Keeping up with technology is central to the capability of generating innovative products: for instance, the use and development of more versatile and sophisticated software. It is this aspect – skills – of keeping up with technology that appears to exercise the concerns of the firms.

Similarly, *innovativeness*, ranked second, is significantly seen as an entry barrier.

Table 6.6 Entry barriers to electronic publishing

Entry barriers	*No. of firms*
Keeping up with technology	11
Innovativeness	9
Lack of financial resources	7
Marketing	5
Difficulty with finding employees with right skills	4
Uncertainty of payback	4
Collection and maintenance of data	3
Establishing brand names and track record	3
Lack of industry knowledge	3
Lack of reliability of product/delivery	3
Lack of entrepreneurial skills	2
Piracy	2
Lack of good management	1
Difficulty of obtaining easy credit	1

Note
$n=31$

Respondents seemed to regard differentiating products as the key to a robust market for electronic publications. The differentiation lay in distinguishing between a good-quality product and an innovative product. A good-quality product could only include high-quality content; an innovative product requires a high degree of interactivity and imagination, for instance. Interestingly, many firms felt that, although the United Kingdom has a successful publishing industry, this has not been translated into more innovative electronic publications. Many firms considered current publications to be mostly 'unimaginative'. The *lack of financial resources*, ranked third, is a more conventional entry barrier – although it is of some importance, it ranks behind the factors already mentioned. As with the resources required for undertaking electronic publishing and the difficulties involved in establishing market presence, knowledge and skills feature importantly in entry barriers for new firms. Keeping up with technology not only entails cost and financial resources, but also demands the requisite skills for *using* the technology. The knowledge base needs are also reflected in *innovativeness*, *marketing* and *finding employees with the right skills*. Curiously, *lack of management* is not perceived as a significant entry barrier. This suggests that entering the electronic publishing business is initially perceived as primarily a problem of technical and product-related skills. It is also possible that smaller firms are not usually saddled with unwieldy bureaucratic procedures, and hence do not treat management capability as a priority requirement.

Significantly, Table 6.6 indicates that *piracy* is not perceived as a significant entry barrier to the sector – only two of the firms declared its significance. This might be thought especially odd, given that most of the intellectual property and innovation are created in-house, and constitute the largest part of operating expenses. Curiously, four firms declared that, if their publications were pirated, they would regard it as a 'compliment', since piracy of their products implies that their products had 'made it in the market'.

Exit from the industry

The factors that are regarded as promoting exit from the industry were elicited indirectly through requesting the main difficulties of remaining in the industry. They are listed in Table 6.7. The *cost of development* was most often noted as the biggest problem for remaining in the business, followed by *keeping up with technology* and *innovativeness*. 'Knowledge-based activities' and skills of both employees and management (*business acumen*) are clearly pivotal to maintaining market presence and avoiding exit. Again, these reflect the predominance of technologies (including product development) and administrative functions, with a lesser though still appreciable contribution from marketing.

The role of *piracy* in affecting the continued operations of electronic publishers (just five crediting it) is again rather revealing. One firm did, however, assert that piracy had nearly forced the company to cease its operations. The relatively low priority accorded to piracy implies that it is not a material threat to most businesses, even though the firms interviewed are small businesses that create most of their IP out of a budget that allocates a substantial portion to the creation and innovation

Table 6.7 Factors promoting exit

Factors impeding incumbency	*No. of firms*
Cost of development	15
Keeping up with technology	14
Innovativeness	10
Business acumen	9
Distribution	5
Piracy	5
Marketing	3
Bandwidth	2
Maintaining quality of customer support	2
Segmented market	2

Note
$n = 31$

process. The next section reviews their perceptions on the recent legal reforms to the copyright regime. This was asked for in order to elicit further their views on how they were managing their IPR and the conditions for entry and exit, and as another means of confirming their earlier views on these two issues.

Views on strengthening IPR

The firms were asked whether they believed that current European Commission directives on *Copyright and Related Rights* and the *Legal Protection of Computer Databases* (see above) would benefit the industry. Remarkably, 24 of the 31 firms said no. Among the seven firms who said yes were a few who admitted to very little knowledge of the content of such directives. The majority of the firms were only vaguely aware of legislative reforms to copyright, and several remarked on a 'management weakness' in their lack of knowledge of these matters. Somehow this acknowledgement did not seem to engender a sense of urgency. Only seven of them claimed to have in-house capabilities in legal matters. Despite the difficulties involved in prosecuting pirates and receiving compensation for damages, all firms but one maintained that the (current) law is still adequate as a deterrent against piracy.

Some warned against 'excessive tampering' with the law, as legal changes might make it even more complicated and difficult for SMEs to understand and comply with it. As it stood, many firms did not seem to be too familiar with the 'arcane' aspects of IP law. Furthermore, legal reforms seemed to imply that there could be an increased cost for copyright clearance and additional complications, and this would inevitably increase the cost of exploitation of IP and transaction costs. These possibilities were regarded with a considerable degree of unhappiness. Since the production of electronic publications is, in large part, dominated by SMEs, as explained above, increased cost could well stifle the growth of the industry and restrict choice.

In sum, the respondents believed that the present legal reforms could positively disadvantage the industry. The main point the survey illustrates is that IPRs are principally about creativity and resources. Piracy is not a material threat to investment in electronic publishing, as is widely posited by industry. Given the general structure of the electronic publishing industry, imitability is thus quite hard, contrary to the views of the policy-makers and their lobbyists. How can, or should, policy-makers help the industry? The next section addresses some suggestions for government 'intervention' in the industry.

Policy suggestions for government intervention

Most firms stated that they had not really considered government help for their businesses. Instead, government assistance was perceived in terms of minimal support and overwhelming bureaucratic obstacles. Firms declared that small companies do not have the time or manpower to understand and fill in the application forms required for government aid and grants. Many were not aware of government programmes for SMEs, such as the Information Society Initiative of the DTI, and the few that were aware of them felt that information on them was vague and of little help. Government grants are usually a 'one-shot deal' and firms considered these as inadequate for start-up companies in a rapidly evolving industry, especially as one of the factors for growth and remaining in the electronic publishing industry is 'keeping up with technology'.

Many also argued that civil servants, especially those of the DTI, did not fully understand technological developments and the needs of small publishing firms; instead, firms felt that the DTI's interests were often biased toward larger electronic publishing companies. A few firms, however, alleged that the over-emphasis on assistance for small companies disadvantage medium-sized firms. However, many acknowledged that publishing SMEs were partly responsible for their own lack of input into government programmes, as they were not organised within themselves to present their collective interests to government. As a corollary, most of the firms admitted that they were not members of any trade associations as they were dubious of the benefit of these organisations.

Others felt that civil servants were generally not business-minded, even though they provide help and guidance to industry. An example of the lack of business sense on the part of government officials is their lack of understanding that businesses that require technological upgrading need a different kind of financial assistance. In particular, this should address more sustained funding or more aid for technology procurement.[29] On the whole, the firms agreed that a main role of government, especially that of the DTI, was to ensure 'fair play' in the industry, by prudently considering the interests of all sizes of companies.

To sum up, the suggestions advanced for the government's role in the electronic publishing industry were:

- to provide *sustained* funding for capital equipment and development;
- to provide *sustained* funding for educational use of multimedia equipment and products;
- to ring-fence funds for multimedia development;
- to provide useful information on the developments and the implications of

legislative developments in copyright on government schemes, and reliable information on the electronic publishing industry; and
- to provide more tax incentives for SMEs.

Conclusion

The study finds a basic divergence between the views of the industry and those of the policy-makers concerning the main threats facing electronic publishing (and similar IT-based service industries). National and international bodies see this as an industry with easy replicability and imitability, and accordingly would like to protect it through the development of tight IPRs, yet those in the industry seem to suggest a contrary situation characterised by difficulties in replication and little need for a further tightening of IPRs.

Copyright reforms and a plethora of technical systems of protection are the main political responses to the increasing prospects of piracy. Apprehensions about piracy as a 'growth industry' are becoming part of received wisdom. Yet this fear does not appear to be widely shared among the producers in the survey. Pressure to intensify the defence of IPRs could actually make the situation worse for the bulk of the industry being studied, which is composed primarily of SMEs. This is because what is required for creating and marketing electronic publishing products is often in conflict with what appears on a priori grounds to be required for protecting it. The legal and economic arguments for defending IPRs are largely 'static' in nature, in that they assume a product to be already in existence and with market presence, and as a result they tend to ignore the issue of first generating and selling the product.

The paramount concern of electronic publishers is instead getting the product rapidly to market, despite the industry's overall consternation about the growth of digital piracy and their consistent use of legal forms of protection. According to the admittedly limited sample, how electronic publishers are creating and managing their intellectual property and innovations indicates concerns far beyond that of piracy.

Research, and primarily in-house research, is the most frequently cited factor in *creating* IP. The factor of 'innovativeness' shows up especially in *managing* IP and as an *entry barrier*. Respondents to the survey clearly identified this factor with linking technologies to the on-time development of marketable products. Innovativeness in electronic publishing is necessary for the vitality of this industry because a wide assortment of largely similar electronic publications will not readily find market acceptance, thereby retarding growth. Innovation, whether in the form of interactivity, 'user-friendly' interfaces or 'smart' functions, underpins the success of these products. Retaining competence in keeping abreast of technologies and in viable product development head the list for *avoiding exit* from the industry. It is from these various dynamic resource-based and resource-linked capabilities that firms aim to appropriate maximum returns on their investment and ensure that their electronic publications are not easy prey to electronic marauding.

It should be noted that customers are crucial not just for the market acceptance of the product, important as this is. They are also seen as exerting considerable influence on the acceptability of tightening legislation and IPRs. In general, the survey indicates that entrepreneurs do not want stricter IPRs if, as they presume, the latter are likely to drive customers away. On balance, they would prefer imitation or piracy rather than losing their customer base. In this sense, there is an emphasis on the need to interlink all the functions of the firm – technologies, processes, products and administration. The creation of IP and resources required for this industry warrant in-house provision of most of these functions, even in very small firms. In managing IPRs, technical means of protection have to some extent to be traded off against market means and customer needs.

In sum, the threat of piracy is much alleviated by the industry's dependence on internal knowledge-based resources like innovativeness. By comparison, the levels of static resources like fixed investments and quasi-static ones like levels of R&D or advertising budgets, which can be important determinants of large firm sizes, are less important relative to the resources highlighted by the smaller electronic publishers. The reliance of many on market niche and on trust for protecting IPRs also shows their attitude towards piracy. The IPR or economics literature has paid scant attention to these forms of protection. Further investigation into these issues could perhaps be extended to other industries experiencing rapid change and development.

Notes

1 On originality and creativity, see *California Management Review* (1997).
2 The music and software industries were excluded on the basis that these two activities could not be adequately dealt with in this project, *Managing Intellectual Property: Electronic Publishing SMEs*, which was funded by the UK Economic and Social Research Council in 1996–7.
3 According to a database of electronic publishers created for this project, the results of which this chapter is based upon, small and medium-sized firms comprise more than 80 per cent of the sector. See also Mansell and Tang (1994).
4 Please note that the low percentage figures of Tables 6.1 and 6.2 are a result of the lower number of firms (24) responding to these issues, which was mainly a result of the lack of time during the interview.
5 Tang, Powell and Von Tunzelmann (1997).
6 Electronic Publishing Services (1993).
7 See Mansell and Tang (1994). There is little reason to believe that the United Kingdom's leading position has changed since 1994, although the publishing trend in Germany and Italy appears to be growing. Recent comparative figures are, however, not readily available.
8 *Guardian*, 4 September 1997, p. 8.
9 Industry analysts contend that it will be virtually impossible to distinguish DVD movies from the original; see Bell (1996).
10 See Millê (1997).
11 European Commission (1996).
12 Business Software Alliance (http://www.bsa.org) visited 1997.
13 Copyright industries generally refer to those involved in publishing, motion-picture-making, musical recordings, public performance, software, multimedia products, photography, sculpting and painting.
14 Samuelson (1996a, 1996b). See also Shapiro and Varian (1999) and Tang (1998).
15 (http://www.dbs.cordis.lu) visited 11 April 2001.
16 For an overview of current US IP law, see Lemley, Menell, Merges and Samuelson (2000).
17 See Puay Tang (1999).

18 Union for the Public Domain, *Proposals to Regulate the Public's Rights to Use Information Stored in Databases* (1996): (http://www.public-domain.org/database/database.html) visited 1997.

19 Laddie (1999).

20 Jacob (1997).

21 Firms were selected on the basis on location and attempts were made to include each type of electronic publisher, i.e. CD-ROM producers and on-line and off-line producers of a variety of publications, from throughout the United Kingdom. Although interviews were conducted with these firms, informal discussions were held with two leading multinational publishers who have started to publish electronically. Their opinions on the capabilities for electronic publishing, the threat of piracy, the need for further tightening of IPRs and the use of other means of IP protection do not fundamentally diverge from those of the smaller firms. However, both firms agreed that they would have to consider more thoroughly the increasing prospects of illegal use and replication of their electronic publications.

22 This company ceased its operations in 1998.

23 See, for instance, Klevorick *et al.* (1987), Klevorick *et al.* (1995).

24 For conditions for copyrightability, see Edenborough (1993).

25 Encryption entails a scrambling of the embedded digital content into unintelligible language, which can only be unscrambled by means of a 'key' that only the user (as in the case of a CD-ROM) or receiver (as in the case of on-line services) possesses.

26 Teece *et al.* (1997).

27 Kay (1993); see especially Chapter 7.

28 Freeserve™, owned by the electronics company Dixon, was the first company to offer free internet access. Up until then access was by subscription. Free access is now widely available, but usage is still metered and paid for.

29 One firm did attest to the benefit it had obtained from a DTI scheme for SMEs in the form of a financial grant.

References

Bell, A. E. (1996) 'Next Generation Compact Discs', *Scientific American*, 275 (1), 28–32.

Business Software Alliance (http://www.bsa.org).

California Management Review (1997), 40 (1), special issue on 'Creativity in Management'.

Edenborough, M. (1993) *Intellectual Property Law*, Cavendish, London.

Electronic Publishing Services Ltd. (1993) *Electronic Publishing in the UK*, a report prepared for the British Library Research and Development Department, London.

European Commission DGIII/F6 (1996) 'Technical Mechanisms for IPR Management in the Information Society', EC, Brussels.

Guardian, The (1997) 4 September, 8.

Jacob, The Hon. Sir R. (1997) 'Industrial Property – Industry's Enemy?', *Intellectual Property Quarterly*, 1, 3–15.

Kay, J. (1993) *Foundations of Corporate Success: How Business Strategies Add Value*, Oxford University Press, Oxford.

Klevorick, A. K., Levin, R. C., Nelson, R. R. and Winter, S. G. (1987) 'Appropriating the Returns from Industrial Research and Development', *Brookings Paper on Economic Activity*, 783–831.

Klevorick, A. K., Levin, R. C., Nelson, R. R. and Winter, S. G. (1995) 'On the Sources and Significance of Interindustry Differences in Technological Opportunities', *Research Policy*, 24, 185–205.

Laddie, The Hon Mr Justice (1999) 'Copyright: Over-strength, Over-regulated, Over-rated?' *European Intellectual Property Review*, 18, 253–60.

Lemley, M. A., Menell, P. S., Merges, R. P. and Samuelson, P. (2000) *Software and Internet Law*, Aspen Law and Business, New York.

Macauley, S. (1992) 'Non-Contractual Relations in Business: A Preliminary Study', in M. Granovetter and R. Swedberg (eds) *The Sociology of Economic Life*, Boulder, CO, Westview Press, 265–84.

Mansell, R. and Tang, P. (1994) *Electronic Information Services: Competitiveness in the United Kingdom*, Department of Trade and Industry, London.

Millê, A. (1997) 'Copyright in the Cyberspace Era', *European Intellectual Property Review*, 19, 570–7.

Samuelson, P. (1996a), 'Intellectual Property Rights and the Global Information Economy', *Communications of the ACM*, 30 (1), 23–8.

Samuelson, P. (1996b) 'Regulation of Technologies to Protect Copyrighted Works', *Communications of the ACM*, 39 (7), 17–22.

Shapiro, C. and Varian, H. (1999) *Information Rules*, Harvard Business School Press, Boston, MA.

Tang, P. (1998) 'How Electronic Publishers are Protecting against Piracy: Doubts about Technical Means of Protection', *The Information Society*, 14, 19–32.

Tang, P. (1999) 'Innovation, Electronic Publishing and the Management of Intellectual Property: What of Digital Piracy?', *Information, Communication and Society*, 2 (1), 45–68.

Tang P., Powell, D. and Von Tunzelmann, N. (1997) *The Development and Application of New Information Technologies in the Next Decade*, a report prepared for Scientific and Technical Options Assessment, European Parliament, Luxembourg.

Teece, D. J., Pisano, G. and Shuen, A. (1997) 'Dynamic Capabilities and Strategic Management', *Strategic Management Journal*, 18, 525.

Union for the Public Domain (1996) *Proposals to Regulate the Public's Rights to Use Information Stored in Databases* (http://www.public-domain.org/database/database.html).

7 Controlling intellectual property across the high-tech frontier

University spin-offs, SMEs and the science base

Andrew Webster, Brian Rappert and David R. Charles

Introduction

Since the science park boom in the early 1980s, universities in the United Kingdom and worldwide have been exhorted simultaneously to exploit their intellectual property (IP) base, and to contribute to economic growth and job creation through the formation of new small firms. Universities also make many other contributions, both economic and social/cultural in nature, to their localities (Goddard *et al.*, 1994), but commercialisation and spin-offs have a particular appeal to policy-makers in times of seemingly accelerating technological change, strikingly uneven regional economic performance and tight budgets for higher education. It is hardly surprising then that a number of recent policy documents have called for further efforts by universities to commercialise their knowledge (House of Commons, 1994; Scottish Enterprise/Royal Society of Edinburgh, 1996; Department of Trade and Industry, 1998; European Commission, 1996). This is currently being intensified through new programmes such as University Challenge and Science Enterprise Challenge, and a significant increase in the numbers of university spin-offs (USOs) is a target of the DTI's competitiveness strategy (DTI, 1998).

Universities are increasingly being recognised as having a key role to play in the regional development process. The development of an increasingly 'knowledge-intensive' economy – not only in terms of the expansion of the knowledge sector itself but also in terms of the increasing role of information and knowledge in all sectors and activities – suggests that this role can only increase (Lundvall, 1992, 1994; Florida and Cohen, 1999). As one of the key traditional centres of knowledge production and distribution, universities have more or less enthusiastically deepened their engagement with regional development issues and the regional development community. As part of this development, universities themselves are becoming more centrally managed institutions which require new organisational structures and processes.

This chapter examines the role of the university in the formation of spin-off companies, and how this reflects different regional contexts. In addition we sketch out a conceptual framework to help understand how USOs stabilise proprietary claims to knowledge, and translate such knowledge into a form that can be appropriated. In the appropriation of knowledge the ability of the university to exert control over intellectual property (IP) is central: the commercialisation or commodification of knowledge is dependent on the exertion of ownership rights over the knowledge developed within university research.

University (and other) knowledge can be appropriated at three different spatial levels: international, national and local. A common concern of national policy-makers, and the prime reason for the introduction of more formal mechanisms that control IP within the university system, is the desire to prevent free appropriation on an international level. Different mechanisms can be used to attempt to control the location of the benefits. If IPRs are managed by the university and traded in return for revenue, then the university can control the location of exploitation to some extent, but the interests of the institution may be best served by international exchange and higher licence fees. For national government or regional interests this may be undesirable, and local appropriation either through an existing local company, or a new spin-off, may be preferred. The location of benefits, and the ability of the ultimate funder of the research to control that location, depends on the negotiation of the interests between the various parties: firms, individual inventors, universities, national government and regional interests.

Regimes of appropriation, governance and stabilisation

Central to our desire to examine the benefits of the appropriation and commodification of university knowledge at national and regional levels is a framework for understanding the production and reproduction of knowledge. In an earlier paper, Rappert and Webster develop such a framework which has three main elements: a regime of appropriation wherein social actors capture economic rents from innovation; a local regime of governance concerning the way individual academics are encouraged to pursue commercialisation; and stabilisation strategies and procedures whereby actors attempt to manage the context through which knowledge is produced, exchanged and disseminated (Rappert and Webster, 1997: 117).

The concept of the regime of appropriation directs attention to the external environment governing the ability of various actors to capture the benefits or profits generated by an innovation (Teece, 1986). Central to this is the legal framework of intellectual property rights[1] and their protection, but also the character of the innovation and the ability of it to be codified in such a way that legal protection may be obtained. In the context of knowledge generated within universities, codification is often seen as essential in securing rents from third parties, hence the emphasis in the literature on patents, and the means by which universities can secure patent rights. However, in many cases such IPR is not appropriate and other forms of strategy are needed such as copyright, know-how licences, or even ownership of the means of exploitation. Whilst some aspects of this framework are internationally agreed, national variations in the legal rights of universities to own IPR, invest in commercial ventures, or benefit from appropriation lead to significant variations in the overall regime of appropriation for university-generated knowledge.

Even within a national regime of appropriation there will be differences in the ways in which individual institutions negotiate with researchers concerning the balance of commercial and academic goals at both an institutional and individual level. Such regimes of governance cover the diversity of regulatory mechanisms which link the activities of individuals and organisations. Academics must operate within various forms of authority such as departmental politics, national research assessments, peer review, university regulations and administrative practices, etc. As individuals they must engage with these various regulatory and negotiating frameworks in making sense of their own positions as academics, and building their positions within institutions with a keen sense of hierarchy and value. However, alternative governance regimes also impinge on academics where they engage in boundary-crossing activities such as commercialisation. Taking out a patent, for example, places the academic in a different form of governance for the evaluation of that knowledge claim, where 'value' depends on wealth-creation potential and novelty relative to 'prior art' (Webster and Packer, 1996). Moving further, in setting up a spin-off company the individual is placed in a complex web of governance regimes through which they must negotiate: academic values, market and commercial governance, and the more specific frameworks whereby university authorities manage and seek to derive rents from commercialisation activities. Company founders seek to gain some control over the way these various forms of authority impinge on their new enterprise, in order to generate wealth for themselves, expand their firm or achieve whatever other personal goals they have.

The third element of our framework, stabilisation strategies, concerns the process by which the actors manage knowledge and its appropriation within a context of power relations, as set out via regimes of appropriation and governance. Stabilisation is a central feature of the sociology of scientific knowledge, in that new knowledge claims must be embedded in a particular institutional 'ordering' before appropriation can take place. The new knowledge must be translated into a form that can to some extent be codified, at least in the form of a product, so that it can be de-localised and hence appropriated – rents can only be realised if the knowledge can be repeatedly sold outside of the university.

Stabilisation processes involve the enrolling of other actors as supporters of the knowledge claim, and in the context of academic science this process of enrolment and translation takes place within a regime of appropriation and governance that carries certain assumptions. Processes of publication, peer review and the replication of experimentation provide a mechanism by which knowledge claims can be subjected to trials of strength, and in which stabilisation can be managed (Latour, 1987). However, in the commercialisation of knowledge claims we see a different process of building networks involving suppliers, customers, government regulations, distribution channels, production facilities, etc. for the stabilisation and ultimately the de-localisation of the 'product'. A core concern here is with the problems inherent in translating knowledge claims between two different regimes of appropriation and governance, with different approaches to exchange and trust, and hence we are concerned with the strategies that are developed by the universities and individual researchers in protecting their respective academic and commercial interests in managing the stabilisation process.

Policy and regimes of appropriation and governance

There are several stakeholders in the process of developing potentially exploitable IP within universities – the members of the research team that take the inventive step, the university which employs the individuals and may exert rights through contracts of employment, the funders of research (often government through general university funds and also specific programmes, but also charities and other bodies), and the local community served by the university. Leaving aside the issue of contracts from companies which exert rights to the IPR, the question of ownership is central to appropriation and whether society in the form of the state, local community or the university benefits from the commercial exploitation (Charles and Howells, 1992).

During the 1980s there were major shifts in policy in the United Kingdom concerning the routes by which IP could be exploited, although the basic rights were largely unchanged. Prior to 1985, rights of first refusal on publicly funded research IP went to National Research Development Council/Business Technology Group (NRDC/BTG), and royalties were split with the university. Universities could, however, exploit anything that NRDC refused. Subsequently, with the abolition of the NRDC/BTG monopoly, universities were free to develop their own strategies for commercialisation, but could still use BTG as one route, although BTG would only take on a licence for exploitation if they felt it was commercially advantageous to them. BTG have also been very much concerned with the international exploitation of patents as formal IP, and as such have only formed part of the overall framework (Charles and Howells, 1992; Harvey, 1996).

There has also been the development from the early 1980s of industrial liaison officers (ILOs) and the parallel development of science parks and other incubators, university companies, and consultancy organisations, all of which have played different roles in the exploitation of academic knowledge, mainly on a more local scale (Charles *et al.*, 1995).

An example of the perceived importance of this issue to regional agencies can be seen in Scotland, where Scottish Enterprise and the Royal Society in Edinburgh published the report of an enquiry into the commercialisation of public sector science and technology (SE/RSE, 1996). In order to meet Scottish Enterprise's objectives of increasing employment, prosperity, competitiveness and economic growth, attention has been focused on the commercialisation of the science base, both in support of existing firms, and through the establishment of new spin-off firms. The enquiry suggests that by increasing the number of spin-offs from a rate of 60 over the past ten years to 150 in the next ten years, an additional 3,500 to 4,500 jobs could be created. The primary mechanism for this is through a range of proactive support policies, but also through more structural changes within the university system.

The regional and institutional setting for USOs

Our analysis here is based on research in two regions[2] in the United Kingdom: East Anglia and North-East England. The regions represent different contexts for the examination of regimes of IP appropriation. In each region we examined IP policies, interviewed relevant university staff and carried out interviews within selected USOs.

East Anglia includes the Cambridgeshire area which is the focus of our study: one of the fastest growing sub-regional economies in the United Kingdom with a booming small high-tech firm sector (Cambridge County Council Research Group, 1996). The region has benefited from the presence of the University of Cambridge, with high levels of public sector expenditure on public research, but due to the recent economic success of the area has received little support for economic development, and underlying policies have if anything been restrictive of economic growth.

The 'Cambridge phenomenon', typically defined in terms of the growth of small-scale high-tech firms in and adjacent to Cambridge, has assumed a mythical status in commentaries on economic development. Indeed, Cambridge is the site of one the most dense concentrations of 'high-tech' firms in Europe. The total number of such firms grew from 769 in 1988 to over 1,300 in 2001 employing approximately 33,000 people. While these firms' failure rate is lower than those in the manufacturing sector, they also have low incremental growth and are small in size. Numerous studies have been undertaken to confirm, elaborate or dispute the myths surrounding Cambridge (see, e.g., Keeble, 1989; Garnsey and Cannon-Brooks, 1993; Lumme *et al.*, 1994).

Cambridge has been described as an 'innovative milieu': that is, a place of networking characterised by both vertical sub-contracting chains and horizontal linkages that provide financial, technical, training and marketing services. Keeble (1989) suggests that most firms were started by indigenous entrepreneurs, and though these were usually not life-long residents, Cambridge University and its research labs play a significant role in research linkages and recruitment. He also argues that the Cambridge phenomenon developed spontaneously rather than being planned. Its origins are primarily due to the residential attractiveness of the area, the proximity (and yet distance) from London and the quality of local research.

Just as harnessing university research has been a focus in public policy, so has the significance of Cambridge University in the growth of local high-tech firms. Commentary on the university often portrays it as a place where academic freedom and pure research are more important than other policy goals. The university is known for its 'laissez-faire' attitude in terms of central administration as well as decentralised collegiate structure. There is no on-going strategy seeking to maximise the commercialisation of research. The structure places few formal constraints on individuals in terms of commercialisation. While researchers have to meet the demands of contributing to teaching and academic research, consultancies are not monitored and researchers are on a honour system in reporting the use of facilities for outside work. Employees are still bound by the constraints of research councils and other grant-funding organisations. Assistance in commercial activities can be sought through the Wolfson Cambridge Industrial Unit and commercial exploitation can take place through the university's commercial exploitation company, Lynxvale Limited.

The IP policy is seen as a key element in harnessing entrepreneurial activities for the good of wealth creation (NBEET, 1995). As an employer the university has the policy of not taking IPR on inventions or appling for rights in the name of the university. In the case of financially successful exploitations conducted on research council grants, though, the university does expect the benefits to be divided between the inventor, the department and the university (see Sherman, 1994). The relaxed structure means it rarely seeks to catalogue commercial potential or to monitor commercial exploitation. This policy is often justified by those outside and inside the university as prudent, because it requires the researchers to be willing to facilitate commercial exploitation and provides an incentive for the diffusion of research. According to Richard Jennings, the director of Cambridge University Industrial Liaison and Technology Transfer Office in 1995, the policy actually developed in an ad hoc fashion with little rationale in terms of meeting some objectives.

In contrast, the *North-East* is a peripheral region, primarily industrial in character, but having suffered relative decline for most of the twentieth century. The economic problems of the region have been recognised by the continuous availability of high levels of regional assistance for almost all of the region, and by the development at the regional scale of a cohesive partnership of agencies and local authorities. The region's economic problems are known to have originated in a legacy of declining traditional industries, but throughout most of the twentieth century there has been an active regional policy, seeking to diversify the region's economic structure through an exogenous development strategy based on new branch plants. The continuing emphasis on large workplaces and external management skills is thought to have reinforced a climate of low levels of firm formation rates, especially in high-tech and new forms of services.

The North-East has no strong history of university spin-offs, and by the early 1980s the 'old' universities of Newcastle and Durham[3] had adopted traditional structures as red bricks. Neither had strong internal pressures to collaborate more closely with local industry or stimulate spin-offs, but both were enrolled by local development lobbies in different ways. Durham was encouraged by English Estates to develop a science park on a greenfield site on the edge of the science campus, Mountjoy Research Park, initially as a incubator building, but more recently expanded with new blocks developed with private capital. Associated with this development was a facility for local firms to gain access to university equipment and facilities, and an industrial liaison office. Other than these, though – and they were physically semi-detached from the university – the only other strong linkage with local industry was in the Durham University Business School, which focused on the development of small firms and the encouragement of entrepreneurship. The university encouraged spin-off firms to develop in Mountjoy, and the university's ILO was its manager, but there were relatively few spin-offs established and several chose to locate in more traditional industrial premises. Newcastle had always been the more regionally embedded of the two old universities in the region but, again in the 1980s it needed to be re-enrolled in economic development by local interests, this time in the form of the local authorities. Two key initiatives were both assisted by Tyne and Wear County Council.

First, a company was established as a joint venture between the university,

Newcastle Polytechnic (now the University of Northumbria at Newcastle) and the county council to undertake training and research in IT. The Microelectronics Applications Research Institute (MARI) was initially formed as an enticement to the government-owned Inmos semiconductor company to locate in the North-East, but after this was not achieved, MARI developed as a major training organisation for IT skills, and a research-based company with a stunning record of success in European collaborative programmes. MARI was a company limited by guarantee, but eventually it split from the founder organisations and became a private employee-owned company in around 1990, at which time it employed around 300 people, and had offices in a number of different locations.

Second, and perhaps more important here, the same combination – university, polytechnic and council – established the Newcastle Technology Centre to encourage commercialisation activities and spin-offs. This later evolved into the Regional Technology Centre and relocated to Sunderland, but was replaced at university level within Newcastle University by Nuventures Ltd, a standard university commercialisation company.

The three new universities or former polytechnics in the North-East have had much less success with spin-offs and have only recently formalised policies to develop such firms. Sunderland has perhaps done most, largely though the development of consultancy operations outside of the normal academic faculty structure. One early such operation providing EMC testing services was sold off to an international company, but currently there are several small businesses operating through the university's Industry Centre, itself a holding company and physical building for such ventures, but importantly not a general incubator. The university's ability to pursue this strategy has been partly based on the availability of European Regional Development Fund support, both for the construction of the centre, and for capital and revenue subsidies for the new companies established. A number of these 'firms' are primarily involved in delivering publicly subsidised consultancy, and hence would perhaps be more internalised within departments in a different governance regime in another university. The remaining two universities, Teesside and Northumbria, have both experimented with joint-venture, commercialisation companies, although Teesside is more active at present, especially in IT. Neither has a strong record of spin-offs, although some exist where individuals have left the institution to form a company without university involvement.

These two regions, therefore, can be seen as providing contrasting contexts within which the negotiations between university and regional agencies, between university and spin-off firms, can be examined.

Categorisation of USOs

In examining the experiences of USOs in our two case study regions, we must first be attentive to the great variety of forms of USO that can be found (see earlier attempts at typologies,.e.g. Stankiewicz, 1994). Not all spin-off companies from universities embody intellectual property of a technological or scientific nature – nor do they exclusively emerge from the various science and technology faculties.

Entrepreneurs may emerge in sectors relating to cultural activities, publishing and so on. The research here focused on USOs in three sectors: *IT*, *scientific instruments* and *new materials*. Strategies for the appropriation of IP are not only institutionally and regionally varied, but also vary to some extent by technology sector. While all the USOs in each sector were most dependent on preserving their control over the core design and experimental and test data relating to their product(s) (apart from the shell firms), the three sectors varied in terms of firms' knowledge base, typical inter-firm patterns of linkage, product life cycle, time to market and so on. These differences appeared to influence the sort of IP protection and appropriation strategies the firms deployed. So, for example, the IT sector is characterised by a knowledge base marked by rapid incremental change, typically associated with the development of technologies (IT systems) that embody highly codified and accessible forms of knowledge typically embedded in and dependent on software systems that reflect high levels of path dependency and 'lock-in'. Not surprisingly, this creates an innovation environment with strong linkage between suppliers and users, a high level of outsourcing, and a dependency on dominant operating systems, platforms and hardware. IT products here tend to have short product life cycles, need to be taken to market quickly and rapidly lose market control unless, by definition, they can secure themselves as a 'gateway technology', through which many others must 'pass'.

In this broad context, IP generated within firms has to be managed in very specific ways: first, given the accessibility of the knowledge base to other, dominant systems, the firms found it difficult to secure, in any meaningful way, core protection for their system(s), other than to build in some form of technical security (e.g. through controlling access to the source code) over the actual software configuration on which their products depend. The key to success here is the mobilisation of software into and across the market as quickly as possible: as a result, non-exclusive licences were reported as a preferred option, while, in a rather ritualistic way, some firms sought the protection of copyright, acknowledging, however, that this was virtually impossible to police.

Based on our interviews with USOs we have developed a typology of firms in terms of their relationship with the host or former host university. This reflects the differing degree of separation between the founders of the firm and the institution, and is in part an outcome of the success of each side in managing and negotiating IP ownership and subsequent benefits to meet their respective objectives. Assessment of the position of USOs within this categorisation may be made through six variables which allow us to map the characteristics of the firms and visually represent each form.[4] The variables are:

- the institutional distance between the university and the USO;
- the significance of linkages (formal and informal);
- the relative 'hardness' of the USO's product;
- the commercial ambitions and opportunities for the USO;
- the degree of geographical separation between the USO and the university;
- the degree of university control over the USO.

These variables are selected on the basis that certain attributes of the business will tend to lead to a distancing from the university, particularly the 'hardness' of the product, commercial ambitions, geographical separation and an absence of linkages. Institutional distance and university control relate more to the strategy of the university to seek returns on its IP investments. Collectively these variables represent a series of dimensions in which the universities and firms negotiate their relationship.

On the basis of these variables, we identified four main types of USO:

- those committed to independence from the university;
- spin-offs retaining some informal links with the university;
- spin-offs retaining formal ties in the form of ownership links or joint staff appointments;
- university-based companies, which act as 'shell companies'.

Although these categories may be regarded as a spectrum which is developmental in nature, we found little evidence of migration along the spectrum. Many of those firms set up as university-based companies remain in that position, and there is a tendency for many to be short-lived – to exist only to exploit a short-term opportunity then dissolve at the end of their natural life. Conversely, those individuals wishing to set up companies that are independent of the university often move to this option at the outset, cutting off links as the company is formed, perhaps only retaining some informal links for a transitional period.

The experiences of USOs

Let us now discuss in more detail the variety of experience found among the different types of firm.

Companies committed to independence from the university

An important sub-group of USOs established themselves through a complete split with the former host university, usually with no IPR relations.

Company founders provided many reasons for distancing themselves from their former universities, usually on the basis that they either felt driven out of the university, or the university was unhelpful, or that their ambitions were to develop a commercial business which they felt to be incompatible with the culture of a university. Attitudes towards the university were sometimes quite hostile:

> I've never got any support whatever from the Department for this project – it's a personality thing, it's not because of the technical side . . . I used to advocate in the Department that they enter this area as a legitimate area of research and it fell on deaf ears . . . There was a lot around within [the] University that they never ever understood. As a Department they never understood the potential of what I was talking about.

In another case:

> We got the company up to a turnover of several hundred thousand before we left the University. It got to a point where it was becoming increasingly uncomfortable – what we were doing was upsetting people. Other people in the University I think were jealous of our success – they wouldn't have minded very much if we were failing but we were succeeding and we were earning money.

In other cases sectoral dynamics meant that a break with the university was inevitable, especially likely in both IT and scientific instruments firms which require strong user–supplier links: whilst the university founder may have drawn on academic knowledge in the formation of the firm, the principal need was for knowledge from the commercial environment.

> The theory of (. . .) is well understood and well established. So, if you like, the technical underpinning of what the products do, in that respect, is defined. Anything else is what we feel [we] can do with it, to improve it for our customers. So there is nothing else there . . . I was aware that XXX were doing a joint venture with the civil engineering department about looking at getting some kind of metrics for risk and whatever else, but it is too abstract for us. We are a small company and we can get easily distracted and spend a lot of time and effort . . . so we are insular or focused depending on how you look at it.

The question of which party – the USO or the university – controlled the IP was not significant for this type of firm, either because the firms were established at a time when universities were less concerned about IPRs, or more importantly because the knowledge base used was highly tacit, or built upon scientific principles which were in themselves not patentable. In both regions there was no real attempt by the universities to prevent the distancing of the USOs, and indeed the firms felt themselves to be pushed out in some cases. Yet despite the absence of on-going links, some of these firms were successful in the market and were able to generate considerable employment. It is also perhaps indicative of a certain organisational culture that they also sought little assistance from their local agencies.

Spin-offs retaining some informal links with the university

Some spin-offs were keen to retain links with the university even if there were no formal ownership or IP agreements. Whilst the typical case of spin-off reported in the literature usually involves tenured staff, many of the more recent examples involve staff on short-term contracts and only tenuously connected to the university. There can be little option for such staff in retaining a part-time position in the university whilst setting up the company, nor is there likely to be much willingness on their part to offer any IP rights to the university. However, there are benefits from a close relationship with the former department, and some university commercialisation agencies see the assistance of such firms to be well within their remit, especially if some income can be gained from the provision of services or premises.

One company exemplifies this mutual benefit:

> There have been a couple of instances whereby we have sub-contracted work to the Department and vice-versa when each of us has been involved on larger projects. The Department was used for some software expertise whilst I was brought in to help the Department with some coding work . . . There's also quite a lot of little things – we'll get postgrads in particular from the Department helping out and getting experience in return, we've done that on quite a lot of occasions. The firm asked Departmental staff to participate in some training courses the firm ran in 1995.

The company had been assisted by the university's commercialisation arm at foundation, although due to changes in the nature of the of the administrative support service offered by that company the spin-off found themselves having to develop their own administrative functions. The commercialisation unit encouraged the company out of a desire to see it as a route for technology transfer and income for the department (and its own operations), but it seems that there were no formal IP agreements, nor did the university seek to take any equity in the firm. Despite a close relationship with the department, the spin-off founders had a more distant relationship with the central administration of the university and tried to avoid formal IP deals where possible.

Typically there was an element of opportunism on the part of the firms:

> The last thing you want to do is go to a new town and figure out how to get the photocopying done. There are a lot of hidden resources in the university and if you already know the ins and outs, who is who, what is what, then if you are exploring ideas then that is a good seed bed to exploit them. There are almost informal relations which could help you picture what is useful or not.

Such firms were often as close to the university as those with formal links, but there was a specific strategy of distancing from the administrative systems, either because the firm wanted to avoid disputes about IPRs or because the university itself was not interested in pursuing IPRs. This was especially true in the case of Cambridge.

Spin-offs retaining formal ties

These include firms where the university retains some equity, or has a licence arrangement, or where there are staff links, usually with one of the founders retaining a staff position in the university whilst serving as a director of the company. The existence of an equity stake is usually based on some form of repayment for IP invested in the company rather than recognition of financial investment by the university. Few universities are prepared to make a financial investment, and Newcastle is reluctant even to take an equity stake in return for IP. Some form of royalty payment for IP is often regarded as a less risky option, if the company can be persuaded to pay the IPR costs. As noted earlier, though, Newcastle participated in a non-profit company, MARI, in the early 1980s as part of a local partnership. Although the company later decided to convert to an employee-owned plc, its initial remit was less one of commercial success as regional development. The university did, however, benefit financially when the group moved into private ownership.

Firms in this group fell into two main types: those where the university link was related to the exploitation of some previous IP agreement, and was usually purely financial; and those where the formal link was based on a continuous mutual benefit. In the first type the relationship was often quite complex:

> The initial patent was owned by the inventors plus the university. But then it was realised that sitting on the patent was not going to do much, if the technology was going to happen and money was going to be generated then a company had to be formed. And so, in 1992 [the company] was formed as a holding company, basically a place to assign the IP. But, and this is unusual, the university gained equity in the company, not just for the IP but for agreements for any future IP in the area to be assigned to the company. And that is where we are now. Any IP generated from the university is assigned and owned by [the company].

So one option used in a number of cases is where a company is formed to exploit some IP, and external staff are brought in to manage the company, with the academics acting as consultants or subcontractors, and the university perhaps participating through equity or royalties on the IP invested.

By contrast, when there is no direct financial relationship or IP agreement with the university, it is still possible for there to be a satisfactory agreement. An instrument firm which was a spin-off from a university, and employed the key academics as scientific consultants, built close relationships with the department in everything but formal IP. The department functioned as a basic research facility, using the company as industrial leverage to gain other external resources, whilst the firm developed the basic knowledge of products. Here a mixed regime of appropriation and governance allowed for some mutual benefit to accrue at the local level. In such cases a claim for the ownership of IP would be so weak, perhaps because the IP relates to an area of basic research or a technique where patenting would disclose without achieving protection, that the establishment of a strategic alliance with non-monetary benefits is preferable.

University-based (shell) companies

The final core group are those firms which operate as companies but have never left the campus, and in many cases remain wholly owned subsidiaries of the university. This is not merely those companies like commercialisation companies that are established principally for taxation reasons, to protect the university's status as an educational charity exempt from corporation tax. Some companies operate commercially as service or product companies, but channel the income into the university. One interesting form of tension that developed in some of these cases was a conflict between the objectives of the commercialisation company to encourage spin-offs, and the desires of the university staff to keep their USO within a university framework. A regime of governance based on corporate interests might be seen as an essential means of addressing the needs of IP management and contractual obligations to partners, as well as managing the relationship of the university to commercial activities. However, the motivation for the income-generation activities was in some cases to fund research in the host department, and hence the establishment of the company was seen by the founders as merely one mechanism amongst a range of industrial liaison and contractual arrangements. This led at times to conflict between the university's central commercial arm and the USO. The aims of the department and the centre may run counter to each other:

> I think the other problem was that [the university's central arm] was a trading company with a requirement to make a profit and basically it was to do that by exploiting other people, basically a parasite. It's okay if you have got a lot of flesh on what you are doing. If there is a lot of money there you can do that kind of thing, but a small company just starting up, I don't think it could stand a lot of overheads and one of the criticisms they made of us was that we, although we constantly made a profit, we never made enough to grow and they wanted to grow us, and their approach to growing a small company was to invest in management services, consultancy, marketing, promotion, without actually putting a great deal into the technical input. They had the view that a business was a pyramid where the technical resources was at the peak and very small and outside there was a huge marketing device.

The vision of the founders was much more within the traditional view of the university as a research community:

> the products are not just products . . . they have a lot of research and development content. What we do now is that we put the money back into the University to employ research associates to carry out the activity so the company still owns the IPR, it's a shell company but the funding that comes in from the sale of the products to develop them is granted to the University in order to maintain research staff in here through normal University contracts, so we've gone a long way from the SME model if you like and I think this leads to a much better way of working. So there are the benefits of the department being able to carry out the research we wanted to do, the benefits of doing it within the University framework, and people have the benefits of being able to move between projects and do more basic research or more applied research depending on what they want to do.

One of the motivations for establishing the company was to regularise the employment contracts of researchers who had been seen as marginal to the University.

Regional-level benefits and feedback into USO policies within higher education

In the light of these case studies, what then are the benefits arising to the universities and their regions from these emerging regimes of appropriation and governance in their consequences for spin-off firms? Concern over the management of the mobility of knowledge from both a university and firm perspective is core to the question of benefits from IPR and spin-off policies. For the universities, there are parallel needs to encourage the flows of knowledge through networking amongst academics and with firms, but also a need to appropriate knowledge, albeit within the different academic and commercial regimes. So the question is how to structure that mobility. For instance, Cambridge University has a quite open policy in regards to its IP. No doubt this has its benefits to the researchers and the relevant companies involved. In terms of the university, though, the benefits are much more indirect and difficult to quantify. Such a system might have very good overall benefits, but at the level of an organisation such as a university, it is more difficult to prove. Yet the consequences for the region are more significant, in that the undoubted benefits of considerable national research investment in Cambridge leads to opportunities for spin-offs, and the development of agglomeration advantages, that ultimately feed back into the attractiveness of the university and its prestige.

IP strategies may be established either to raise revenue or encourage regional development, but the practice leads to conflict between the exploitation company and the wider interests of the institution. In Newcastle this has repeatedly led to a restructuring of the IP exploitation function. Furthermore, spin-offs (and academics) have tended to view commercialisation mechanisms as self-serving, and in a conflictual relationship with both the spin-off and the department. Current policy on IP exploitation within the universities focuses much more on control than hitherto, and many institutions have introduced auditing procedures and incentives for academics to report any likely exploitable technologies, so they can be protected. A decision to establish a spin-off firm then becomes a more managed process involving the university as the owner of IPRs, the provider of core business services and incentives, and as a potential shareholder. But managing the process more tightly may not guarantee greater benefits, as the potential for spin-off opportunities to emerge do seem to vary. Although it is well understood that Cambridge is a fertile source of spin-offs, within the North-East the majority of firms we could identify emerged from Newcastle University, with fewer from Durham, despite its science park, and almost none from the new universities. The pattern seems to be highly related to research performance, raising questions over investment in IP management in any but the most research-intensive universities. Even here, though, unless the institution is extremely fortunate in investing in a rapid-growth firm, the main benefits are more likely to come from continued research links, with collaboration also helping the university to access public funds. One might question whether such an investment strategy should focus on spin-off firms particularly. Newcastle University is reluctant to take an equity stake in spin-off firms in case it is regarded as endorsing the product and thereby taking on shared liability. Licensing the product gives more opportunity to distance the university from any subsequent liability. However, if an institution was seeking to invest in high-tech firms to maximise revenue alone, then it would not make sense to restrict this policy to USOs.

From the regional perspective, especially in an area like the North-East, with a dearth of successful entrepreneurs, regional agencies are keen to encourage spin-offs regardless of the IP arrangements and potential returns to the universities. Here, though, the regional benefits measured in terms of jobs created is modest. We estimate that all of the spin-offs in the North-East since 1980 have created no more than 1,000 jobs. This is considerably less than the jobs created within the universities themselves over this period. Again, as for the universities, the potential payback is random and comparable to buying a lottery ticket, although the more that is invested in terms of research funding the more likely the universities are to win.

Firms also have a concern to ensure the mobility of knowledge, although again with concerns about their ability effectively to appropriate that knowledge whilst denying access to other firms. It was instructive that even USOs often regarded universities as leaky with regard to company IP, and so were very cautious about the nature of links. One of the cited strengths of Cambridge was the availability of skills, not just from universities but as a result of a greater circulation/mobility of high-tech staff between SMEs and a high level of recruitment from within the region. Along with this was a greater sense of mobility of knowledge across networks. This is supported by the work of Lawson *et al.* (1997) on Cambridge and Oxford firms, which indicates that the possible loss of IP or IPR because of linkage with other firms was regarded as a low risk. This may be because of the greater mobility of knowledge and the problems that would attend controlling it, rather than because Cambridge firms are more adept at controlling IP/IPR. It may also be the case that Cambridge firms understand that the release of knowledge (through the movement of people or other firms of dissemination) should not be tightly controlled because this movement benefits them all in the end.

Not surprisingly, then, it was discovered that firms in the North-East found formal links of greater importance than informal links, in contrast to Cambridge firms. In reviewing the cases and number of links in each region, the focus on formal links was not due to a higher absolute level of formal links (because of easier access to government sponsorship), but to a greater propensity for Cambridge firms to engage in informal links. This raises the question of whether the greater importance of formal links might limit the utility of university links.

Discussion and conclusion

We have described above a quite complex institutional ecology wherein are found distinct types of USO with different relations to their parent university, different capacities for growth and different strategies for securing and stabilising their respective IP. This means that debates over the 'benefits' of commercialising university R&D will depend on the sort of investment – scientific, financial and institutional – made in a USO and the priorities that lie behind it. Moreover, despite the development of a national funding system for higher education in the United

Kingdom, there remain considerable regional variations and variation in types of university, with consequent effects on the patterns of appropriation that are found. It may well be possible to suggest ways of formalising distinct regimes of appropriation according to this variation. Such different models may have considerable implications for the level of establishment of USOs, the promotion of university linkages, the commercial pay-off for universities, and the diffusion of benefits at different levels. These models might include the following:

1. Universities as centres of excellence. This has many of the overtones of 'traditional models' of universities. Here university researchers strive for excellence in furthering the knowledge base rather than considering the commercial potential of their research. Here commercial work is very much something that happens on the margins and only when it is convenient and furthers the pursuit of knowledge. At a broad level, the allocation of funding might be directed to areas depending on the strategic importance of the work, but by and large the universities are left to their own devices. Some supporting infrastructure might be necessary to enable academics to go commercial when it is prudent. This sort of model would be more sophisticated than a 'laissez-faire' approach in recognising that the greatest contributions academics make to industry in formal and informal links is their expertise and in providing general and specific assistance (see Faulkner and Senker, 1995). Links could be made globally or nationally, depending on where the best 'knowledge' opportunities are.
2. Universities as businesses. Quite a different model is where generating external income is a key objective of universities. Obviously it is unrealistic to suppose universities would ever be able to act just like businesses in this sense, but a considerable amount of policy is taking them in that direction today. Here universities should be very protective of their IPR, they should try to market themselves, and academics should be proactive in searching out commercial work. This has implications for the organisation of universities (the marginalisation of some subjects) and the wider commercial world (competition in the private sector). Links are fostered on the basis of commercial considerations, and USOs are a way of generating income.
3. Universities with an explicit regional focus. Here the model is of universities as a part of the regional development infrastructure. Key concerns would be in the creation of a qualified workforce, but universities would have a role to play in regard to formal and informal links. Links would be fostered, in part, dependent on their 'regionalness'. So some emphasis might be placed on helping SMEs, but the regional role could also be interpreted as developing USOs as new businesses.

In conclusion, the research here would suggest a need on the part of government at both national and regional levels to be much more sensitive to the complex ecology within which different types of USOs operate. At the same time, those that argue that small firms – such as USOs – are poor protectors of their core IPR need to recognise that the form and level of IP appropriation will be determined in relation to a number of factors such as sectoral location, scale of market, capacity to defend IPR, relations of trust, and the perceived relationship between, and relative priority given to, the production of public as opposed to private knowledge.

Notes

1 It is worth pointing out a distinction between intellectual property, which we regard as multiple forms of knowledge over which an actor may wish to exert ownership and appropriate benefits, and intellectual property rights, which are legally defined rights exerted by an actor often for a limited period of time. Thus an expired patent remains intellectual property although no rights can be exerted. Similarly some intellectual property may be tacit in nature and cannot be legally protected through IPR, although other strategies such as secrecy clauses on employees may be used to restrict its mobility.

2 The research also included the North-West of England but this is not included in this chapter.

3 The two universities can trace their origins back to the 1830s with the establishment of Durham University and a separate College of Medicine in Newcastle. The two were then merged into a collegiate university which developed on two sites until formal separation in 1966 with the creation of the University of Newcastle. However, throughout much of this period, Newcastle was the larger of the two parts, and more regionally oriented, with a strength in medicine and engineering.

4 The detailed results of the mapping of variables is reported elsewhere in Webster *et al.* (1998).

References

Cambridge County Council Research Group (1996) *The Hi Technology 'Community' in Cambridgeshire*, CCC, Cambridge.

Charles, D. R. and Howells, J. (1992) *Technology Transfer in Europe: Public and Private Networks*, Belhaven Press, London.

Charles, D. R., Hayward, S. and Thomas, D. (1995) 'Science Parks and Regional Technology Strategies: European Experiences', *Industry and Higher Education*, 9, 332–9.

Department of Trade and Industry (DTI) (1998) *Our Competitive Future: Building the Knowledge Driven Economy*, Cm 4176, The Stationery Office, London.

European Commission (1996) *First Action Plan on Innovation in Europe*, Office for Official Publications of the European Communities, Luxembourg.

Faulkner, W. and Senker, J. (1995) *Knowledge Frontiers*, Oxford University Press, Oxford.

Florida, R. and Cohen, W. M. (1999) 'Engine or Infrastructure? The University Role in Economic Development', in L. M. Branscomb, F. Kodama and R. Florida (eds), *Industrialising Knowledge: University–Industry Linkages in Japan and the United States*, MIT Press, London.

Garnsey, E. and Cannon-Brooks, A. (1993) 'The Cambridge Phenomenon Revisited: Aggregate Change Among Cambridge High Technology Companies Since 1989', *Entrepreneurship and Regional Development*, 5, 179–207.

Goddard, J. B., Charles, D. R., Pike, A., Potts, G. and Bradley, D. (1994) *Universities and Communities*, Committee of Vice Chancellors and Principals, London.

Harvey, K. (1996) 'Capturing Intellectual Property Rights for the UK: A Critique of University Policies', in A. Webster and K. Packer, *Innovation and the Intellectual Property System*, Kluwer Law International, London.

House of Commons, Science and Technology Committee (1994) *The Routes through which the Science Base is Translated into Innovative and Competitive Technology, First Report*, Vols. I to III (Session 1993–4, 74–I to III), HMSO, London.

Keeble, D. (1989) 'High Technology Industry and Regional Development in Britain: The Case of the Cambridge Phenomenon', *Environment and Planning C: Government and Policy*, 7, 153–72.

Latour, B. (1987) *Science in Action*, Open University Press, Milton Keynes.

Lawson, C., Moore, B., Keeble, D., Lawton-Smith, H. and Wilkinson, F. (1997) *Inter-Firm Links between Regionally Clustered High Technology SMEs: A Comparison of Cambridge and Oxford Immovation Networks,* ESRC Centre for Business Research working paper 65, Cambridge University, Cambridge.

Lumme, A., Kauranen, I. and Autio, E. (1994) 'The Growth and Funding Mechanisms of New Technology-Based Firms: A Comparative Study between the United Kingdom and Finland', *Finnish Journal of Business Economics,* 44 (1).

Lundvall, B.-Å. (ed.) (1992), *National Systems of Innovation. Towards a Theory of Innovation and Interactive Learning*, Pinter, London.

Lundvall, B.-Å. and Johnson, B. (1994) 'The Learning Economy', *Journal of Industry Studies,* 2, 23–42.

National Board of Employment Education and Training (NBEET) *(1995) Maxtmising the Beneflts,* Australian Government Publishing Service, Canberra.

Rappert, B. and Webster, A. (1997) 'Regimes of Ordering: The Commercialization of Intellectual Property in Industrial–Academic Collaborations', *Technology Analysis and Strategic Management*, 9,115–30.

Scottish Enterprise/Royal Society of Edinburgh (1996) *Commercialisation Enquiry – Final Report*, SE/RSE, Edinburgh.

Sherman, B. (1994) 'Governing Science: Patents and Public Sector Research', *Science in Context,* 7, 5 15–37.

Stankiewicz, R. (1994) 'Spin-Off Companies from Universities', *Science and Public Policy*, 21(2), 79–87.

Teece, D. (1986) 'Profiting from Technological Innovation: Implications for Integration, Collaboration, Licensing and Public Policy', *Research Policy*, 15, 285–305.

Webster, A. and Packer, K. (1996) 'Patenting Culture in Science: Reinventing the Wheel of Credibility', *Science, Technology and Human Values*, 21, 427–53.

Webster, A., Rappert, B., Charles, D. R. and Windrum, P. (1998) 'University Spin-Offs, SMEs and the Science Base: The Effective Use of Intellectual Property', ESRC End of Award Report L325253035, Swindon.

8 Worlds apart

Patent information and innovation in SMEs

Stuart Macdonald and Bernard Lefang

Introduction: the patent system of SMEs

The patent is the instrument of the intellectual property system best known and most closely associated with innovation. The patent is the outcome of a bargain between the inventor and society by which society grants the inventor certain rights to his invention in return for the inventor's disclosure of whatever it is he has invented (see Taylor and Silberston, 1973). Without these rights, it is argued, the inventor would be unable to reveal his invention for fear that others would steal it. Consequently, the inventor would have little incentive to invent and society would forgo the invention and its benefits. Thus the patent system neatly allows the inventor to exploit his invention, and provides society with an invention it would not otherwise have had.

In theory at least, the system is particularly appropriate for encouraging invention by small firms and independent inventors. While large organisations often have the internal resources to develop their inventions and so can keep the information of invention to themselves, smaller organisations must generally seek these resources outside and so must reveal all. In practice, though, the protection the patent system affords the weak against the strong may be illusory. Most obviously, the patent affords protection only when the patentee can afford to enforce his rights, which may mean that the poor have no protection at all (see Mansfield, Schwartz and Wagner, 1981). As the journal *Nature* (1929) noted long ago: 'the consideration for which patent rights may be enjoyed is nowadays not so much the introduction of a new invention as the possession of exceptional wealth'.

The problems SMEs encounter in protecting their inventions through the patent system are widely acknowledged. There is much less concern with what advantage they and their innovation might reap from the other part of the patent bargain: the information the patent system makes available. SMEs cannot depend on vast R&D departments to generate the information required for invention; they must look to external sources for this information and one of the richest of these would seem to be patent specifications.

Information for innovation

Of the screeds that have been written about the patent system, the vast bulk is concerned with the rights of the inventor over his information; very little is concerned with the rights of society to this information. Most of the information required for innovation is gathered rather than created, no matter how strong the firm's R&D. And most of the information required for innovation is to be found outside the firm rather than within it (Macdonald, 1998). Technology builds on technology in a cumulative manner, reflecting two characteristics of information. Information cannot be exhausted, it cannot be destroyed, but its quality can be enhanced by adding new information to existing stock. And since the cost of production of information is independent of the scale of information use, it may pay an industry as a whole to share information as widely as possible.

Silicon Valley is outstanding in that the participants in its high-technology industries have acknowledged, at least tacitly, that external information is fundamental to innovation, and have accommodated mechanisms appropriate to its flow (Rogers, 1982; Rogers and Larson, 1984). These include informal networks, highly mobile experts and second sourcing. Though the pace of innovation is less furious in other industries, innovation in even the largest and most self-contained of firms in the most sedate of industries is still dependent on information from beyond the firm's own boundary (von Hippel, 1988). The nature of information dictates that informal mechanisms are often more efficient in acquiring this information than formal ones (Macdonald, 1996). The patent system, of course, depends entirely on formal mechanisms for the dissemination of its information.

The patent specification is primarily a legal document, not a source of information for innovation. One respondent to a survey of professional engineers who had taken out patents encapsulated the situation nicely: 'I could barely recognise my own inventions in legalese'; 'I also feel that it is difficult to gain any information from filed patents as they are written in legal terms rather than engineering terms and therefore extremely hard to understand for people with engineering education' (Mandeville, 1982: 12). Furthermore, 'A company's patent lawyers can protect the company's proprietary position without giving away too much in the application process' (Labich, 1988: 30). Basically, the information contained in patent specifications is available only to those who consult them directly, or who pay others more adept at arcane classifications and the language of lawyers to do so (Liebesny, 1972). Moreover, the delay between the filing of an application and the publication of a specification may be far greater than the pace of change in some industries. In addition, the criteria by which patents are granted pay no heed at all to the contribution the patent information might make to innovation. Details of inventions which can make no conceivable contribution are frequently published, as are those of patents designed to mislead or obstruct (Schmookler, 1957). There is no public benefit from such publication. It has been calculated that patent information is worth about three-quarters of 1 per cent of firms' research and development (R&D) expenditure, and thus an infinitesimal proportion of total innovation costs (Taylor and Silberston, 1973: 212). This may help explain why there is such toleration of the poor dissemination of patent information; it is just not worth the spreading.

The patent in the innovation of SMEs

To test the use that SMEs make of the patent system, and especially patent information, in their innovation, two postal surveys were carried out in October 1996.

- *Survey 1 Innovation in patenting SMEs*. The sample was taken from the Patent Office's own database of those UK SMEs (employing between 10 and 250 people) that had been granted at least one patent in the United Kingdom or Europe in 1990. Some 615 questionnaires were despatched, from which 218 usable replies were received – a response rate of 32 per cent.
- *Survey 2 Innovation in SMEs*. Questionnaires were sent to 2,000 manufacturing firms throughout the UK with between 10 and 250 employees, the sample being taken from a commercial database. Some 774 replies were received, of which 687 were usable – a response rate of 35 per cent.

Innovation in SMEs

The survey firms were given every chance to identify themselves as innovative, a very broad definition of innovation being adopted, and any innovative activity over the last decade being the qualification. Innovation was perceived as technological innovation, defined as any product the company had produced new to the company or the market, or any process new to the company. Add to these criteria the general desire of respondents to perceive their own firms as innovative and it is perhaps not surprising that 69 per cent of all these SMEs declare that they are innovative. What is much more interesting is that even more – 83 per cent – report that they are engaged in investigative activities that they consider to be R&D. Among patenting SMEs, the tendency is even more marked – 94 per cent declare that they have innovated in the last ten years, and 90 per cent that they conduct investigative activities (Figure 8.1).

Sources of information for innovation

Innovating firms, even those which perform a great deal of R&D, are generally heavily dependent on external information for their innovation. In particular, they look to customers, suppliers and competitors for information about the latest developments in their industry and market. So, too, do these SMEs: 58 per cent of the non-patenting group find customers useful sources, and about 40 per cent declare suppliers and competitors useful. These proportions are massive compared with the contribution of information from other external sources (Figure 8.2(a)). In fact, all other likely sources of external information vie with each other in their uselessness for innovation in SMEs, which is interesting in that many of these sources take some pride, and expend considerable public resources, in their efforts to provide information to SMEs. Most successful in this unenviable competition are government sources and the patent system. Roughly 80 per cent of the non-patenting SMEs declare both these sources to be of little importance as sources of information for their innovation.

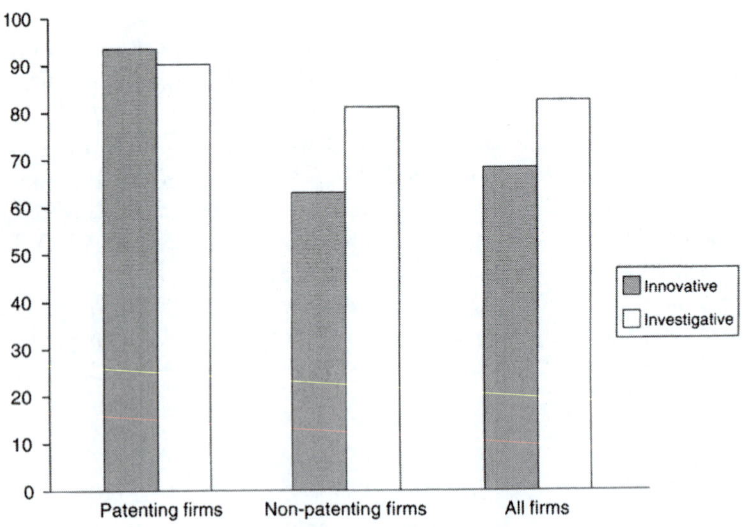

Figure 8.1 Firms that have innovated and that carry out investigative activities (%).

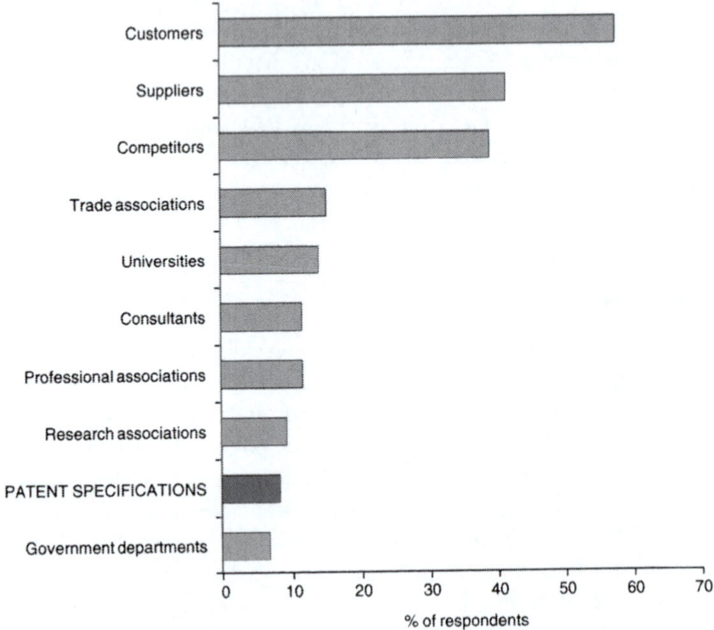

Figure 8.2(a) External sources of information rated important for innovation (non-patenting firms).

The pattern is very similar for patenting SMEs (Figure 8.2(b)). Again, they look to customers, suppliers and competitors for information, though slightly less so than the major group of SMEs. And, again, they find all other sources of information to be of little importance. As might be expected, they declare the patent system to be somewhat less useless than do SMEs in general, but the positive side is not encouraging for those who feel that the patent system is obviously a major source of information for innovation in SMEs: while just 8 per cent of the non-patenting SMEs think patent information of some importance, only 12 per cent of SMEs that have patented, and that therefore have some familiarity with at least the protective side of the system, consider patents are of some importance as a source of information for innovation.

There is, then, evidence that innovation in SMEs is the sort of activity which is carried on in isolation from all but their immediate contacts in the outside world, which is almost entirely dependent on the company's own resources. This is reinforced by what the surveys reveal about the means by which information is acquired. By far the most important of these means is the firm's own R&D (specified as such). The only other means of any significance is the technical and trade press (Figure 8.3(a)). Once again, there is intense competition among the means least useful for the innovation of these non-patenting SMEs (Figure 8.3(b)). Means that

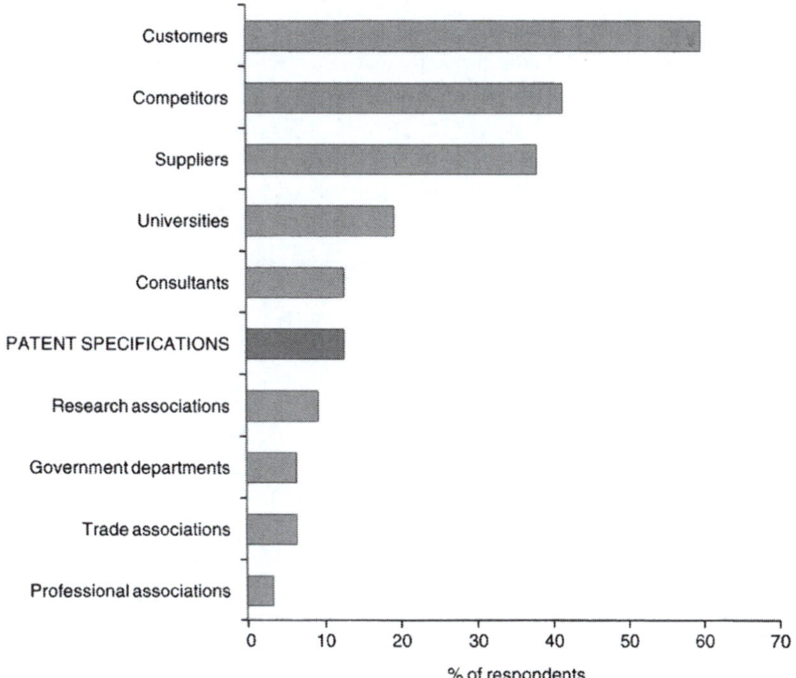

Figure 8.2(b) External sources of information rated important for innovation (patenting firms).

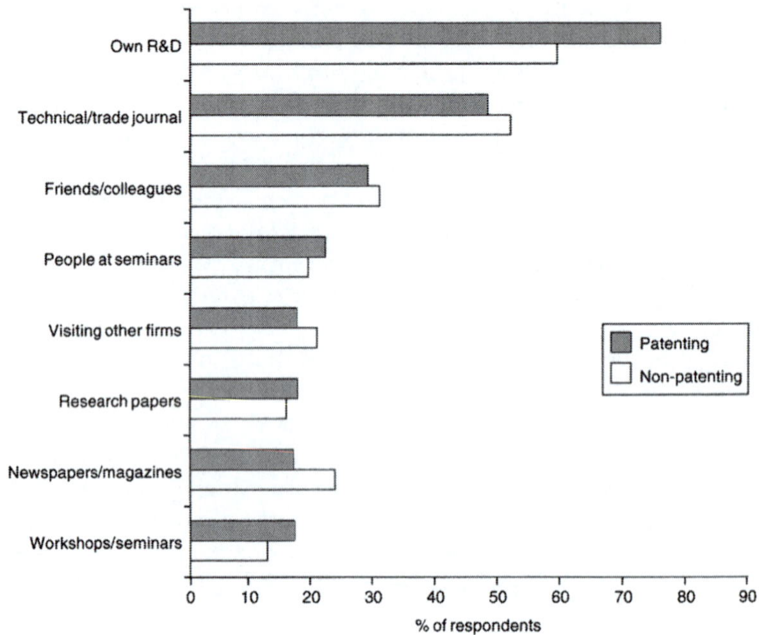

Figure 8.3(a) Means of acquiring information for innovation considered important.

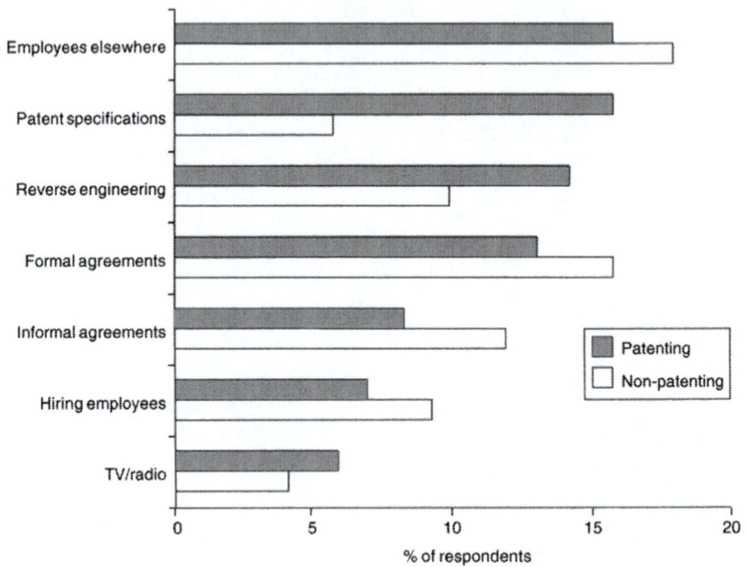

Figure 8.3(b) Means of acquiring information for innovation considered less important.

are characteristically important for innovation in larger firms, such as formal and informal agreements with other firms, are of no importance for this group. Means that have been found to be important in industries with rapid innovation, such as hiring employees from other firms, are similarly insignificant here. But, once again, one of the least useful of all is consulting patent specifications. The pattern is very much the same for patenting SMEs. Technical and trade journals are far and away the most important means of acquiring external information for innovation, but even this means pales into insignificance alongside reliance on the firm's own R&D. A full 77 per cent of patenting SMEs reckon this an important means of gaining information for innovation. Just 16 per cent see patent specifications as an important means of acquiring information for innovation, which exceeds the 6 per cent of non-patenting SMEs.

Involvement with intellectual property rights

It is often argued that the other forms of intellectual property protection – registered designs, copyright and trademarks – are of more practical use to SMEs than patents. This would seem to be questionable. These SMEs do not consider any form of intellectual property protection as important to their innovation. What is most remarkable is that even those SMEs that have patented, and therefore have some knowledge of the system, are only slightly more likely to see the other forms of intellectual property protection as benefiting their innovation (Figures 8.4(a) and 8.4(b)). In both cases, trademarks and trade secrets are a little more valued than copyright and registered designs, but the difference is marginal and is overwhelmed

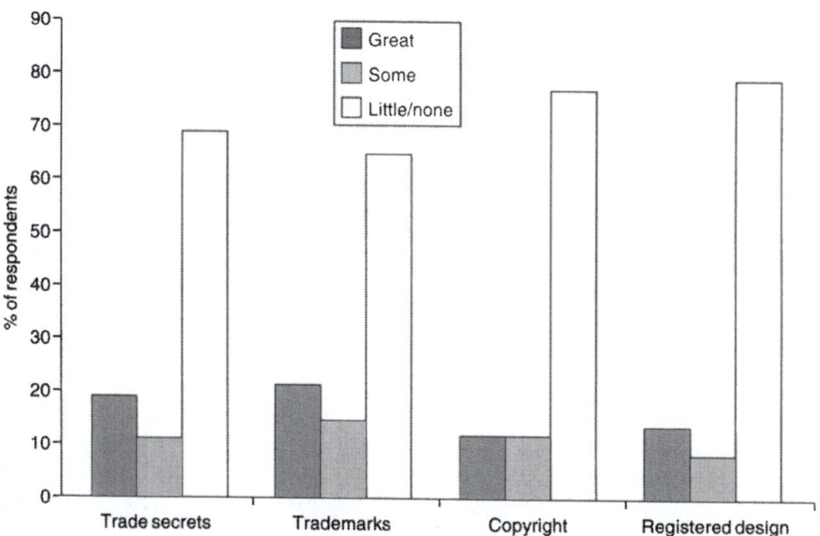

Figure 8.4(a) Benefits to innovation from other forms of intellectual property protection (non-patenting firms).

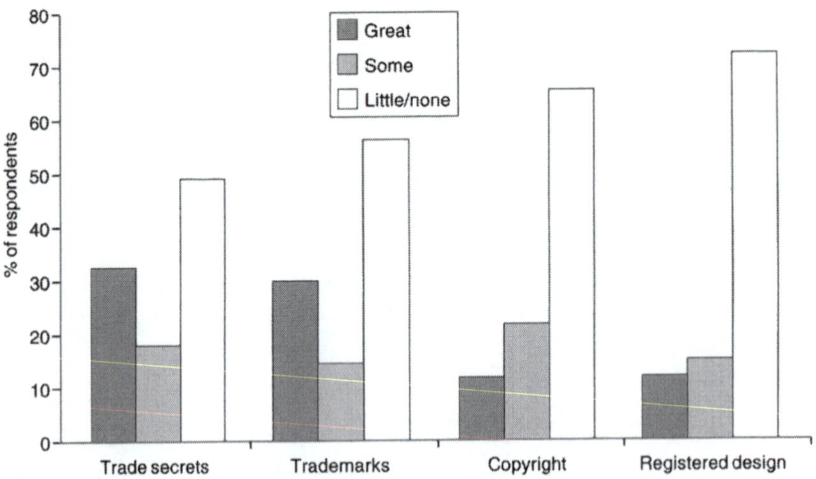

Figure 8.4(b) Benefits to innovation from other forms of intellectual property protection (patenting firms).

by the vast majority of all these SMEs considering that all forms of intellectual property protection are of little importance for their innovation.

Most of the firms surveyed because they had been granted a patent in 1990 had since acquired other patents – but not many. On average they had been granted but one other patent, and only 13 per cent had more than 10 patents. This does not necessarily mean that they are not innovative: it does suggest that they have reservations about the value of a patent. About half did not apply for patents on inventions they thought were patentable. Two-thirds have developed their invention since patenting it in 1990, but 87 per cent would have developed the invention even without a patent. Predictably, development is almost exclusively in-house rather than in partnership with others. Licensing the patent to others is not a popular course; 81 per cent have not done so. Nor has the vast majority of firms licensed patents from anyone else over the last ten years. Not a single firm could boast that it frequently licensed patents from others. Of the few firms that did license, most gained know-how as part of the agreement, but the licence also restricted what they could do with the technology. Most common among these restrictions are agreements not to sell outside a geographical area, not to dispute patents, not to sell competing products, and agreements to buy parts from the licensor and to license back improvements.

These patenting SMEs were asked the obvious questions: why take out a patent? The response is equally obvious: simply to protect the invention. About half also want to prevent others patenting, but there is little sympathy with the argument that a patent can assist in the development of an invention. More revealing still are the patent-searching practices of respondents. About half regularly conduct patent searches and almost all of these pay a patent attorney to search on their behalf. As Figures 8.5(a) and 8.5(b) show, the most important reason for doing this is to keep

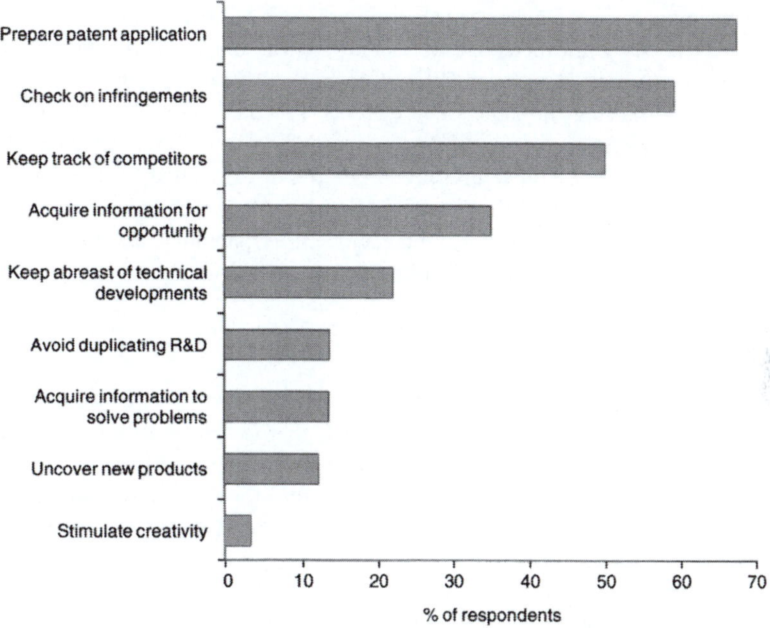

Figure 8.5(a) Why patent searches are conducted (non-patenting firms).

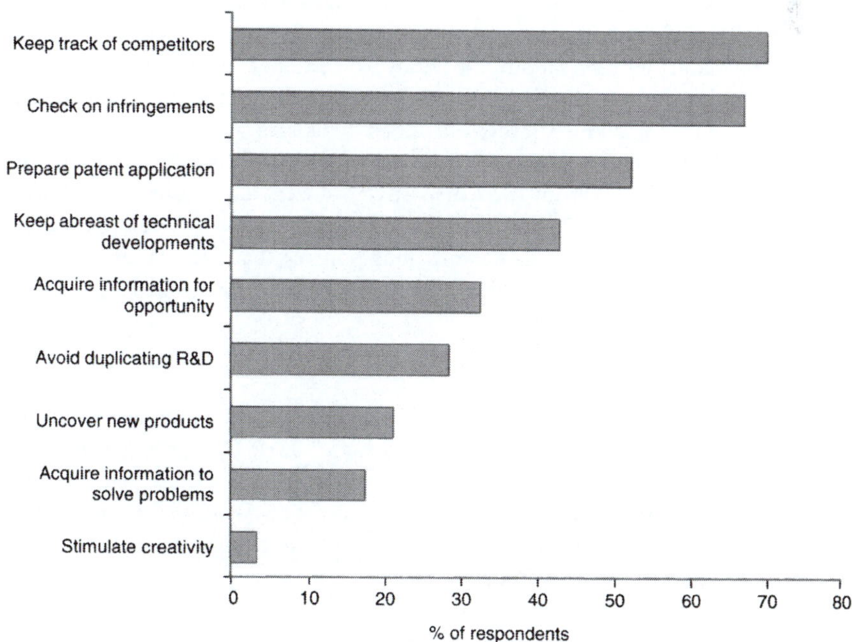

Figure 8.5(b) Why patent searches are conducted (patenting firms).

track of competitors, but the next most important reasons are to check on potential patent infringements and to prepare patent applications. It has been noted by others that some of the most significant uses to which the patent system is put are demanded by the patent system itself (Australian Patent Office, 1980). When this happens, the patent system is serving not the requirements of innovation, but its own requirements. Given that about two-thirds of those SMEs which do regularly search patent specifications seek no other information than that demanded for the patent system itself, it may be assumed that many SMEs which do search to keep track of competitors are actually keeping track of their competitors' patenting, and that this is why patent attorneys are so generally employed to do the searching.

Observations on the surveys

The two surveys paint a somewhat depressing picture of SMEs that are isolated from the external sources of information for innovation that larger firms and firms in rapidly innovating sectors find so important. These SMEs seem to rely very heavily on their own resources. There is a range of likely reasons for this, but basically they come down to managers of SMEs having few resources available to search for information in the outside world and to use the information acquired there. In a small firm, everyone is needed for day-to-day operations, and perhaps for survival.

Yet these are not stagnant firms. They declare themselves to be avid innovators. But because they rely to a singular extent on their own resources, they run a real risk of reinventing the wheel with every effort to innovate, and certainly of innovating with more trouble and expense than might be necessary (see Pettersson, 1983). There is, of course, a vast range of policy measures designed to help small firms acquire information for innovation. The performance of these tends to be assessed in terms of firm involvement in these programmes rather than in terms of benefits to the firms' innovation. The surveys described here step well back from these programmes and their customary performance measures to look at innovation as SMEs themselves see it. From this perspective, no external influence has much impact on their innovation. Patent protection is little valued and innovation is rife in its absence. And among a host of information sources that SMEs might use for innovation and rarely do, patent information is distinctive in being used least of all.

Models of innovation

An invention is a discovery: an innovation is a product or service that is new to the market, or simply new to the adopter (see Schott, 1981). Of the total resources required for innovation, only a small proportion come from invention; the majority come from design, production, marketing and so on. This assumes, of course, that every invention contributes something. It does not. Most inventions, patented or not, make no input to any innovation.

> Although most innovations can be traced to some conquest in the realm of either theoretical or practical knowledge that has occurred in the immediate or remote

> past, there are many which cannot. Innovation is possible without anything we should identify as invention, and invention does not necessarily induce innovation, but produces of itself . . . no economically relevant effect at all.
>
> (Schumpeter, 1939)

Society may want innovation from its patent system very much indeed, but the patent system is really concerned only with invention (Kingston, 1987). This desire for innovation has produced two models in justification of the patent system. Though they are not incompatible, they are seldom presented together (Merges, 1988). Both are rooted in the supposition that invention would not take place if it could be purloined by anyone so inclined.

The first model emphasises development: the patent system gives an incentive to invent because it allows the inventor to reap a reward from his invention, either through developing it himself or by selling it to others for them to develop. The second model is less contingent on development and emphasises information: it is that a bargain has been struck between the inventor and society by which society grants property rights, with which the inventor may do what he will, in return for giving society the information of his invention (Merges, 1988). In the first model, society allows the inventor to make his information public: in the second, society demands that he make his information public. The first is a linear model in that it supposes that patent information leads directly to the innovation which is society's reward. The second is a model of innovation that sees patent information adding to a social store of information in which information for innovation may be found, and – with the owner's consent – used. In this case, information is society's reward.

Innovation in the world of patents

Although the patent system is insignificant in the innovation of the vast majority of SMEs, it is important in the innovation of a few. However, these few are often presented as if they were the many, or rather what the many could and should be. If the patent system is especially suited to SMEs, and if SMEs should innovate, then SMEs should use the patent system. This is not a logical progression of which SMEs themselves are fond; rather it is one beloved by those with greater interests in the patent system. It is much more important for them that SMEs use the patent system than it is for SMEs themselves. Indeed, much of the perpetual discussion on how the patent system may be improved is formed in terms of innovation in SMEs, which is odd considering how little connection there is between the two (Kahaner, 1983). Discussion, of course, is not about wholesale change to the system. The system has been around for a long time and it is not about to disappear.

> If we did not have a patent system, it would be irresponsible, on the basis of our present knowledge of its economic consequences, to recommend instituting one. But since we have had a patent system for a long time, it would be irresponsible, on the basis of our present knowledge, to recommend abolishing it.
>
> (Machlup, 1958: 80)

Instead, discussion is about appropriate tinkering – rewarding employee inventors, for example (Littler and Pearson, 1979; Orkin, 1984) – which tinkering has long distracted attention from what should be done to what can be done (Polanyi, 1943).

While the longevity of the patent system is usually attributed to a persistent inability to devise anything better, the resilience of the institution is also related to its accommodation of perceptions of innovation that are readily acceptable to existing social and economic systems. A view of innovation as the outcome of procedure – as something contained within, and controlled by, the organisation – readily finds room for that part of the intellectual property system that is concerned with the ownership and control of information. It is, however, much less compatible with that part of the intellectual property system intended to encourage the dissemination of information. For the patent system ever to become a serious source of information for innovation would require general acceptance of another model of innovation altogether.

Linear models dominate perceptions of technological innovation. New technology is depicted as the product of process, with innovation emerging from a series of steps in the industrial management of technology. It is presented as axiomatic that science must precede technology, invention innovation. In its classic form, the linear model endows research not just with the importance of coming first, but with a mystic quality: research is the mind of man challenging the laws of nature: 'Technological advances are possible only because of major investments in research and development' (Girifalco, 1983).

In academic studies of innovation, the linear model has long since been dismissed as unrealistic and unhelpful, yet it endures (Macdonald, 1986). In part, this is because of an essential simplicity, which is attractive in any model. There is also a vague and general feeling that if innovation happens – which it obviously does – then it must have started somewhere. For every omega there must have been an alpha. In addition, there is a basic organisational requirement to deny the reality, and certainly the virtues, of disorganisation. It is all very well to allow that disorder produces unfavourable outcomes, but the favourable – amongst which is innovation – must be claimed as the product of good management, good decisions, good organisation. Amidst the uncertainty of innovation – often the chaos (Kantrow, 1980) – linearity provides the comforting assurance of order and direction: 'the very idea of a patent law is something of an oxymoron: it is a hybrid of two opposing principles, change and order, that live always in tension with each other' (Kass, 1982: 43).

Society needs innovation, but the need may actually be more important than the innovation itself. Society as a whole, and more particularly certain elements within it, has reason to welcome a degree of retardation in innovation. Rampant innovation is disruptive; it raises the level of uncertainty. For organisations with capital sunk in existing ways of doing things, rapid and unpredictable change is not welcomed wholeheartedly, especially when it is forced on them by the innovation of competitors. The very nature of organisation, social or economic, is antagonistic to rapid and unpredictable innovation. Consider a world in which such change is normal: a high-technology world extended to all other activities. Such a world would be extremely disconcerting for most people and for all organisations. The patent system may actually slow down the pace of innovation (Takalo and Kanniainen, 1997), which is the cost of exercising some control over the rate and direction of innovation. Without at least the illusion of control, our attitude towards innovation would be even more timorous than it already is.

Those who seek reassurance in the patent system find themselves allies of those who take the patent system seriously because it is very much in their interest to do so. This is an uneasy alliance, entwining value from the general impression of order bestowed by the system, with value from specific exploitation of its parts. Scientists, for example, while craving order at least as much as the rest of us, are not wholly opposed to the notion that their efforts are responsible for technological innovation; nor are managers to the control the linear model lets them feel they exercise over innovation (see Greiner and Barnes, 1970); nor policy-makers to the idea that innovation can be driven by the programmes they implement.

Government policies and programmes to encourage innovation are virtually universal, the unaided market being reluctant to replace the old and familiar with the new and uncertain. Innovation programmes require specific aims and objectives, means of monitoring and evaluation. Above all, they require justification. It is important to believe not only that the public resources devoted to innovation actually produce innovation, but also that they give value for money. There is no room for doubt, much less failure, when public money and political reputations are at stake. The policy-maker is instinctively and pragmatically in tune with the patent system, with the notion that resources go in and innovation comes out, that the process is contained, and that public institutions and the market should work together to produce innovation (see Griliches, 1989).

These same policy-makers are especially eager to measure the innovation that arises from their programmes. This is no mean task, and they must generally resort to measuring what goes into innovation rather than what comes out. Worse still, they must content themselves with measuring what goes into research – typically money and manpower – rather than into all the activity responsible for innovation. Patents are a godsend because they are one of the few output measures of research available. The use of patent statistics to measure innovation rather than simply to count patented inventions says much more about the perceptions of the users than the statistics say about innovation (see Rosenberg, 1974; Wyatt, 1977–8; Sciberras, 1986). Just as tinkering with the patent system implies that the system itself is worthy of the tinkering, so the countless caveats that accompany conclusions emanating from the esoteric manipulation of patent statistics affirm that counting patents really is worthwhile.

The pharmaceutical industry also likes to see innovation as it is portrayed in the patent process. The pharmaceutical and chemical industries are the patent system's biggest users: about 22 per cent of the world's patent applications are in these fields (Johnston and Carmichael, 1981). Much of the pressure for extension of the patent term came from the pharmaceutical industry, arguing that if society insists on costly and lengthy development, it must also allow the developer of the innovation sufficient time to recoup these costs. For many years, the industry insisted it deserved extra patent protection because pharmaceutical innovation is different from innovation in other industries. More recently, the pharmaceutical industry has argued that pharmaceutical innovation is typical of innovation generally, and consequently that the whole patent system should be reinforced for the sake of national competitiveness.

> Since, today, it takes an average ten years and over $100 million to develop a new drug, only seven or eight years are left for the product to recover its entire investment before manufacturers who made no R&D investment at all are free to copy and compete with it. In the United States, the 1984 Patent Restoration Act has added up to five years of life to a pharmaceutical patent to make up for some of the time lost in the governmental approval process . . . If the United States is to avoid further erosion of its competitive position, a new framework for growth must be envisioned . . . in which intellectual property rights are protected and in which investment and innovation are encouraged.
>
> (Miller, 1988: 88)

The pharmaceutical lobby is a potent force in the patent system. Business strategy is thoroughly focused on making the whole patent system as powerful as possible. Certainly the pharmaceutical industry is quite unashamed in its lobbying to strengthen the system (Miller, 1988; Porter, 1989); it is also quite ruthless: 'We are most interested in a strengthening rather than weakening of the Australian patent law, especially for pharmaceuticals. Substantial weakening might prompt us to drastically shortcut investments in Australia' (Mandeville and Bishop, 1982: 16). The real strength of the industry's argument lies not in logic, but in the match between its innovation practice and the view of innovation embedded in the patent system.

It is now more than a decade since Mansfield published his classic table illustrating the importance of the patent system to the innovation of various industries (Table 8.1). It shows some industries to be very much more reliant on the patent system than others. Basically this is because invention in these industries is highly codifiable

Table 8.1 Inventions that would not have been developed in the absence of patent protection (%)

Pharmaceuticals	60
Chemicals	38
Petroleum	25
Machinery	17
Fabricated metal products	12
Electrical equipment	11
Primary metals	1
Instruments	1
Office equipment	0
Motor vehicles	0
Rubber	0
Textiles	0

Source: Mansfield (1986).

(Levin, Kevorick, Nelson and Winter, 1987). The difficulties normally associated with information transactions are easily overcome, allowing information to be acquired and used by competitors. Put another way, the precision of a chemical or pharmaceutical patent specification makes the patent particularly easy to defend and thus enhances the value of the intellectual property (Tapon, 1989). As Taylor and Silberston (1973: 231) concluded more than two decades ago, the 'pharmaceutical industry stands alone in the extent of its involvement with the patent system'. The pharmaceutical industry has done much since then to ensure that the patent system meets its own requirements: basically the requirements of large companies, operating with highly codified information on a route to innovation made linear by government regulation and social expectation.

> Strong multi-million dollar organisations will patent to protect without any desire to allow a product onto the marketplace – 'preventive patenting' – this can seriously damage real innovation.
>
> Patents are used as a device by large companies to attempt to prevent smaller companies from innovating.
>
> In many cases, large corporations use the patent system to safeguard their research and to intimidate smaller companies with IPR litigation – other large companies may be in a position to 'deal' or fight but not small ones!
>
> (SME survey respondents)

Innovation in the world of SMEs

Linear models struggle to explain the innovation of SMEs (Rothwell, 1986, 1992). They reveal only that much of this innovation is different from the innovation of linearity, a revelation from which it is all too easy to conclude that the innovation of SMEs is somehow inadequate: indeed, that SMEs themselves are inadequate as long as they remain SMEs.

There appears to be an assumption in much of the literature that SMEs need to innovate to grow and prosper: 'Companies that introduced new technologies at least once a year were three times as likely to forecast an increase or rapid increase in turnover than those that never introduced new technology' (Marsh, 1996). Of course, many managers of SMEs have no ambitions to manage large companies, and the economy is dependent upon the part that SMEs play in it – as SMEs (Rothwell, 1989).

It should come as no surprise that SMEs are highly innovative; their innovation is a necessary response to competition and the fluidity of their markets. The vast majority of SMEs report customers to be the dominant source of external information for their innovation (Rothwell, 1991), and suppliers and competitors are also significant sources. But we find little evidence of any network behaviour, and considerable evidence of firms shackled to a very few obvious information sources. There is little benefit from government programmes, there are few qualified scientists and engineers, and innovation is regarded as essential to survival rather than as the means to prosper and grow.

> Really, our business is to subcontract as 1st/2nd tier supplier to the automobile business. We don't therefore produce 'our own' products.
>
> Process innovation is such an automatic activity in our company that we forget that we are being innovative!
>
> My company makes products to other people's designs. Our customers hold the patents if appropriate.
>
> We have had patents which resulted in expense and no real protection. We now rely on simply being the first.
>
> We have had patents. There is no purpose, it is very expensive, difficult to police and therefore not practical to us. We rely on being first then leading by innovation progress.
>
> (SME survey respondents)

Our findings – that customers, suppliers and competitors are the most important sources of external information for innovation – are reminiscent of those of von Hippel (1988), and might raise suspicions of the information-trading that he and others have found elsewhere (von Hippel, 1987; Carter, 1989, Schrader, 1991). But the networks of these SMEs are not the networks of equals typical of high-technology firms. They are networks of dependence in which the powerful help the weak only as long as they are of use, and equals compete to be used. According to a recent Department of Trade and Industry (DTI) survey of innovation in SMEs, nearly a third earn more than half their turnover from their three largest customers (Marsh, 1996). Such networks do not necessarily facilitate innovation, which is presumably why SMEs perform so much of their own R&D, and look to their own resources for development. Inevitably, these resources are limited and often inadequate. The result is often frustration, not just with failure in innovation, but also with government exhortations to succeed that are based on a linear understanding of innovation. Programmes to increase the involvement of SMEs in the patent system are merely symptomatic of this misunderstanding.

> In our business, we have to develop new ideas with our customers and move quickly. Our products have been copied – but there is no point in patenting them – as any slight production variance invalidates the patent and is therefore not worth pursuing.
>
> I used to use patent information extensively at a previous company but in my present business, we have to respond in weeks or months with new developments and these will be out of date within a year or so.
>
> (SME survey respondents)

Neither our survey evidence nor the argument presented here gives any support to policy-makers who would resort to the patent system to encourage the innovation of SMEs (e.g. Inter-departmental Committee on Intellectual Property, 1995). Those who do so allow their own perceptions of innovation to outweigh the evidence. The patent system will remain, of course, because there is nothing better to replace it, but also because it serves the needs of specific interest groups – including policy-makers – very well indeed, and because it is so thoroughly compatible with a neat and ordered view of innovation. But for most innovation in most SMEs, the patent system is at best an irrelevance and at worst an obstacle (see Rothwell and Zegveld, 1982). If there is scope for policy, it is in reducing not so much the impact of the patent system on SMEs, for that would mean altering the whole system, but rather the expectations that SMEs have of the patent system and consequently the disappointment they experience when it proves largely irrelevant to their innovation (see Rothwell, 1983).

> Once got involved in trying to get a patent. Hopeless – very expensive, very tedious. Would not bother again – ever.
>
> Over the lifetime of our business, I've protected the innovation of the company with two patents in two fields of activity. The risk of taking out patents has grown considerably and now is almost out of reach of a small company.
>
> Generally too expensive to initiate and too expensive to police.
>
> Cost and complexity of patents make them non-viable . . . for us to consider patenting anything because we could not afford to go to law. Several of our customers have gone to the wall trying to defend patents against larger firms.
>
> We have found the patent system overly costly and as a result avoid using it!
>
> (SME survey respondents)

Concluding thoughts

The notion of the patent system existing as much to disseminate information as to protect it has been further obscured by a new relationship between the patent system and innovation. No longer is the patent simply an indicator of invention, or even of innovation; the patent is increasingly being seen as almost the equivalent of innovation. This new world of patent-orientated innovation offers both the dangerous illusion that all innovation can be rendered tidy, and also distinct advantages for those industries, those companies, those academics, those administrators and those policy-makers who are comfortable with the idea of a neat and ordered world. But for innovation as a whole, the new order brings only problems. Innovation is not usually a linear process; anything that helps affirm this error is a deterrent to understanding how innovation generally does occur, and therefore to innovation itself.

> Patents are expensive to obtain and maintain and one would expect, expensive to defend. I wonder, therefore, whether their value is more psychological than real.'
>
> (SME survey respondent)

Any strengthening of the patent tilts the balance of the system in favour of seeing the benefit to society not in terms of making information available for innovation, but in terms of the protection it gives, and then not to invention but to innovation itself. This shift is evident in a growing tendency in the United States to regard the commercial success of innovations as a major determining factor in the granting and upholding of patents (Merges, 1988). Thus is the patent system extended from mere invention to encompass a host of factors – production, distribution systems, service networks, advertising, marketing and whatever – which contribute to the success of innovation, factors in which SMEs have a decided disadvantage.

> When intellectual property rights are protected, *innovators* are able to recover the costs incurred in research, product development and market development. This cost recovery . . . is essential for stimulating the future research and development that is necessary to maintain America's competitive edge (emphasis added).
>
> (Silverman, 1990: fn. 110)

> . . . an overemphasis on successful innovation, coupled with reduced attention to the presence or absence of a true invention, reinforces only one of the dual policy goals of the patent system: providing incentives to inventors. It ignores the goal of encouraging inventors to disclose technical information.
>
> (Merges, 1988: 876)

It would seem that whatever advantage patents once gave SMEs in facilitating the external development of their invention is being eroded. It follows that there is also less interest in the argument that it is incumbent on the inventor, and the patent system, to broadcast the information of invention as widely as possible. To SMEs at any rate, the public good arguments traditionally presented by patent offices to support the dissemination of information begin to sound, if not exactly hollow, then increasingly out of tune with the times.

> Patent specifications are a source of valuable technical information, readily available and much of it *free* for the taking. It is a pity that *so few* manufacturers, engineers and scientists seem to be aware of this. So next time you have a technical problem, check to ensure that it has not been solved already. Even if you don't find a ready solution, you may pick up some good ideas for use in your current or future design (original emphasis).
>
> (Australian Patent Office, 1981: 2)

> Each patent specification is a detailed disclosure of the invention and it is this

aspect of course which is particularly valuable as a rich source of technical information.

(Blackman, 1994: 47)

Acknowledgement

The research on which this paper is based was funded by a grant (L325253021) from the Economic and Social Research Council under its Intellectual Property Programme. An earlier version of this chapter was published in 1998 by the authors as 'Patents and Policy in the Innovation of Small and Medium Enterprises: Building on Rothwell' in Ray Oakey and Wim During (eds), *New Technology-Based Firms in the 1990s*, vol. 5, Routledge, London, 185–208.

References

Australian Patent Office (1980) *Pilot Study of the Users of Patent Information and their Needs*, Canberra.

Australian Patent Office (1981) *Patent Literature, a Source of Technical Information*, AGPS, Canberra.

Blackman, M. (1994) 'Taking Patent Information Services to Small and Medium Enterprises', *Intellectual Property in Asia and the Pacific*, 40, 44–67.

Carter, A. (1989) 'Knowhow Trading as Economic Exchange', *Research Policy*, 18, 155–63.

Girifalco, L. (1983) 'The Dynamics of Technological Change', *Economic Impact*, 42, 54–9.

Greiner, L. and Barnes, L. (1970) 'Organization Change and Development' in G. Dalton and P. Lawrence (eds), *Organizational Change and Development*, Irwin-Dorsey, Homewood, IL, 1–12.

Griliches, Z. (1989) 'Patents: Recent Trends and Puzzles', *Brookings Papers: Microeconomics*, 291–319.

Inter-departmental Committee on Intellectual Property (1995) *Use and Exploitation of Intellectual Property by Small Firms*, Patent Office, London.

Johnston, R. and Carmichael, S. (1981) *Australian Science and Technology Indicators Feasibility Study – Private Enterprise. Final Report*, Australian Department of Science and Technology, occasional paper 4, Canberra.

Kahaner, L. (1983) 'Changes Pending for the Patent System', *High Technology*, 3 (12), 48–57.

Kantrow, A. (1980) 'The Strategy-Technology Connection', *Harvard Business Review*, 58 (4), 6–21.

Kass, L. (1982) 'The Right to Patent', *Dialogue*, 58 (4), 42–5.

Kingston, W. (ed.) (1987) *Direct Protection of Innovation*, Kluwer Academic, Dordrecht.

Labich, K. (1988) 'The Innovators', *Fortune*, 6 June, 27–32.

Liebesny, F. (1972) 'Patents as Sources of Information' in F. Liebesny (ed.), *Mainly on Patents*, Butterworth, London, 117–19.

Levin, R., Klevorick, A., Nelson, R. and Winter, S. (1987) *Appropriating the Returns from Industrial Research and Development*, Brookings Papers on Economic Activity, 3.

Littler, D. A. and Pearson, A. W. (1979) 'The Employee Inventor and the New Patents Act', *Planned Innovation*, 2 (10), 335–8.

Macdonald, S. (1986) 'Theoretically Sound: Practically Useless? Government Grants for Industrial R&D in Australia', *Research Policy*, 15, 269–83.

Macdonald, S. (1996) 'Informal Information Flow and Strategy in the International Firm', *International Journal of Technology Management*, 11 (1-3), 219–32.

Macdonald, S. (1998) *Information for Innovation. Managing Change from an Information Perspective*, Oxford University Press, Oxford.

Machlup, F. (1958) *An Economic Review of the Patent System*, Studies of the US Patent System 15, US Senate Sub-committee on Patents, Trademarks and Copyrights, US Government Printing Office, Washington DC.

Mandeville, T. (1982) 'Engineers and the Patent System: Results of a Survey of Members of the Institution of Engineers', in T. Mandeville, D. Lamberton and J. Bishop (eds) *Supporting Papers for Economic Effects of the Australian Patent System*, Australian Government Publishing Service, Canberra.

Mandeville, T. and Bishop, J. (1982) 'Economic Effects of the Patent System: Results of a Survey of Patent Attorneys', in T. Mandeville, D. Lamberton and J. Bishop (eds) *Supporting Papers for Economic Effects of the Australian Patent System*, Australian Government Publishing Service, Canberra.

Mansfield, E. (1986) 'Patents and Innovation: An Empirical Study', *Management Science*, 32 (2), 173–81.

Mansfield, E., Schwartz, M. and Wagner, S. (1981) 'Imitation Costs and Patents: An Empirical Study', *Economic Journal*, 91 (364), 907–18.

Marsh, R. (1996) 'Innovation in Small and Medium Sized Enterprises, 1995 Survey', *Economic Trends*, 516, October, 24–41.

Merges, R. (1988) 'Commercial Success and Patent Standards: Economic Perspectives on Innovation', *California Law Review*, 76, 805–76.

Miller, W. (1988) 'Productivity and Competition: A Look at the Pharmaceutical Industry', *Columbia Journal of World Business*, Fall, 85–8.

Nature (1929) 'The Grant of Invalid Patents', 9 November, 713.

Orkin, N. (1984) 'Rewarding Employee Invention: Time for Change', *Harvard Business Review*, 62 (1), 56–7.

Pettersson, E. (1983) 'Description of the Way Transfer of Scientific and Technical Information of SMEs is Organized in Sweden' in P. Degoul and J. Gibb (eds) *Regional Industrial Information Transfer*, Frances Pinter, London, 196–9.

Polanyi, M. (1943) 'Patent Reform', *Review of Economic Studies*, 11 (1), 61–76.

Porter, V. (1989) 'The Copyright Designs and Patents Act 1988: The Triumph of Expediency over Principle', *Journal of Law and Society*, 16 (3), 340–51.

Rogers, E. (1982) 'Information Exchange and Technological Information' in D. Sahal (ed.) *The Transfer and Utilization of Technical Knowledge*, Lexington Books, Lexington, MA, 105–23.

Rogers, E. and Larson, J. (1984) *Silicon Valley Fever*, Basic Books, New York.

Rosenberg, N. (1974) 'Science, Invention and Economic Growth', *Economic Journal*, 84 (333), 90–108.

Rothwell, R. (1983) 'The Difficulties of National Innovation Policies' in S. Macdonald, T. Mandeville and D. Lamberton (eds), *The Trouble with Technology*, Frances Pinter, London, 202–15.

Rothwell, R. (1986) 'Reindustrialisation, Innovation and Public Policy' in P. Hall (ed.) *Technology, Innovation and Economic Policy*, Philip Allan, Oxford, 65–83.

Rothwell, R. (1989) 'Small Firms, Innovation and Industrial Change', *Small Business Economics*, 1, 51–64.

Rothwell, R. (1991) 'External Networking and Innovation in Small and Medium-Sized Manufacturing Firms in Europe', *Technovation*, 11 (2), 93–112.

Rothwell, R. (1992) 'Successful Industrial Innovation: Critical Factors for the 1990s', *R&D Management*, 22 (3), 221–39.

Rothwell, R. and Zegveld, W. (1982) *Innovation in the Small and Medium Sized Firm: Their Role in Employment and Economic Change*, Frances Pinter, London.

Schmookler, J. (1957) 'Inventors Past and Present', *Review of Economics and Statistics*, 39, 321–33.

Schott, K. (1981) *Industrial Innovation in the United Kingdom, Canada and the United States*, British North American Committee, London.

Schrader, S. (1991) 'Informal Technology Transfer between Firms: Cooperation through Information Trading', *Research Policy*, 20, 153–70.

Schumpeter, J. (1939) *Business Cycles*, McGraw Hill, New York.

Sciberras, E. (1986) 'Indicators of Technical Intensity and International Competitiveness: A Case for Supplementing Quantitative Data with Qualitative Studies in Research', *R&D Management*, 16 (1), 3–13.

Silverman, A. (1990) 'Intellectual Property Law and the Venture Capital Process', *High Technology Law Journal*, 5 (1), 157–92.

Takalo, T. and Kanniainen, V. (1997) 'Do Patents Slow Down Technological Progress?', paper presented to the conference 'New Developments in Intellectual Property: Economics and Law', Oxford, March.

Tapon, F. (1989) 'A Transaction Cost Analysis of Innovations in the Organization of Pharmaceutical R&D', *Journal of Economic Behaviour and Organization*, 12, 197–213.

Taylor, C. and Silberston, Z. (1973) *The Economic Impact of the Patent System*, Cambridge University Press, Cambridge.

von Hippel, E. (1987) 'Cooperation between Rivals: Informal Know-How Trading', *Research Policy*, 16, 291–302

von Hippel, E. (1988) *The Sources of Innovation*, Oxford University Press, Oxford.

Wyatt, G. (1977–8) *The Determinants of Inventive Activity Reconsidered*, working paper 2, Department of Economics, Heriot-Watt University, Edinburgh.

9 Barriers to the use of patent information in SMEs

Matthew Hall, Charles Oppenheim and Margaret Sheen

Introduction

This chapter is about how small and medium-sized companies (SMEs) can make use of the information contained in patents. It goes on to examine what barriers may be preventing the wider use of such information within this sector. Much of what we now know about this area comes from a study we undertook recently which was supported by public funding (see acknowledgements).

There is no doubt that patents can be a valuable source of both important technical and commercial intelligence. Patents not only disclose detailed technical descriptions of inventions, but they may also give away commercially useful information since they contain the names of inventors and applicant organisations. Indeed, patents may be the *earliest* if not the *only* source of information in the public domain. However, it is the level of *detail* required by the law that makes them potentially of such value as this level of detail is rarely found in publications elsewhere.

The fact that many small companies do not use patent information does not mean that patent information could not be useful to them. Indeed, if patents are potentially such an rich or significant source of information then one is curious as to why there is such an apparent anomaly. In 1994, the European Patent Office (EPO) published findings that supported what anecdotal evidence had said for some time: that company size is an important factor in the level of patent information use. Small and medium-sized companies apparently do not use patent information as often as large companies. In an address to the EPO Patent Information User Meeting in 1995, the president of the EPO, expressed his concern that: 'there are many compelling reasons to believe that the SMEs' situation in the new world order will deteriorate rapidly, if they do not make better use of patent information' (Braendli, 1995). What this does not tell us, however, is what proportion of SMEs actually could benefit from use of patent information. So, while other studies may have shown *relatively* how few companies regard patents as being of any use to them in the conduct of their business, this does not answer the key question, which is: *In those companies where patents could yield useful intelligence*, are there significant barriers preventing acquisition of patent information?

From the policy angle, there is considerable interest in SMEs, as they are a major employer and are now thought to be the main engine of economic growth. Many SMEs, however, are thought to be lagging in performance. Anything that can improve their competitiveness should make a contribution to economic development and growth. In most advanced economies, policies to stimulate innovation and competitiveness are major themes of industrial policy. It is much more difficult, however, to obtain data and measures on such phenomena. Part of the difficulty stems from treating SMEs as a 'sector', which can be highly misleading. Furthermore, while patent activity may be a crude indicator of the inventiveness of a nation, very little is known about how good firms are at finding and using ideas in patents as a stimulus to their own creativity. This whole topic can be likened to the dark side of the moon, and it was our task to examine it.

The academic literature on use of patent information by industry is extremely sparse. In a study covering companies of all sizes, Stephenson (1982) found that even in companies claiming to avail themselves of patent protection, a lack of awareness of the information patents could provide was evident. It is, perhaps, not surprising that most studies assume that patent information is of use to SMEs (Blackman, 1995; Schmoch, 1990; Koch, 1991) and therefore focus more on how such information might be promoted to SMEs. Apart from a report from the UK Patent Office Interdepartmental Committee on Intellectual Property (1995) suggesting that cost might be the key factor, no study has really examined in depth what the barriers to use of patent information actually are.

A survey commissioned by the EPO and carried out by the Munich-based Roland Berger Forschungs-Institut in 1994 across 2,000 companies in 17 European countries, found that patent information is of little importance to companies that do not apply for patents (European Patent Office, 1994). Such a result is hardly surprising in view of Stephenson's findings. If firms actually owning patents lack awareness of the potential usefulness of patent information, what chance is there that the rest will do so?

What none of these studies have done, however, is to examine in more depth *why* firms behave in the way the do, across different sectors with different propensities for patenting activity. Only then can one begin to draw some conclusions as to what might be done, if anything, to stimulate increased innovation through the better use of patent information.

This chapter is organised under seven main headings following this introduction. In the next section we discuss our approach to the study, where we describe how we identified companies and profiled SMEs in the sectors examined. Following on from this we look at patenting behaviour, then examine how patent agents may act as an information filter between the patent literature and a company. This sets the scene for exploring what expectation companies have of information found in patents. Having thus established the foundations of knowledge, attitudes and behaviour in different companies, we are then in a better position to discuss the barriers to the use of patent information. On the basis of these observations we can interpret these results and see a pattern emerging, from which we begin to group companies according to a 'learning' curve. In conclusion, putting this information together with sectoral characteristics, we are then in a position to suggest what strategies public bodies might employ to raise the usage level of patent information amongst appropriate SME segments.

Scope of the study

It will help to start with a brief description of how the study was conducted and to give a sense of its scope. Our starting point was that the companies where patent information might be most useful would be found in sectors where patenting is most prevalent. These areas include chemicals, pharmaceuticals and the machine and instrumentation fields. Interestingly, the reason why these two areas are relatively heavily patented would appear to differ.[1] We ruled out the software sector where patenting is still a relatively new phenomenon and restricted our study to SMEs which are deemed to fall under the following SIC (Standard Industrial Classification) codes:

Code 28: chemical and allied products;
Code 36: electronic and other electrical equipment and components, except computer equipment;
Code 38: measuring, analysing and controlling instruments, photographic, medical and optical goods;
Codes 3511 to 3569: industrial and commercial machinery and computer equipment;
Code 7391: research and development laboratories.

Our main aim in the first phase of the project was to screen companies by questionnaire so that we could obtain a profile on each company, find out if they had sought or obtained patent protection and whether or not they were users of patent information. The search was run using Dun and Bradstreet's database of UK companies, selecting both by the SIC codes shown above and by number of employees (5–250). For our own convenience we limited our enquiries to two regions in the United Kingdom – the Midlands and Scotland. This search was run in 1997, resulting in 2,500 questionnaires being sent out. As is expected in such circumstances there was a low response rate (17 per cent – which in itself may indicate a lack of interest), but at least the returns gave us 390 replies to work on, the main purpose being to select from this companies for interview. In the second phase of the study we conducted 23 interviews which gave us the deeper insights discussed later on in this chapter.

The initial screen, however, did serve to confirm some of the issues that other studies had suggested. In the sample as a whole, and assuming that our questionnaire had reached the right person (in small companies this is less of a problem), we found that patent information does not appear to be a major activity: 44 per cent of companies never use patent information and 80 per cent of the companies conducting patent searches are doing so just once a year or less often than that. As we will see later on, if firms do not themselves interact with the patent system and use a third party to do this for them, this in itself may be a cause of their lack of apparent interest.

As with larger firms, size is also a factor amongst SMEs. Overall, smaller companies make less use of patent information than the larger ones. Over 85 per cent of the medium-sized companies (50 to 250 employees) conduct patent searches, whereas over 50 per cent of the small companies do not. Patent information also increases with the level of turnover. These findings, therefore, point to the possibility of a resource barrier to the greater use of patent information.

The survey also confirmed the link between a company's use of patent protection and its propensity to use patent information. Companies that have been involved with patent protection are 15 times as likely to conduct a patent search than companies that have never been involved with patents. This was not surprising when their reasons for conducting patent searches were examined; it was found that most companies which use patent information do so in order to prepare for their own patent applications. SMEs appear uninterested in the technological information content of patents, which in theory should be of use to all technology-based companies irrespective of their own interest in patent protection. Only one in ten companies conducting searches did so solely to benefit from the technological information which patents contain. Most companies gave the reason of 'not useful or relevant' as the main reason they did not look at patent information. While this evidence might *seem* to support the lack of relevance of technical detail found in patents, such figures may be misleading. One also needs to examine the role of the patent agent or other intermediary coming between the firm and patent information.

We found that nearly two-thirds of companies using patent information only do so through the use of intermediary services and do not access patent information sources directly themselves. Therefore, while the use of intermediaries may be a way to overcome the constraints posed by lack of time and expertise, the need to use intermediaries may prove to be a barrier itself. Some corroborative evidence of this is that where companies have *direct* access to patents, they are more interested in the technological information content.

Both this last piece of evidence, and the fact that only a third of respondents in the survey perceived the patent system to be about providing information, point very strongly in the direction of the need to delve more deeply into behavioural patterns. Knowledge and attitudes are not necessarily good predictors of behaviour. Behaviour depends also very much on cost and benefits or rewards. For behaviour to be understood, more in-depth research was necessary.

On the basis of the company profiles we were then in a position to conduct the second phase of the project, which was to go out and interview companies from all four of these sectors and include in our sample both companies with and without a background in patenting. Many of these firms, we discovered, were engaged in 'design', i.e. putting together standard technologies, many with electronic control giving scope for additional customisation and improved performance. We also encountered a sizeable proportion of new/high-technology-based companies. However, only four of the 23 companies interviewed could actually be said to be conducting any 'scientific' research – all of the work was very applied or developmental. Even companies at the leading edge of their technologies described themselves as 'doing up technology'. What can be described as developmental and what is 'design' would appear to be activities with considerable overlap.

Nearly all the firms we interviewed are serving international markets which can best be described as global niche markets, but where the niche is so specialised and narrow as to offer little prospect of rapid growth. Some firms might be described as verging on 'lifestyle', i.e. profitable to the extent of maintaining present staff in work, not ambitious, and comfortable with their current level of trading. However, even within the group interviewed we found two companies who exhibited an unusual capacity for growth, having identified a large but underdeveloped market need. Another company had made what may be described as an 'architectural' invention, i.e. a radically new product altering the basis of competition. Given the diversity encountered there was little opportunity for grouping according to market, product or technology. Our approach was to look at where companies exhibit similar patterns of behaviour and to seek some deeper explanation in terms of both their internal situation and their external competitive environment.

Patenting behaviour

Enough has been said already to suggest that patent information use is an important corollary of patenting behaviour. So it was important to find out more about why people in firms sought patents and what they did to obtain a patent. Logically, one might expect to find patents in areas where a patent would afford tight legal appropriability (see note 1). It would seem pointless to pay to advertise to the world something which others could copy in a roundabout way that would avoid the legal constraints.

In practice, other factors such as patenting tradition, marketing strategy or even individual egos may precipitate companies into patenting. Several firms we came across in what might be described as the more traditional 'mechanical' sector have had some experience of patenting. A picture emerged, especially in 'equipment' rather than 'widget' manufacturers and those with a long family tradition or history, of a 'patenting tradition'. In fact 'pat. pending' would be closer to the truth since such companies might go as far as filing for a patent but would not follow through to completion. It seems as if patents are being used more as a marketing tool than a means of protecting intellectual property. Indeed, some firms seem not to make any distinction between patents and trademarks.

The majority of firms we interviewed are operating in global niche markets where the costs of maintaining a patent portfolio with worldwide coverage is simply not cost-effective. Given the fact that many products are highly customised and that there are relatively few competitors, then the economic theory of markets is inappropriate. Competitive edge is not achieved by merely giving temporary monopoly rents – in such markets, customer relationship is key. That said, however, firms still have to adhere to rules of 'competition' set by their other competitors. In some sectors, German, Italian and Japanese firms are very keen on patenting.

So, while regime of appropriability *should* be a main consideration, there are other factors such as resources, competitive position of rivals, and position in the supply chain which also need to be taken into account. Large companies which have more resources to patent may well use this capacity to block off areas to other potential competitors. Their very size and clout is a threat to smaller companies. As one technical director of a company producing high-tech instrumentation said:

> I have had examples with bigger companies that really have stolen our ideas and they have said to us: '...well we have got more lawyers and you sue us! That will keep you busy for years!' At the end of the day a small company cannot afford to do that . . . in small companies you have got to save your technology by keeping it in house and wrapping it up and hoping that you have got a lead – because particularly in high tech, the lifetime of new ideas and new product ideas is quite limited – maybe a 5 year life cycle . . . It takes all that time to get your patent up and granted so you might as well keep it secret and carry on!

Small companies may well be nibbling at the edges of market sectors served by larger companies and could well be infringing their patents. While some large companies may not bother with the minnows, clearly others are willing to take action. We found several small companies that had been drawn into litigation. Nonetheless, few small companies would appear to live in fear that they may be infringing others' patents. They say that since litigation is so expensive, most settlements will occur out of court. Others said that it was only in the courts that a patent could be really challenged and, if that situation were to arise, then it would not be difficult to dig up some *prior art* which would invalidate the patent's claims.

Whether these views are substantive is perhaps less important than the fact that patents were not seen as a stumbling block to wider creativity. This was also borne out by the fact that few companies use licensing as a strategy. That said, it should be noted that while this may be the view held amongst the *majority*, nevertheless there can be the more rare case where licensing in and licensing on is the platform upon which an entire firm's strategy has been built. Such an example was in the area of second-generation pharmaceuticals; in this case, drugs for which patent protection has expired are being piggy-backed onto patented delivery systems. The deliver system is a material that will allow an administered dose of drug to be released slowly. The whole package is then being licensed back to the pharmaceutical industry. Pharmaceuticals form a very distinctive and virtually unique sector. Even with second-generation drugs, development costs are still high, and such that no firm would make the commercial investment without first legally securing the intellectual property.

A more typical statement, not in the specialist field of drugs, illustrates how ambivalent many firms are about searching for information they might prefer not to know about:

> I would be worried about digging up something and finding that somebody else was doing it, because you may think 'Oh dear we can get a licence from that man and that's very good, he's done that already' – but you're much more inclined to think: 'Oh dear! We have to find a way round that'. I'm not sure whether that is the right stance.

One has the impression from statements such as this that many firms do not want to examine what they are doing too carefully, and they prefer to go on in 'blissful ignorance'. Even when they are paying a high premium to maintain patents they do not really need, it is much easier to follow normal company practice than to ask any awkward questions. It may be only when a company is bought out that questions such as the legal aspects of what intellectual property the firm owns and whom they might infringe come under the microscope.

Experience with the patenting process and all that it entails also depends very much on how a firm manages its intellectual property and how much of that process and responsibility is contracted out to a patent agent. The patent agent him/herself may well be a moderating influence on a company's attitudes to such matters.

Sources of patent information and the influence of patent agents

Patent agents perform a variety of tasks for companies. Not only do they undertake the task of developing a patent application, they will also give advice on the benefits of doing so and, where necessary, will assist in the defence of a patent. Some will also give commercial advice. All will undertake to get patent searches done, though many will contract this on to a patent searching agency, such as the Patent Office's own Search and Advisory Service. Patent agents also frequent the dozen or so regional libraries in the Patent Information Network which are supported by the Patent Office in order to fulfil its obligation to provide free access to patent information. Very few of the companies we surveyed or spoke to actually use these libraries themselves, and those that did talked about the apparently anachronistic system for classifying and storing patents which acts as a disincentive to searching through them.

As for other methods of accessing patent information, there are specialist patent information providers such as Derwent (which is the major commercial player in the United Kingdom), who will undertake patent searches, and on-line hosts through which Derwent's services can be accessed directly. Business Links (government-sponsored) and Industry Associations will also offer patent search services. More recently, IBM has made US patents available on line from their website and the European Commission is in the process of making European patents more accessible. With the huge expansion of information technology, access is going to be made increasingly easier.

The patent agent, however, is the main source of information concerning whether something is patentable, or whether a company is infringing someone else's patent. The patent agent may not be an expert on how important patenting is in a certain sector – that is a commercial judgement. It is our impression from visiting patent agents, that top city-based patent firms can give very sound advice of both a technical and a commercial nature. Many patent agents who are working on their own or in small local practices (which SMEs located outside big cities often find via the *Yellow Pages*) cannot be expected to offer such a wide range of expertise.

The majority of companies we spoke to did have some experience with a patent agent at some stage. Few said they used a patent agent regularly and the level of knowledge about what their agent(s) could offer seemed to depend on how much they used them. One firm brings their agent into their company for more than one day a week, but this was exceptional. This firm will probably do what another firm has already done, which is to employ their own in-house patent agent. Both of these firms, unsurprisingly, are in the pharmaceuticals business.

Companies where patents are not mainstream to business strategy tend to use patent agents much more intermittently and view the service as very expensive and not value for money. Those at the higher-tech end tend to view cost as a necessary evil if it saves the time of their own technical staff.

It was also informative to find out what tasks firms use patent agents for. Some firms will only do searches (via their agent) prior to making a patent application. Some patent agents advise writing up the patent without a search and then leave it up to the Patent Office to do a 'patentability' search, which is a standard part of the application process. Clearly this is an area where not only the preferences of the patent agent come into play, but also those of the client. Some 'inventors' like to carry out a patent search before they embark on some innovation. Many (and they are probably in the majority) do not, because they think it might 'channel their minds' or narrow their thinking. Furthermore, to make a search and use someone else's ideas might also threaten their status amongst colleagues as a 'wizard'.

Many companies do not seem to have learnt the knack of using a patent agent constructively. The way that claims are written up depends upon how well the client and agent can communicate with each other. Overall, if we were to take a view on how small companies view their patent agents, then it would be fair to say that many had a very limited understanding of what they could offer. Many felt that they did not offer value for money and were therefore best avoided.

Expectations of patent information

Expectations of the value of information that can be obtained from patents has to be set within the context of what other intelligence a company gathers, how easy it is to access, and how good this information is. In the small firms we were dealing with, most obtain intelligence from customers and competitors products via their sales force. Some actively strip down competitors' products. Trade shows, exhibitions and conferences are also a major source of intelligence. Most companies find themselves inundated with the literature that they receive from industry associations and other trade journals. The impression is that firms receive more information than they have time to assimilate. Neither do most appear to have any systematic approach to intelligence-gathering. This is hardly a surprise given that even the largest firms with the most sophisticated systems for external surveillance are far from perfect in this respect (Sheen, 1992). It seems to be only leading-edge and the more science-related technology firms that consult academic journals.

In addition to the comparative richness of other sources of information and the relative ease of access, there is also what might be called a 'patenting climate' which firms in a similar line of business will operate under. To quote from one interviewee on this subject:

> I think that you might find that varies from industry to industry and technology to technology. There are some which traditionally have made little or no use of patents and occasionally there is a change in a given industry. I think that if one looked 25 years ago at digital electronics you might have found that there was surprisingly little use made of patents and I don't know why that was. There are other industries where, quite frankly, one could consider that the patent system has been overused and it is the scene of a great deal of rather unnecessary skirmishing between competitors.

From the broad spectrum of technology-based companies we interviewed, those that considered themselves to be at the leading edge of their market were also those that were the most outward-looking, and the most keenly aware of their competitors. If patents were an important competitive weapon, they had acquired the means to monitor the technology of their closest rivals and were using patents as one amongst other sources of information. These companies, however, were in the minority. Most had not explored what patents could provide. Interestingly, one company which had recently taken on a marketing assistant, has begun regularly to monitor competitor companies. This, in turn, has triggered an enormous interest from the development department which has now become an avid consumer of the technical content in the patents. In another company, however, the chief 'inventor' of the development department would not countenance what he considered would be a challenge to his personal 'prowess'. Personalities and individual dispositions are disproportionately influential in the smaller company. Engineers in particular came under criticism, and the following comment was typical:

> I mean the engineers – it's a difficult time for them. They assume they will conjure up something that will do, rather than go for the best – and so they will reinvent the wheel! So, I said to them: 'Don't reinvent the wheel. Go and do a patent search and find out!'

This, of course, is part of the underlying reason why governments support a patent system – because it is supposed to prevent duplication of effort and waste of scarce resources. While our findings could not confirm that the system was working in the way intended – simply because so few firms actually use the patent literature – what we did find were some instances which indicated how it could work:

> I believe that patent searches add value to what I'm trying to innovate and it will make you aware of much more different ways of doing things, different ways of skinning the cat. Personally all I need is an abstract and a picture and that's it. . . . I can't say I've been hampered, because we're never short of ideas, so I always have a solution. But have I got a better solution because I have read the patents?

Note that this interviewee did not say that he needed to get good ideas, but rather he indicates that it is about making *better* innovations. Also, the technology may be used in a different product context. One can appreciate, therefore, that expectations and barriers are something that exist in people's minds as much as in company strategies – explicit or non-explicit, rational or irrational. So, before going on to discuss the barriers to use of patent information, it may be useful to describe the benefits that firms in this survey could gain from searching patents.

1 *For technical information.* There are situations where patents can be highly educational when the reader starts from a zero knowledge base:

> So I learnt a lot about their technology; it was beautifully written and I learned a lot from that. They were disclosing an incredible amount, so I went from a zero base to rather, quite an expert in their technology just by reading the one patent and then I took in a couple of other patents that were cited in that one to get a view of what was available and you can very, very quickly home in . . .

Most people do not start from scratch and one of the dilemmas any inventor is faced with is at what stage information searches should be carried out – whether to leave it to the Patent Office or to look before inventing. Again this can be a purely personal preference. As one engineer said: 'I also want to be aware of what's there, so I can create the bit in the middle.'

2 *For finding out if something is patentable.* This is the most common reason for conducting patent searches. However, this is not normally the firm doing the search, but writing up a brief on the invention and passing it on to a patent agent.

3 *For competitive positioning.* Only a small proportion of small firms would appear to continuously monitor the patent literature. It seems to be really only those that are at the leading edge both technically and commercially.

4 *To check they are not infringing patents owned by others.* Some firms do search patents so that they can keep themselves in the clear, but many put their heads down and just hope that they won't ever come to the attention of larger companies who would have the resources to take action. This does happen and can result in the closure of a firm. Where the field is specialised and there are few players, then continuous monitoring makes good sense: 'I am sure we would be sued a lot more times if we were not aware of what was out there'. The alternative scenario is that a firm might wish to monitor patents specifically to find out if their own patents are being infringed by other patent applications. This would seem to be more theoretical than actual. No companies in our sample were searching patents for this reason, although several said that they has seen competitors' products in the market where their patented invention had been copied.

5 *For finding new areas to get into/opportunities for licensing in.* Two biotechnology firms said that they regularly conduct searches to look for things already patented which they could license in and develop up.

6 *For 'inventing around' other patents.* Although this is a perfectly legitimate use of patents, not many companies will admit to such behaviour, perhaps because they believe it is unethical. 'Inventing around' a patent is where they will pick up

the main idea, but make a slight modification so that the claims of the original patent are not infringed. We believe that this is fairly common practice in some areas like mechanical and electrical engineering where there are complex products.

7 *For costing/pricing intelligence.* The following is an example of how information found in patents can be useful if a firm is a supplier to another company:

> we are supplying antibodies to a company which has developed a new kit . . . We were trying to work out the value to them of our reagents – because we know how much it costs to make them and we have invested a huge amount before there was ever a product . . . so we got out their patent for this new test method and looked up exactly how they were doing it. We worked out how much reagent would go into each test. That kind of thing you could get from a patent that you would be unlikely to get from a publication.

8 *For problem-solving.* We gained the impression that firms would normally only go to the lengths of searching the patent literature when the problem they needed to solve was a major barrier to progress, and that would only be in firms which knew their way round the patent literature. The patent literature can be the source of solutions to practical problems not recorded in any other place. For example, one firm found out how to bond two materials.

9 *For information about manufacturing processes.* Processing generally embodies a good deal of 'know-how' or tacit knowledge which a firm, even when it holds a patent, will try to keep to itself. One interviewee commented that he was surprised about how honest people were in revealing details which people like him could use.

10 *For improving the quality and success rate of a firm's own patent applications.* Firms that are knowledgeable about patents claim that it improves the drafting of their own patents, it helps them to protect themselves against events which they would not otherwise foresee, and it means that they can pre-empt any prior art which might otherwise preclude them from a successful application. Also, it would appear from the biotechnology-based firms that new methods disclosed in patents can enhance their own R&D productivity.

11 *For avoiding R&D costs.* Other firms said that they could not have avoided duplicating R&D costs by using the patent literature. However, this attitude may have been either due to the field they were in, or because there was little depth of experience underpinning their comment.

Several of the companies we visited were 'on the edge' of increasing their patent-searching capability. Although it would be unwise to place too much reliance upon a few examples, nevertheless the impression gained was that the interest in patent information was growing, especially in less traditional sectors. Much of this growing interest is also associated with getting direct access to information through the internet.

Clearly what the situation looks like today is not what it will be tomorrow. Quite a few of the firms interviewed are gearing up their computer technology and experimenting with the internet. The fact that both US and European patents have become available on-line is greeted with considerable enthusiasm although, with little experience, it is still too early to judge how easy people will find it to access the information they need. As we will see, access is not the only barrier to the wider use of patent information.

Barriers to the use of patent information

Many firms do not use the patent literature as a source of information because they have no or little expectation that it can be useful. If they are not sure what they will get for their effort, then any difficulty – however minor – will deter them. The following comment demonstrates an attitude that is not unusual:

> Yes, the immediate barrier is how do you get information? You write to the Patent Office and they send you these things and they talk about the Search and Advisory Service, but it all costs money and if you don't really know what you're going to get . . .

As we indicated above, once firms have obtained information of real value to the firm, then their whole outlook changes and some turn into avid users. One suspects that the sense of achievement is greater when the firm has done this all on their own and not through a patent agent.

Patent agents themselves may sometimes present a professional barrier rather than an enabling function – at least to those who do not understand how best to use their services. Firms may ask patent agents to do things which they could well do for themselves. When they get charged a full professional fee, they balk at the charge and decide never to return. It is also better if the patent agent chosen has some knowledge of the technical area. Here again firms can make a poor decision, and the less they can do for themselves, the less likely they are to ably assist in developing the patent specification. Patent agents will tell you that there are firms, even small firms, that always have something going on related to their patent portfolio. Over the years they build up a close working relationship with their client. Sadly, such firms are in the minority; most of the work coming from SMEs is ad hoc in nature and expectations are often unrealistic.

Patents are often criticised by lay people for their use of obscure legal terminology. This terminology is intended to be very precise. However, from the applicant's point of view, the whole purpose of a patent is to make the broadest possible claims but to reveal as little as possible. This difficulty with the language is how a client may also perceive the agent and can have the effect of distancing a client from his agent.

Underneath the language there lie the legal and technical aspects. Patent claims may be written up as 'not obvious', but technologically qualified people seem able to get into the technological detail with little difficulty. Technical jargon only becomes a problem where the searcher is not from a similar background. However, it appears that the legal aspects do present some considerable difficulty. This is where the patent agent has his/her uses. But it is in the cases of possible infringement where the communication and comprehension gaps between agent and client are most put to the test. The agent must have in-depth knowledge of the technology before s/he can be quite certain of the legal claims. Equally it is a good thing if the client can see things from the legal side. The following comment shows that some people find this easier than others. This quote is from a biotechnology company which employed its own in-house patent agent:

> It can be a problem for some people on the research side, who are not maybe used to reading an awful lot of patent specifications, but it is something that is generally overcome with practice and with instruction, and sometimes a lot – how to read patent claims is something which some find very easy and others don't. Some only need to be told once, others don't pick it up at all.

SMEs typically operate very close to the limits of profitability and are often working below the level at which scale benefits come into play; hence they have little or no spare capacity in terms of time, resources or of cash. Lack of time is one of the greatest problems of small companies – combine this with not knowing how to get into the patent system and it is a powerful deterrent:

> there is always plenty to do and not knowing a quick and easy way to do it . . . show me the door and I will go and open it, but if you have to find six doors before you find the right one . . .

There is no doubt that gathering patent information in the traditional manner is a very costly process and will, to some extent, require a degree of expertise – especially if searching is on a deeper and more exploratory basis. So even those that do understand the process, and are within easy striking distance of a patent library, may hesitate before getting involved.

Like the firm quoted below, whichever route is chosen – either the DIY or via the patent agent – cost is a big deterrent:

> The thing that I have always had a problem with is it's a very expensive process in terms of man power and in terms of the resources outside the company that you need, like the patent agents etc. Consequently I suppose the other thing we fall foul of is quite often we might develop a completely unique process, but to us it's so blindingly obvious that you can't believe it isn't already covered by prior art. Now to actually get to the stage of actually finding out whether it is covered by prior art or not, is effectively a very expensive process. So, though we have done patent applications, I must admit it's something which I don't undertake lightly at all, because there is such an enormous amount of work required to actually get to the stage when we could say this is something that is patentable. Seriously, including internal resources and external resources, you could easily

> eat up £2,000, £3,000 or £4,000 just getting to the stage of finding: is this patentable?

According to another company, sheer overload of information in some areas is making searching quite impractical:

> Typically on most of the patents I have come across, if you've got say 20 to 30 claims on the front of the patent, it can easily take you half an hour to strip through those claims and actually understand what the claims are about. Let's say that in my industry there are about 10 patents a day being granted . . . 3,000 a year . . . it's a full-time job. There is no way you can possibly keep track of what out there is currently being patented.

This interviewee goes on to say that over the past six years they have probably had at least 50 patentable ideas, but have not had the resources to confirm that they are patentable. A further disincentive is that they are operating in such an advanced area of technology that, even if they did have the resources, they would not be able to find anyone to do the work for them:

> every patent search I have ever seen from the Patent Office normally comes up with half a dozen absolutely irrelevant pieces of information and they will miss something that I actually know exists that is very relevant because it's borderline as to whether your information is built on top of this other invention or not. Therefore to me that is information that should definitely appear in a patent search whereas it doesn't.

For the majority of companies we interviewed, patenting is a purely ad hoc affair and no budgets are set aside for this kind of contingency. One firm claimed that when they asked their patent agent to do a search, he sent someone 'down to London' to do the search. For them, as others, the cost seemed 'outrageous'. Yet without any real experience of what they were asking for, firms had no real gauge as to whether they were getting value for money, or indeed setting the criteria for search appropriately.

A particular difficulty for SMEs who operate in global niche markets, as most of our sample did, is the high cost of getting worldwide coverage and, since our focus was on *barriers to use of patent information*, the potential difficulties on accessing intelligence might seem to be equally challenging. However, such information is available, with translation when required, and we found little evidence that firms were particularly worried about this aspect. If it was important to them, then they developed strategies to deal with the problem. Such strategies do not normally include buying in the information from service providers unless these services are provided by their trade association.

Interpretation

What constitutes the under-use of patent information by SMEs is conditional upon a number of factors ranging from unawareness to avoidance. Our findings suggest that we may be able to differentiate between different segments of the SME population according to the types of benefit each segment can obtain from patent information and the barriers presenting themselves in each case. This results in what we call a behavioural segmentation. Clearly cost is a factor that most companies find a major burden. Cost becomes an insurmountable barrier when firms cannot be clear about the benefit they will obtain. There is no doubt that having on-line access will considerably lower the cost of access. Even so, we suspect that here too, there will be differences according to how sophisticated companies are about their needs and we would expect each of the following segments to show a different response:

- *Irrelevant:* The vast majority of SMEs are in this set, including technology-based firms where there is no relevant technical information to be gained and where patenting is not the general practice – either because the legal regime of appropriability is low, or because patenting is not a feature of their competitive environment.
- *Unaware:* These firms are in a relevant set but have had no expectation of gaining any real benefit. Many technology-based firms are still in a state of relative ignorance as to what benefits are to be found in the patent literature.
- *Aware:* The aware set can be further broken down into several sub-sets:
- *Avoiders:* This segment includes firms that are aware but are disaffected; many firms have had bad experiences with the patent system and especially with patent agents. Others exist in some degree of apprehension that they might be infringing others' patents but prefer to do nothing about it. For others, cost is the main barrier.
- *Offloaders:* Such firms are partially aware, but by contracting out their patent searches either to the Patent Office (when applications are first filed) or to patent agents or other information providers, the knowledge benefits are largely lost.
- *Defenders:* These firms use patent information merely for defensive purposes and thus also fail to gain the maximum benefit available to them.
- *Learners:* Firms that have begun to interact proactively with the patent literature in such a way that they are beginning to learn what they might do better. Thus they obtain real benefits and this in turn begins to alter their behaviour towards gaining further information.
- *Professionals:* Very few SMEs come into this category; they can be characterised as strategic and having intelligence-gathering activities that are highly systematised; they may even employ their own in-house experts.

The usefulness of such a segmentation, though still tentative, is that it emphasises the diversity of behavioural patterns – both individual and organisational – which govern the use of patent information in small companies. This study has demonstrated the diversity both of SME 'types' and of learning styles within them, and such a recognition is obviously going to necessitate different approaches to stimulating patent information use in different SME 'communities'. Understanding how and why these behavioural communities interact with patent information – and how that will be affected by overall patent usage in a range of market and technological environments – are important steps in targeting the information effectively: having defined more accurately the target market, then it should be possible to tailor messages and assistance in a more meaningful way to a more specific audience.

Concluding remarks

The concern that SMEs under-use patent information and that this in turn may lead to a severe loss of ability to compete in the future, seems to be only partially substantiated. For the vast majority of SMEs, and even a fair proportion of technology-based SMEs, the patent system is not relevant to their needs either with regard to establishing legal rights over intellectual property or in obtaining useful information.

That said, there is another sector which is not making the most of information available to them in the patent literature. We have begun the process of sub-dividing this section into what we called *avoiders*, *defenders*, and *offloaders*. Avoiders would seem to have a very negative view of the system and may have more than one psychological barrier to overcome. Many in this segment, *even if intellectual property rights were not directly applicable to them,* might find the technical content illuminating. If these barriers can be removed then it is probable that such companies will become *learners* and the more benefits they find, then the keener they will become. *Defenders and offloaders* do already interact with the system in one way or another. However, it may be less easy to shift them into the *learner* sub-group if they feel that they already have a system in place for dealing with patents, and therefore they may be less receptive to incoming prompts.

To sum up, we hope that the findings from our study have not only deepened insight into SME attitudes and behaviour, but also that the tentative segmentation outlined above can become the foundation of a more targeted and strategic approach to stimulating interest in patent information among relevant SMEs.

Note

1 We have found it helpful to view the effectiveness of patent protection in terms of Teece's concept of the 'regime of appropriability'. According to Teece (1986): 'a regime of appropriability refers to the environmental factors, excluding firm and market structure, that govern an innovator's ability to capture the profits generated by an innovation. The most important dimensions of such a regime are the nature of the technology, and the efficiency of legal mechanisms of protection. For example, a regime of *high* or *tight* appropriability is where the innovator has an iron clad patent or where the nature of the product is such that it cannot be reverse-engineered to find out how it works.'

References

Blackman, M. (1995). 'Taking Patent Information Services to Small and Medium Enterprises'. WIPO Asian Regional Seminar on the Use of Patent Information by Industry, World Intellectual Property Organization, Geneva, 75–98.

Braendli, H. C. P. (1995) 'Small and Medium-Sized Industry and Patent Information', EPO Patent Information User Meeting, European Patent Office, Munich, 2.1–2.8.

European Patent Office (1994) *Utilisation of Patent Protection in Europe: Representative Survey Carried Out on Behalf of the European Patent Office Munich*, European Patent Office, Munich.

Inter-departmental Committee on Intellectual Property (1995) *Use and Exploitation of Intellectual Property by Small Firms*, HMSO, London.

Koch, A. (1991). 'Patent Information to Stimulate Innovation in Small and Medium Sized Companies, *World Patent Information*, 13 (4), 201–5.

Schmoch, U. (1990) 'Disclosure of Patent Information for Small and Medium Sized Enterprises', *World Patent Information*, 12 (3), 158–64.

Sheen, M. R. (1992) 'Barriers to Scientific and Technical Knowledge Acquisition in Industrial R&D', *R&D Management*, 22 (2) (April), 135–42.

Stephenson, J. (1982) 'The Use of Patent Information in Industry', *World Patent Information*, 4 (4), 164–71.

Teece, D. J. (1986) 'Profiting from Technological Innovation: Implications for Integration, Collaboration, Licensing and Public Policy', *Research Policy*, 15, 285–305.

Index